DEMOCRACY AND THE POLICE

Critical Perspectives on Crime and Law
Edited by Markus D. Dubber

DAVID ALAN SKLANSKY

Democracy and the Police

STANFORD UNIVERSITY PRESS

STANFORD, CALIFORNIA

Stanford University Press
Stanford, California
© 2008 by the Board of Trustees of the
Leland Stanford Junior University.
All rights reserved.

Printed in the United States of America on acid-free, archival-quality paper

Library of Congress Cataloging-in-Publication Data
Sklansky, David A., 1959–
    Democracy and the police / David Alan Sklansky.
        p.   cm.—(Critical perspectives on crime and law)
    Includes bibliographical references and index.
    ISBN 978-0-8047-5563-4 (cloth : alk. paper)—ISBN 978-0-8047-5564-1 (pbk. : alk. paper)
    1. Police—United States.   2. Police-community relations—United States.
3. Rule of law—United States.   4. Democracy—United States.   I. Title.

HV8139.S55 2008
363.20973—dc22   2007026215

Typeset by Westchester Book Group in 10/14 Janson

For Jack Sklansky and in memory of Gloria Joy Sklansky

Contents

Acknowledgments

Half a decade ago, when I became interested in the relationship between policing and democracy, I knew I had a lot to learn. Having worked as a prosecutor and taught criminal procedure, I felt reasonably knowledgeable about law enforcement but utterly unsophisticated about democracy. I realized I needed tutoring in the broad interdisciplinary field that has come to be known as "democratic theory." As it turned out, I seriously underestimated my ignorance: I had as much to learn about the police as about democracy. I knew what judges, lawyers, and law professors have had to say about law enforcement, but I was familiar only in broad outline with the incredibly rich body of work that social scientists have produced about the police over the past half century. I needed an education in that field, as well.

My dual, belated course of study in democracy and policing became a great pleasure, largely because I was blessed with wise and generous teachers. On the democracy side, I am especially grateful to Stephen Gardbaum, Sandy Muir, and my brother Jeff Sklansky. On the policing side, I owe particularly large debts to Malcolm Feeley, Jonathan Simon, Jerry Skolnick, the late Eric Monkkonen, Sandy Muir (again), and Frank Zimring. Each of these scholars offered patient guidance and kind encouragement as I worked to learn the rudiments of fields they had long mastered and in many cases had helped to shape. Each also read early versions of some or all of the arguments presented here and gave me much-needed criticism.

I deeply appreciate, as well, the guidance I received from many other friends and colleagues—too many to list here. I do want to single out for thanks, though, a few individuals whose comments and criticism were particularly valuable: Ann Carlson, Sharon Dolovich, Markus Dubber, Mel

Eisenberg, Jody Freeman, Phil Frickey, Elizabeth Joh, Anne Joseph, Robert Kagan, Jack Katz, Máximo Langer, Monique Marks, Michael Musheno, Carol Pateman, the late Nelson Polsby, Dan Richman, Seana Shiffrin, William Simon, Steve Sugarman, David Thacher, Leti Volpp, Adam Walinsky, and Stephen Yeazell. I want to thank, too, the participants in workshops and symposia at Berkeley, Buffalo, Columbia, Harvard, Stanford, UCLA, and the University of London where I presented fragments of the ideas collected in this book; I benefited greatly from each of those sessions. And I want to acknowledge the large role that my colleagues Norm Abrams, Peter Arenella, Devon Carbado, David Dolinko, Robert Goldstein, Laura Gómez, Angela Harris, Ian Haney López, Erin Murphy, Melissa Murray, Arthur Rosett, Charles Weisselberg, and John Wiley have each played over the years in shaping my understanding of law enforcement and criminal procedure.

I published earlier versions of portions of this book in the following articles: *Police and Democracy* (Michigan Law Review, vol. 103, no. 7, June 2005); *Private Police and Democracy* (American Criminal Law Review, vol. 43, no. 1, Winter 2006); and *Not Your Father's Police Department: Making Sense of the New Demographics of Law Enforcement* (Journal of Criminal Law and Criminology, vol. 96, no. 3, Spring 2006). Student editors at each of these journals helped me refine my thinking.

Without the intelligent input of my wife, Deborah Lambe, this book would be far weaker. Without her love and encouragement it would not exist at all.

The book is dedicated to my parents, my first and best teachers. My mother, Gloria Sklansky, died as the book was nearing completion, but her influence can be found on every page. At least I hope it can. One of the themes of this book is the importance of seeing the police not just as a type or as occupants of a role but as diverse and complicated individuals. I believe my mother would have approved of that: it echoes what she thought about people in general, and what she valued in them. My fondest aspiration for this book is that my mother would have found in it much more to like, and that it honors what she taught me about how to think and how to live.

Introduction

What constraints does a commitment to democracy place on the police? What implications, conversely, does modern law enforcement have for how we think about democracy? What is the relationship, in short, between democracy and policing?

Events of the past few years—particularly, for Americans, the years since September 11, 2001—have given these questions fresh importance. No one would suggest now, as George Berkley did in 1969, that the police pose one of the "least recognized problems of modern democracy." In truth the suggestion was doubtful even then. The "problem" of democratic policing may not have attracted much notice in the early 1960s, but by the end of the decade things had changed. Jerome Skolnick's widely influential analysis of the dilemmas of "law enforcement in a democratic society" appeared in 1966. Two years later James Q. Wilson published his landmark study tying police practices to local political traditions. Three separate presidential commissions were appointed between 1965 and 1968 to address problems associated with the police. By the late 1960s and early 1970s, the special challenges of "policing in a free society" were very much a subject of public debate, and the debate has never really ended.[1]

In two different ways, though, the debate over democratic policing changed radically over the past four decades, even before September 2001.

First, policing itself changed. Civilian oversight, once resisted tooth-and-nail by the police, became unexceptional. The old orthodoxy of police reform, law enforcement "professionalism," gave way to a new orthodoxy, "community policing." The homogeneous law enforcement workforces of forty years ago were diversified dramatically, if incompletely, by the hiring and promotion of large numbers of minority officers and female officers, and smaller but still significant numbers of openly gay and lesbian officers. Even the Los Angeles Police Department—once the very model of an insular, politically independent, starkly homogeneous and self-consciously "professional" police force—no longer bears much resemblance to its old, stylized image—the department dramatized in television shows like *Dragnet* and *Adam-12*. And police departments are no longer local monopolies: more and more policing is carried out by a patchwork collection of sworn officers and private security personnel.

Second, views about democracy have changed. The 1960s were still the heyday of the "pluralist" theory of democracy, an extraordinarily influential set of ideas, elaborated in great detail by social scientists beginning in the 1940s, about the nature and goals of American democracy. Those ideas, which in the 1950s became omnipresent not only among scholars but also in popular discourse, included a deep distrust of mass politics; faith in the leadership provided by responsible elites; and a tendency to see the jostling among interest groups, rather than reasoned discourse, as the lifeblood of democracy. By the late 1960s those ideas were already under sharp attack, and in the decades since then pluralism has been largely supplanted, both within and without the academy, by understandings of democracy that place more trust in ordinary people than in leadership elites and that emphasize participation and deliberation, rather than interest-group competition, as the secret of democratic success.

These two stories—the transformation of American policing over the past several decades, and the dramatic shift during the same period in ideas about American democracy—are almost never discussed together. The thesis of this book, though, is that the two stories are closely intertwined, and that understanding the connections can help us think more intelligently about what "democratic policing" should mean today.

Democratic Theory and the Police

"Democratic policing" still resists easy definition. References to "democracy" and "democratic values" are common when judges, legislators, and local officials set limits on law enforcement, and when legal scholars and social scientists write about the police. Increasingly, moreover, efforts to create or to strengthen democracies overseas take for granted the need to establish police forces that are, in some important sense, democratic. Part of the retraining the American military conducted for Iraqi police officers, for example, involved asking them to come up with "words consistent with 'democratic policing.'"[2] But it is hard to know how that question should be answered. After half a century of talk about "democratic policing," we still lack a clear sense of the precise connections between policing and democracy.

We sometimes talk as though there were a simple trade-off between "democratic values" on the one hand and, on the other hand, security, order, and law enforcement—the objectives of the police. This way of thinking assumes both that we know what "democratic values" policing affects and that the relationship is straightforward. In fact, though, the values at stake and the nature of the relationship are anything but clear.

Sometimes, for example, democratic policing seems identified with procedural regularity and the "rule of law." This was an important part of Skolnick's account, which in turn echoed aspects of earlier arguments by Jerome Hall and Herbert Packer.[3] At other times democracy appears tied to respect for certain substantive rights—right, for example, against unreasonable search and seizure and compelled self-incrimination.[4] (An Iraqi village leader invoked this idea when complaining about home searches conducted by American forces, early in the occupation: "How do these soldiers have the right to come into my home like this? . . . Where is the democracy that the Americans promised?")[5] Sometimes democracy seems tied to popular participation in policing, either through some form of civilian oversight or through police practices that involve "partnering" with or "delegation" to the "community."[6] At other times democracy is said to require placing police departments under a much more thoroughgoing form of community control.[7] Democratic values are sometimes invoked in support of giving police officers *themselves* a degree of control over the nature of their work.[8] (Not surprisingly, some Iraqi police officers took this view.)[9] And sometimes democracy in policing seems simply a matter of dealing with the public in a particular way: what Wilson called the "service style"[10] and now often is lumped together with "partnering," "delegation," and sundry other fixes under the ill-defined slogan of "community policing."[11] (The American officials retraining the Iraqi police may have had something like the "service style" in mind when they talked about "democratic policing"; press reports suggest the Iraqi officers were urged to become more "polite," "kind-hearted," and "service-oriented.")[12]

As for the trade-offs, we sometimes talk as though effective police are like punctual trains: something we need to sacrifice a little if we wish to live in a democracy. The goal is to strike the right balance between letting the police do their job and preserving our democratic liberties. The more of one, the less of the other. This is the assumption that has framed much of the discussion of "homeland security" measures since September 2001. At other times, though, we talk as though democratic policing is the same thing as effective policing—as though "democracies can, so to speak, have their cake and eat it, too," because, with respect to the police, "'democracy and efficiency in public administration are one and the same.'"[13] A good deal of the discussion about "community policing" in recent years, for example, has proceeded from this optimistic assumption. Between the poles of strict trade-off and perfect convergence, of course, lie other, more complicated possibilities. But they remain largely unexplored.

The vagueness of most discussions of democratic policing is particularly striking given the efforts that philosophers, political scientists, sociologists, and legal scholars have made over the past half century to think carefully about the nature of democracy. Since the 1950s, "democratic theory" has been a rich, lively, and sprawling field of interdisciplinary inquiry. The field has attracted more than its share of gifted thinkers and has generated more than its share of arresting, influential work. But little of this work directly addresses the police. And few discussions of policing draw explicitly on democratic theory.

Certainly this is true of criminal procedure, the field of jurisprudence and legal scholarship concerned with how the police carry out their business. In often minute detail, criminal procedure law regulates how and when the police can conduct searches, seizures, and interrogations. Almost everybody appears to believe that these restrictions have important implications for democracy, but the nature of those implications is rarely examined with care, either by judges deciding cases or by scholars reviewing what the judges have done. As a result, invocations of democracy in these settings often seem to be little more than lip service.

Moreover, criminal procedure has almost nothing to say, in any direct fashion, about other questions of apparent pertinence to the relation between policing and democracy, such as the structure of decision making within police agencies and the arrangements by which the police are made subject to or insulated from external, political control. In part, but only in part, this selective silence reflects our collective decision to entrust the development of criminal procedure rules to courts, and our sense, which may or may not be well founded, that courts are ill suited to address questions of systemic design.[14] Because thinking about criminal procedure has tended to focus on the questions taken up by courts, the unfortunate result has been not just that *judges* have largely failed to consider the systemic requirements for democratic policing, but that most of the rest of us have, too.

None of this is to say that democratic theory and criminal procedure have had nothing to say to each other. It is just that the conversation has been largely below the surface. This book unearths that conversation, dusts it off, and then suggests ways to improve it.

Organization of This Book

The eight chapters of the book divide roughly into two halves. The first four chapters trace the connections between the changing ideas about American democracy over the past half century and developments during the same period in how we think about and regulate the police. The second four chapters explore how our notions about the police and our strategies for police reform might change if they were rooted in a more explicit, and richer, set of ideas about democracy.

The first half of the book, the "how did we get here" part, brings together two stories of transformation—two different ways in which democratic policing over the past several decades has been in flux. One is the story of democratic theory: the rise during the 1950s of the pluralist theory of democracy, with its emphasis on the roles of elites, interest groups, and competition in sustaining American democracy; and then, beginning in the 1960s, the gradual shift away from this theory and toward accounts of democracy emphasizing popular participation, community, and deliberation. The other is the story of the police: the triumph in the 1950s and 1960s of the "professional" model of policing, which purposely distanced the police from the communities they patrolled and made police departments insular, homogeneous, and largely autonomous; and then the slow emergence, beginning in the 1970s and 1980s, of civilian oversight, a more diverse and less unified workforce, and the new orthodoxy of "community policing." Telling these stories in tandem will help us see what has too often escaped notice: the important ways in which they are intertwined.

The book therefore begins, in Chapter 1, by describing the emergence in postwar America of a particular understanding of a democracy, an understanding alternately referred to as "democratic pluralism," "analytic pluralism," "pluralist theory," or simply "pluralism." Pluralism in this sense was not at bottom an embrace of diversity. It was not the "noetic pluralism" of William James, the "cultural pluralism" of Horace Kallen and Alain Locke, or the "reasonable pluralism" of John Rawls[15]—although it shared with them, among other things, the taste for multifaceted explanation that so exercised people like C. Wright Mills.[16] Democratic pluralism was a nuanced, interrelated set of ideas about democracy that during the 1950s grew pervasive both among scholars and in popular discussions of American government. Those ideas included a distrust of mass politics, a preoccupation with social stability and the avoidance of authoritarianism, and a focus on group competition rather than reasoned discourse as the engine of democracy.

We will find the police, in an odd way, at the very heart of pluralism.[17] For one way of understanding pluralism is to see it as a reaction against the "police state"—those European systems of totalitarianism that the pluralists took as the polar opposite of democracy and the paramount threat of modern political life. As the very phrase "police state" suggested, the pluralists viewed totalitarianism as the police unbound, and they tended to think of democratic police forces—when they thought of them at all—as, more or less, totalitarianism tamed and controlled.

Given the pluralists' pervasive influence, and their preoccupation with the specter of the police state, it would be remarkable if democratic pluralism found no echoes in police studies and modern criminal procedure, both of which emerged close on the heels of pluralism, in the late 1950s and early 1960s. In fact, the echoes were extensive and profound. Chapter 2 of this book describes how pluralism helps to make sense of several interrelated hallmarks of criminal procedure and police studies in the 1960s, 1970s, and early 1980s. Among the most important of those hallmarks was a strong attraction to police professionalism, a reform agenda which predated pluralism but found new strength with pluralism's rise. Police professionalism dominated progressive thinking about law enforcement in the 1950s and 1960s in part because it fit so well with other themes of criminal procedure and police studies in this period, themes that themselves resonated with aspects of democratic pluralism. Those themes included a focus on the group psychology of the police, a concern with police discretion and a reliance on judicial oversight, an emphasis on personal dignity, a comfort with and attraction to modernity, a high premium on consensus, and a general disregard of institutional structure.

Chapter 3 of the book traces the rise, beginning slowly in the 1960s, of "participatory democracy" and later "deliberative democracy"—theories of democracy that were framed in explicit opposition to pluralism and that rejected most of its premises. The new theories were never as unified or as consistent as pluralism in its heyday, but they tended to include each of the following elements: an embrace of grassroots politics, a distrust of elites, an emphasis on cooperation and collective reasoning, and an appreciation for the intrinsic value of democracy, wholly apart from its utility as a rule of decision. And just as pluralism often took the rhetorical form of a reaction against a particular nightmare of policing—the Gestapo and the NKVD— the turn against pluralism represented, in significant part, a loss of faith in detached technocrats, epitomized in many ways by the kind of heavy-handed, "professional" law enforcement officer long embraced as the ideal by police departments across the country. Sergeant Friday, the aloof, coldly professional hero of *Dragnet*, may not have been pluralism personified, but he came close.

Chapter 4 of the book examines the various ways in which theories of participatory and deliberative democracy made themselves felt in jurisprudential and academic discussions of the police. The aversion to *Dragnet*-style police professionalism was matched by a mounting enthusiasm for community participation, a growing premium placed on transparency, a preoccupation with legitimacy, and a general retreat from modernity. All of these themes resonated with key aspects of the anti-pluralist turn in democratic theory. But criminal procedure jurisprudence and scholarship today also has important points of continuity with the 1950s and early 1960s. Now as then, the police are almost always treated as a breed apart, institutional structure is pervasively de-emphasized, and issues of equality receive relatively little attention. In part these continuing biases are the legacy of particular political battles fought in the late 1960s and early 1970s. In other respects, though, they reflect broader biases that participatory democracy and deliberative democracy, in their most common forms, share with democratic pluralism.

Identifying those biases helps to highlight important constants in our thinking about the police, and neglected avenues of reform. These loom large in the second half of the book. The question pursued there is what implications a richer, more reflective understanding of democracy might have on criminal procedure, and more broadly on our understanding of and expectations from the police.

Chapter 5 begins that inquiry by crafting a purposefully eclectic account of democracy, an account aiming less at elegance and simplicity than at minimizing blind spots. The account I develop incorporates the key insights of democratic pluralism, as well as of eighteenth-century political economy and 1960s-style participatory democracy. It also is sensitive to what the political theorist Ian Shapiro has called "the oppositional traditions of democratic politics"—those dimensions of democracy, that is to say, that have less to do with collective self-government than with ongoing resistance to "arbitrary hierarchy and domination."[18]

The remaining chapters of the book explore the implications of this rounded account of democracy for a range of issues in contemporary policing. Chapter 6 focuses on the relationship between the police and the communities they serve, examining the broad array of programs now lumped together as "community policing," and contrasting those programs with the more ambitious agenda, now aborted, of the "neighborhood policing" movement of the late 1960s and early 1970s. Chapter 6 also discusses the recent, explosive growth of private policing, and the implications that trend may have for police accountability. Chapter 7 turns the focus to issues of equality: the controversy over "racial profiling," the broader problem of biased policing, disparities in the protection the police provide to different communities (exacerbated in some ways by the spread of private policing), and the ramifications of the dramatic but still incomplete diversification of police workforces by minority officers, female officers, and openly gay and lesbian officers. Finally, Chapter 8 addresses what might be called the "internal" dimensions of democratic policing, reassessing the merit of calls made several decades ago for giving police officers themselves a degree of collective, democratic control over the nature of their work. Those calls were rejected in part because the rigidly homogeneous, politically reactionary police forces of thirty or forty years ago seemed exceptionally unsafe places for experiments in workplace democracy. Chapter 8 will explore whether, in the intervening time, police departments have changed enough to warrant revisiting that judgment.

Caveats at the Outset

In pursuing the ways that our ideas about democracy have helped to shape our ideas about the police, and vice versa, this book risks a kind of double myopia, exaggerating the influence in both directions. I am keenly aware of the tendency Ed Zern mocked years ago in his celebrated review of *Lady Chatterley's Lover* for *Field & Stream*: the novel, he said, offered much of interest about "pheasant-raising, the apprehending of poachers, ways to control vermin, and other chores and duties of the professional gamekeeper," but was weighted down with "many pages of extraneous material" that would prevent it from ever "tak[ing] the place of J R Miller's *Practical Gamekeeping*."[19] Policing is about more than democracy, and democracy is about more than the police. I do not wish to suggest otherwise in these pages. But I do want to suggest the two topics are connected more closely, and in more various ways, than we generally acknowledge—and that closer attention to the connections would help us think more productively about the continuing challenge of democratic policing.

Not everyone agrees that careful thinking about democracy today is worth the effort. Plenty of thoughtful people, for example, suspect democracy is no longer, if it ever was, "a sensible tool of analysis or even a coherent ideal,"[20] but has become simply a term of "vague endorsement"[21]—a " 'hurrah' word."[22] That position receives some support from the frequently remarked fact that almost every government in the world today claims to be democratic in some sense or another. Even if the concept of democracy has discernable content, moreover, it may lack modern relevance: it may be too bound up, for example, with the direct democracy of the ancient Greeks.[23] And even if democracy is a meaningful concept, and a concept with present-day relevance, the pursuit of greater democracy may be a mistake.[24] That might be particularly true when it comes to policing. Perhaps the last thing we should want is genuinely democratic policing; perhaps the whole point of constitutional criminal procedure is, and should be, precisely to remove politics from fundamental decisions about law enforcement.[25]

I think these misgivings are unwarranted. I think the careless use of the term "democracy" is no reason to abandon the effort to use it more precisely; I think the concept of democracy has long transcended its classical origins; and I think the concept of democracy is rich enough to incorporate protections against the pathologies of simple majoritarianism. I also think that the concept of democracy has become so central to our thinking about institutions and society—W. B. Gallie called it "*the* appraisive political concept *par excellence*"—that we probably are stuck with it, like it or not.[26] But I will not pursue these matters in this book, at least not directly. My chief task in the first half of the book will be to trace the links between democratic theory and criminal procedure. If, as I conclude, our thoughts about the police have been bound up with our thoughts about democracy, or about things that we lump together with democracy, that seems worth knowing—even if the connections have been largely unhelpful. Much of the motivation for this analysis will be to lay the groundwork for the second half of the book, where I try to think carefully and systematically about what democratic policing should mean today. The various qualms I have described about the analytic usefulness of democracy do indeed throw doubt on this latter project. But each of these qualms amounts to a suspicion that there is no coherent conception of democracy worth pursuing today, at least not in the context of policing. That suspicion can be rebutted most convincingly, if at all, by finding an account of democracy that is useful in addressing modern-day problems of law enforcement. And ultimately we will not know whether there is such an account until we look.

Our Place, Our Time

This book will do most of its looking in the United States, confining itself largely to the relationship between American democracy and the American police. This limited focus obviously carries its own risks of myopia, and not simply because there are important questions about police and democracy elsewhere around the globe. Even for purposes of understanding the American situation, a comparative perspective has many advantages: it lets us see what is truly distinctive about the challenge of democratic policing in the United States, and what aspects of that challenge we share with other nations.[27] I forego those advantages here largely for practical reasons. The American context is the one I know best, and it is quite enough to fill a book.

The American context in the first decade of the twenty-first century plainly includes the horrendous events of September 11, 2001. The terrorist attacks on the World Trade Center and the Pentagon, along with the reactions they produced, have touched virtually every aspect of American life. The effects on law enforcement have been particularly profound. Investigative powers have expanded, particularly at the federal level. Police agencies have shifted their priorities. Public attitudes have changed, too: ethnic profiling, for example, had many more defenders on September 12, 2001, than two days earlier.[28] Many people, including the President of the United States and his Attorney General, thought it obvious that the atrocities of September 11 should alter, permanently or at least indefinitely, our thinking about law enforcement, civil liberties, and the dictates of democracy.

As the decade has worn on, though, the lessons of September 11 have grown less and less clear. The implications of the attacks for policing, in particular, became heavily contested. Opinions increasingly diverge on how and to what extent the threat of terrorist attacks should shape criminal justice policies—especially, perhaps, at the local level, where the bulk of American policing takes place. Some of the escalating uncertainty has to do with the passage of time. Traditional concerns about crime, violence, police misconduct, and workaday law enforcement practices have gradually resurfaced as the events of September 11 have begun to recede into history. But one reason for the uncertainty should have been obvious from the outset. The implications of terrorist threats for law enforcement depend not just on the nature and degree of those threats; they also depend, heavily and necessarily, on our baseline ideas about law enforcement—how it functions, what should be expected of it, and how it intersects with democracy.

No one who thinks carefully about policing and democracy in early twenty-first-century America can ignore the real and continuing threats of terrorism. Protecting against terrorism is not all the police do; it is not even most of what the police do. For local police agencies, in particular, anti-terrorism work remains something of a sideline—important, certainly, but not the mainstay of their work. But rules and practices devised for fighting terrorism can spill over into more run-of-the-mill policing, and vice versa. Some of the spillover may be beneficial. New challenges can spur fresh thinking about old problems.[29] But there are other possibilities, too. Heavy-handed anti-terrorism measures can, for example, wind up alienating groups on whom the police depend for their more conventional, day-to-day work—including, perhaps, groups that also might be important allies in the fight against terrorism. This was one reason many local law enforcement agencies were unenthusiastic about the federal government's dragnet questioning of Middle Eastern men in the wake of the 2001 attacks, and one reason many police departments remain reluctant to participate in crackdowns on illegal immigration.[30]

Sorting through the daunting problems posed for policing by new forms of global terrorism will require, in part, a sophisticated understanding of the terrorists and their tactics. This book will not supply that understanding. But an intelligent response to the law enforcement challenges made horribly manifest on September 11, 2001, will also take a nuanced appreciation of the complicated relationship between American policing and American democracy. That relationship was in flux well before the attacks on the World Trade Center and the Pentagon, and its present contours and possibilities are best approached through a critical examination of its past. Examining that past, and assessing its lessons, are the central tasks of this book.

CHAPTER I

Preventing the Police State

The Rise of Democratic Pluralism

To explore the relationship between democracy and policing critically and systematically, we need to distance ourselves from ways of thinking that have come to seem natural. We need to see the points of contingency; we need to gain some analytic leverage. The best way to gain that leverage is to recover ways of thinking that not so long ago seemed natural but can now seem strange. Ideas about democracy and policing have changed radically over the past half century. "Democratic policing" meant something very different in the 1950s and early 1960s than it does today, partly because policing was different back then, and partly—more fundamentally—because our notions of democracy were different.

Understanding American ideas about democracy in the 1950s and early 1960s means understanding the work of the democratic pluralists: a remarkably influential group of political scientists and sociologists who, beginning in the 1950s, crafted a new and powerful way of understanding American democracy. The teachings of this school were so coherent and so pervasive that they fully deserve to be called an orthodoxy. To an extraordinary degree, American political philosophy in the 1950s and 1960s *was* democratic pluralism. Legal scholars and sociologists of policing, in particular, read and were influenced by the pluralists. Pluralist thought so dominated intellectual discussions of democracy, moreover, that any reader of newspapers and magazines was likely to have encountered, at the least, derivative versions of the theory.

"Derivative versions" is not quite right. Pluralism did not come out of thin air. It drew many of its central assumptions and preoccupations from the larger culture, and that culture itself operated on the mind of anyone who thought about politics or social problems. The pluralists' preoccupations—the threat of the police state, the dangers of mass psychology, the virtues of compromise, the distinctive strengths of the American political system—all of these drew from cultural currents that were, in a sense, prior to democratic pluralism. To a considerable extent, the pluralists crystallized and systematized views that were already widely held. But they also did much to reinforce those views, and their work remains the best point of entry into prevailing ideas about American democracy in the 1950s and beyond.

Unpacking Pluralism

Pluralism did not break cleanly or permanently with the past. There were strong similarities, as we will see, between 1950s pluralism and 1790s Federalism. Moreover, the theories that later emerged to challenge pluralism, chiefly participatory and deliberative democracy, often drew inspiration from writers the pluralists had thought unhelpful, including Aristotle, Rousseau, and the Antifederalists. And both sides found things to like in Tocqueville.

The rise of democratic pluralism in the 1950s was nonetheless a watershed development in several respects. First, the emergence of pluralism marked the beginning of "democratic theory" as a self-conscious, broadly recognized field of interdisciplinary inquiry; it therefore began a tradition of sustained *academic* thinking about the nature of democracy. (Robert Dahl, perhaps the most influential of the pluralists and certainly the most prolific, recalls that that "the term 'democratic theory' hardly existed" when he began his work.)[1]

Second, the theory developed by the pluralists was the first fully developed account of democracy that reflected the dramatic political and social transformations America underwent in the late nineteenth and early twentieth centuries. This period saw the rise of modern regulatory bureaucracies and, relatedly, the demise of party-controlled, broadly participatory electioneering as the lynchpin of American politics.[2] It also saw the epochal emergence of psychological and sociological understandings of collective life—what my brother Jeffrey Sklansky has characterized as "the fall of political economy and the rise of social psychology" as the prevailing "science of American society."[3] Third, there is the matter of influence, already mentioned. Pluralist theory was so coherent, unified, and ubiquitous—and it tapped so strongly into wider cultural currents—that for years the ideas at its core were rarely questioned in mainstream discussions of American democracy; in Theodore Lowi's words, the theory "was considered so fruitful as to be virtually true."[4] Well into the 1970s, pluralism seemed to its critics—who were by then proliferating—to provide "the dominant description and ideal of American politics."[5] The theories of participatory and deliberative democracy that have emerged since the 1950s have been framed largely as responses to pluralism, and the pluralist view itself still has many sympathizers. Fourth and finally, police studies and the modern field of criminal procedure emerged close on the heels of democratic pluralism, and they grew to maturity in its shadow. So there are special reasons to start with the 1950s and democratic pluralism in exploring the connections between ideas about democracy and ideas about the police.

To unpack pluralism, or any other collection of ideas about democracy, it helps to distinguish four separate questions that can be asked about democracy, questions respectively about *purposes, processes, proximity*, and *particularity*. The question of *purposes* concerns the ultimate aims of democracy, the reasons the system is valued. The question of *processes* involves the mechanisms of democracy, the ways in which the purposes of democracy are advanced. The question of *proximity* is evaluative; it asks how close our present system is to the democratic ideal. Finally, the question of *particularity* addresses the degree to which the answers to the other three questions relate to one specific society—say, the United States—or, on the contrary, are universally applicable.

The democratic pluralists of the 1950s sometimes spoke as though they were addressing only the second of these questions, as if they were pursuing a strictly empirical inquiry into the actual workings of modern American democracy. But the questions are difficult to disentangle, and in fact the pluralists answered all four.

Their answers were heavily informed by their era—in particular, the calamitous rise of European fascism and Soviet-style communism. Nazi Germany and the Soviet Union under Stalin came to represent, for the pluralists as for most Americans, everything that democracy was *not*, everything that a healthy political system should be designed to avoid. They came to see totalitarianism as the antithesis of democracy, and democratic stability as the chief protection against totalitarianism. And, as the Cold War progressed, they sought an understanding of democracy that explained and made manifest the political superiority of America to the Soviet Union.

To borrow William Connolly's terminology, totalitarianism became for the pluralists what aristocracy had been for Tocqueville: the chief "contrast-model" for American democracy.[6] As we will see, it was a contrast-model peculiarly bound up with policing, because totalitarian countries were understood as "police states"—systems in which certain inherent logics of policing had run rampant, obliterating all traces of democracy. And it was a contrast-model from which the pluralists drew a series of strong lessons about the dangers of mass politics.

The Police State, Old and New

The term "police state," a translation of the German *Polizeistaat*, gained wide currency in the middle decades of the twentieth century—applied first to Nazi Germany, and then, during the Cold War, to the Soviet Union. But the English phrase dates back at least to the nineteenth century, and the original German term is older still. Originally, *Polizeistaat* referred to the style of governance associated with Prussia in the seventeenth and eighteenth centuries and, by the late eighteenth century, with Austria and France as well. These early "police states" sought to rationalize and to improve society through a tight, comprehensive system of regulation, administered by a disciplined and professional civil service, and overseen by an extensive apparatus of surveillance. The "police" in "police state" referred both to the regulatory system and to the surveillance officers.[7]

Brian Chapman, in his definitive, pluralist-era history of the concept of the "police state," suggested that professional police forces were resisted for so long in England in part precisely because they were associated both linguistically and historically with Prussian-style political systems—systems that seemed fundamentally at odds with the liberal idea of limited government. To avoid those connotations, Chapman noted, advocates of professional policing in Britain intentionally narrowed the meaning of "police," turning it into "a synonym for the constabulary."[8] The older, broader meaning of "police" survives in the American constitutional doctrine of "police power," the broad, open-ended power of states to protect, through regulation, "the security of social order, the life and health of the citizen, the comfort of an existence in a thickly populated community, the enjoyment of private and social life, and the beneficial use of property."[9] But this meaning of "police" is relatively uncommon, even among lawyers. In America as in Britain, "police" today means uniformed law enforcement personnel.

The narrowed meaning is important, because it influenced, in subtle ways, the Anglo-American understanding of totalitarianism—the new "police states" of the twentieth century. Nazi Germany and the postwar Soviet Union were often described, in the middle decades of the twentieth century, as societies in which the methods and mind-set of the police had been, in Chapman's words, "elevated to a theory of the state."[10] The "professional skepticism of policemen," their habitual invocation of "[t]he category of the suspect," their centuries-old "dream" of total knowledge as a tool of social control—all of this was thought to be characteristic of totalitarian systems as a whole.[11] Sometimes the "standards and methods" of totalitarianism were tied more precisely to the "secret police," instead of to the police more generally.[12] But even those who thought in these terms—Hannah Arendt, for example—tended to suggest that the secret police were guided, ultimately, by "the mentality of all policemen."[13]

Totalitarianism, which the pluralists took to be the antithesis of democracy, thus was widely understood in mid-twentieth-century America as a political system in which the logic of policing had run rampant. That suggested that the police themselves were totalitarianism writ small, and that preventing totalitarianism meant keeping the police, and all that they represented, within proper bounds. The hallmarks of totalitarian bureaucracies—"spying, brutality, arbitrary use of power, and preparedness to take the law into their own hands"—were also "integral part[s] of the nature of any police system."[14] Contrasting democracy with the "police state" therefore placed at the heart of pluralism certain ideas about the police, and certain implications about how the police should be "reconciled" with democracy. We will explore those implications in the next chapter. First, though, we need to flesh out the pluralist account of democracy.

Pluralism and the Fear of Mass Politics

The rise of Nazi Germany and Soviet-style communism left the pluralists not only with a visceral horror of totalitarianism, but also with a more specific distrust of mass politics—a distrust that then shaped and was in turn strengthened by their understanding of McCarthyism as a lineal descendant of Populism. They grew to see ideological extremism, which they associated with mass politics, as the paramount political vice; and compromise and moderation, which they associated with elites, as prerequisites for a stable democracy.[15] The "modern police state," they thought, was "the counterpart to passion and idealism in politics."[16]

All of this drove the pluralists toward an understanding of democracy that de-emphasized mass participation while still assuring the dispersion of political power. The chief obstacle to such an understanding lay in the long-standing celebration of grassroots politics in America, the universal "tumult" and "confusion" in which Tocqueville had found, admiringly, Americans of all "ranks" and "classes" engaged in the ongoing project of government.[17] Asking an American to consider only "his own affairs," Tocqueville wrote, would be like robbing him "of half his existence; he would feel an immense void in his days, and he would become incredibly unhappy."[18] Tocqueville saw widespread political participation as America's chief bulwark against despotism, and that view had at least as much surface appeal when the pluralists began writing as it does today. The imagery of the New England town meeting ran deep.

It was that imagery, above all else, that the pluralists rejected. They were not the first, of course. Max Weber had thought democracy in its full and traditional sense an inevitable casualty of the increasing complexity of modern government and the associated rise of bureaucracy.[19] He shared this view with his friend Robert Michels, author of the famous "iron law of oligarchy": "Who says organization, says oligarchy."[20] But Weber and Michels saw this dynamic as tragic. The pluralists, in contrast, thought low participation was not only required by modern circumstances, but a source and a reflection of democratic strength. They celebrated, rather than excused, the dramatic decline in grassroots political involvement the nation had witnessed since the close of the nineteenth century.[21]

The pluralists had nothing but derision for what David Truman, the only one of their number to rival Robert Dahl for influence, called "the myth of omnivigilant citizenship, the picture of the nation as a sort of continuous town meeting with perfect attendance."[22] Truman himself saw "considerable validity" in Joseph Wood Hutch's light essay, *Whom Do We Picket Tonight?*, which asked half seriously, "Wouldn't a really healthy citizen in a really healthy country be as unaware of the government as a healthy man is unaware of his physiology?"[23] Dahl himself was just as emphatic. It "would clear the air of a good deal of cant," he thought,

> if instead of assuming that politics is a normal and natural concern of human beings, one were to make the contrary assumption that whatever lip service citizens may pay to conventional attitudes, politics is a remote, alien, and unrewarding activity. Instead of seeking to explain why citizens are not interested, concerned, and active, the task is to explain why a few citizens *are*.[24]

"In liberal societies," Dahl concluded, "politics is a sideshow in the great circus of life."[25]

The most elaborate statement of this position came from Angus Campbell and his colleagues at the Survey Research Center at the University of Michigan, who in 1960 completed an analysis of election surveys conducted in 1952 and 1956. The results, published under the title *The American Voter*, revealed "an electorate almost wholly without detailed information about decision making in government" and "almost completely unable to judge the rationality of government actions."[26] The authors were neither surprised nor terribly troubled. "For a large part of the public," they supposed, "political affairs are probably too difficult to comprehend in detail."[27] More importantly, even those voters who *could* be well-informed had no reason to spend the time it would take: "It is a rather unusual individual whose deeper personality needs are engaged by politics, and in terms of rational self-interest, the stakes do not seem to be great enough for the ordinary citizen to justify expending the effort necessary to make himself well informed politically."[28]

The hope for democracy, the pluralists thought, lay not in the masses but in responsible leaders. The role of the masses was simply to help keep the leaders responsible.[29] This perspective was hardly new; the pluralists shared it most conspicuously with the Federalists.[30] But the Federalists lived in a different world. They had an Enlightenment faith in abstract moral truths and in the essential unity of human knowledge. They understood human conduct in the terms of political economy, as a fundamentally rational pursuit of individual self-interest. And they saw society as a voluntary assemblage of sovereign, atomistic individuals.[31] This world was as foreign to the pluralists as it is to us today. By the 1950s, abstract moral reasoning had a bad reputation among American intellectuals; it ran counter to the legacy of philosophical pragmatism and to the growing association of "ideology" with frightening exercises in utopianism—exercises that seemed inevitably to drift toward the totalitarian police state.[32] The pluralists thus had no use for Walter Lippman's brand of neo-Aristotelian elitism, which they thought amounted to "a kind of benevolent despotism in the guise of a set of Platonic guardians unhappily subject to the vagaries of popular election."[33] The pluralists' view of human nature was heavily colored by Freudianism, then still in its heyday.[34] And their understanding of society reflected the early twentieth-century triumph of the social science paradigm, which exalted "an ever-widening identification of self and world, individual and society, conceived not as a federation of autonomous agents, but as an indivisible union of interdependent parts."[35]

For all these reasons, the pluralists could not place their trust where the Federalists had placed theirs, in constitutional machinery balancing "ambition" against "ambition."[36] Dahl's *Preface to Democratic Theory*, probably his most influential book, was framed in large part as a critique of "Madisonian democracy," which Dahl found at odds with "modern concepts of behavior" and the findings of "contemporary social scientist[s]."[37] Similarly, David

Truman began *The Governmental Process* by invoking and then rejecting Madison's famous call for institutional guards against "factions."[38] Dahl and Truman, like the pluralists more generally, thought the real prerequisites for a successful democracy were "social" rather than "constitutional."[39] As Dahl put it, the Constitution did not keep the United States democratic; rather, "the Constitution has remained because our *society* is essentially democratic."[40]

To find the essence of democracy, the pluralists turned not to institutions but to the twentieth-century understanding of society. More specifically, they turned to four fixtures of the new social science paradigm: consumerism, groups, consensus, and personality.

Pluralism and Consumerism

First, consumerism. The rise of mass markets in late-nineteenth-century America seemed to call for a new understanding of the relation between individuals and the economy, to replace the old model of the free market as a kind of tumultuous bazaar in which buyers and sellers, comparably situated, negotiated face-to-face bargains informed by the shouting all around them. A new model emerged that acknowledged the passive nature of modern consumption.[41] Demand could be cultivated and channeled; this was what made the mass market useful to society. Rather than independent agents, merchants and customers were part of an interconnected whole. The role of merchants was to promote demand and then to satisfy it; the role of customers was to enjoy the better life made possible by new and cheaper products. The model retained a remnant of the invisible hand: acting *en masse*, consumers presumably set some limits to the pliability of demand.[42] As long as sellers competed for customers, good detergent at the same price should still drive out bad detergent.[43] But the heart of consumerism was the idea that average people found their freedom not in the market itself, but in what the market produced.

The pluralists of the 1950s did not need to extend the theory of consumerism into the realm of politics: Joseph Schumpeter had already done it for them. Writing in 1942, Schumpeter stressed the parallel between mass markets and modern elections. Democracy consisted simply of pitting would-be leaders against each other in "a competitive struggle for the people's vote";[44] "the reins of government" were "handed over to those who command more support than do any of the competing individuals or teams."[45] Political campaigns functioned exactly like commercial advertising.[46] And just as economic competition was generally imperfect but "never completely lacking," so "in political life there is always some competition, though perhaps only a potential one, for the allegiance of the people."[47] The "social function" of democratic politics was "fulfilled, as it were, incidentally—in the same sense as production is incidental to the making of profits."[48]

Like the pluralists after him, Schumpeter argued that the system actually worked better when average citizens stayed relatively uninvolved in politics. The political world was remote from the day-to-day lives of average citizens, so they were unlikely to care much about it or to approach it with a sense of responsibility:

> Normally, the great political questions take their place in the psychic economy of the typical citizen with those leisure-hour interests that have not attained the rank of hobbies, and with the subjects of irresponsible conversation. These things seem so far off; they are not at all like a business proposition; dangers may not materialize at all and if they should they may not prove so very serious; one feels oneself to be moving in a fictitious world.[49]

With respect to political matters, the average citizen was "a member of an unworkable committee, the committee of the whole nation," and therefore "he expends less disciplined effort on mastering a political problem than he expends on a game of a bridge."[50]

Schumpeter's understanding of electoral politics as akin to mass marketing, together with his rejection of the "town meeting" picture of American democracy, heavily influenced the pluralists.[51] Unlike Schumpeter, the pluralists thought elections actually gave voters a significant amount of control over leaders, but they agreed with him that the control was limited and indirect, because "[t]he public's explicit task is to decide not what government shall do but rather *who shall decide* what government shall do."[52] The pluralists also shared Schumpeter's understanding of democracy as simply "a political *method*," not "an end in itself."[53] Democracy was desirable, Schumpeter believed, only to the extent that it can be expected to advance other interests or ideals, such as individual freedom.[54] Schumpeter did in fact think that democracy could be expected to protect individual freedom, although only as a very general matter; the relationship was contingent and far from secure.[55] His legacy to the pluralists, though, included the notion that "the value of the democratic system for ordinary individuals should be measured by the degree to which the 'outputs' of the system, in the form of security, services, and material support, benefit them," and that therefore, "the less the individual has to participate in politics on the 'input' and demand side of the system in order to gain his interests on the output side, the better off he is."[56]

Pluralism and Groups

The pluralists' debt to Schumpeter has so frequently been emphasized that their differences from him are sometimes overlooked. It is good to keep those differences in mind, because they help to bring pluralism into sharper focus. The pluralists shared Schumpeter's consumerist view of the purpose of democracy; they agreed it was simply a method for arriving at good policies. They shared his view that an election was more like a supermarket than a town hall, and they placed the same emphasis he did on "the vital fact of leadership."[57] But Schumpeter took an especially bleak view of the ability of ordinary citizens to think rationally about politics. The remoteness of political questions from everyday life meant not only that most people found it hard to care much about politics, but that, when they did care, they were apt to act foolishly and irresponsibly. The average person, Schumpeter thought, "drops down to a lower level of mental performance as soon as he enters the political field," reasoning "in a way which he would readily recognize as infantile within the sphere of his real interests."[58] And "if for once he does emerge from his usual vagueness" about political matters, the typical citizen "is as likely as not to become still more unintelligent and irresponsible."[59] Public opinions were largely "manufactured" by the political process; this was why Schumpeter thought elections were unlikely to give voters even indirect control of government in any meaningful sense.[60]

Consequently, Schumpeter argued that the success of democracy depended at bottom on a fairly rigid class structure, a healthy dose of "traditionalism," and a great deal of political quietude.[61] It required, first of all, a stable, elite "social stratum" that saw political leadership as its special calling.[62] Next, a separate, intermediate stratum—"not too rich, not too poor, not too exclusive, not too accessible"—was needed to staff a powerful, professional bureaucracy.[63] Certain issues then had to be placed off-limits to democratic politics—by, for example, delegating them to independent agencies.[64]

Most important of all was what Schumpeter called "Democratic Self-Control,"[65] by which he meant much more than broad acceptance of "the rules of the democratic game."[66] Voters and elected officials had to be sufficiently smart and upright to resist "the offerings of the crook and the crank."[67] Backers of particular programs had to be "content to stand in an orderly breadline; they must not attempt to rush the shop."[68] And ordinary citizens had to confine their political activity to voting: "they must understand that, once they have elected an individual, political action is his business and not theirs."[69]

Schumpeter's prerequisites for a successful democracy pretty clearly excluded the United States, even in the relative calm of the postwar period. His model seems to have been Victorian England,[70] augmented by a European-style civil service.[71] He thought civil services of this kind were bound to expand of their own accord, "whatever the political method a nation may adopt"; their growth was "the one certain thing about our future."[72] But if a successful democracy required a stable class system and a politics of "self-control," it was hard to be optimistic about America. Schumpeter himself was comfortable with pessimism. His book amounted to an extended requiem for bourgeois capitalism, which he thought was done in by its own successes—including modern democracy.[73] But to the pluralists American democracy seemed to be thriving. They therefore searched for the ingredients of democratic success someplace other than in social stratification and a culture of restraint.

They found it in groups. Schumpeter's view of "pressure groups" was close to Madison's: he saw them as a kind of democratic disease, aberrational and injurious.[74] The pluralists, in contrast, celebrated interest groups as the lifeblood of modern democracy.[75]

They took their lead here from Arthur Bentley, who described society in 1908 as "nothing other than the complex of groups that compose it."[76] Bentley had hardly originated the notion that groups rather than individuals were the key unit of social analysis. "Group theory," based in part on studies in the newly emerging field of anthropology, was a broad intellectual current in America at the beginning of the twentieth century.[77] Bentley's contribution was to apply group theory, in a particularly uncompromising form, to the study of politics. He wrote at a propitious time: the Progressive Era, as Mark Kornbluh has stressed, saw the "emergence of a wide variety of specialized political associations organized along particularistic rather than geographic and partisan lines," with the result that voters increasingly "found themselves cross-pressured by conflicting forces."[78] Bentley seized on the new political realities. "When groups are adequately stated," he wrote, "everything is stated. When I say everything I mean everything."[79] Politics was competition among groups, no more and no less. Groups meant interests: every group had its interest, and interests manifested themselves only through groups. There was no such thing as the "social whole"; there were only groups working against each other.[80] Government was the balancing or adjustment of group interests,[81] and the eventual resolution inevitably reflected the relative strengths of the underlying groups.[82]

Bentley took his pragmatism as seriously as he took his group theory; the one-sentence foreword to his book declared it "an attempt to fashion a tool."[83] He therefore had nothing but scorn for the notion that government should be detached and impartial. Abstract standards such as "justice, truth, or what not" were simply products and manifestations of group pressures. Reason itself was just one "technique" for balancing those pressures,[84] and an overrated technique at that. Parties would do better to "drop their set, formal, logically coherent policies," and simply give "more efficient expression to the underlying interests they represent."[85]

Unlike the pluralists, Bentley had relatively little interest in the nature of democracy or in the special conditions for its success. In his view all forms of government amounted to the same thing: "interest groups wrestling with one another."[86] But he ventured that perhaps "pure despotism" and "pure democracy" could be understood as hypothetical extremes at opposite ends of a continuum, with despotism "consisting of an individual who passes personally on every group antagonism at its inception and allays it by appropriate action"; and democracy involving "a government in which every interest would be able to find a technique for organizing and expressing itself in a system in which every other interest was equally represented on 'fair' terms, so that in the final course of action all interests would get their 'due' weight."[87] And he suggested in passing that the dispersed form of interest adjustment found in "governments like that of the United States" was remarkable "for the trifling proportion of physical violence involved considering the ardent nature of the struggles."[88]

Bentley's account of government through interest groups received little attention until after World War II, when the pluralists picked it up and ran with it.[89] They embraced his view of society as a complex of groups, they liked his notion that logrolling and lobbying were the very stuff of governance rather than a degradation of some pristine ideal, and they were intrigued by his suggestion that democracy might be stabilizing and pacifying. Like Bentley, the pluralists viewed group conflict as the essence of politics. And like Bentley, the pluralists were struck by the scattered, multiplicitous adjustments of those conflicts in the United States. They came to see the diversity of interest groups in the United States, and the diversity of mechanisms for the balancing of group interests, as signal strengths of American democracy.

This was the "pluralism" in democratic pluralism. It should not be minimized. For all their discomfort with mass politics, the pluralists had no touch of pastoral traditionalism. They placed their faith in precisely those aspects of modernity—industrialization, urbanization—that people like Ortega y Gasset found so threatening.[90] Old affiliations might be swept aside, but new ones arose in their place.[91] The image of the town meeting left the pluralists cold, not just because it seemed inapplicable to national politics; the image smacked of nostalgia for small-town life, and the pluralists were moderns. They shared the broad tendency of intellectuals in postwar America to associate democracy with "the intricate, many-faceted, cultural life of the metropolis,"[92] and more specifically with a freewheeling, distinctly urban cosmopolitanism, expressed through "a culture that denied absolute truths, remained intellectually flexible and critical, valued diversity, and drew strength from innumerable competing subgroups."[93]

Adding together interest-group lobbying and electoral control, the pluralists arrived at a much rosier view than Schumpeter regarding the ability of average citizens to exert meaningful control over government. Individuals might not have many ways to influence government policy, but groups did. David Truman suggested "the outstanding characteristic of American politics" was its "multiplicity of points of access," its "decentralized and more or less independent" loci of influence over government decision making.[94] Robert Dahl also praised the "decentralized" nature of American politics, which made it likely "that any active and legitimate group will make itself heard effectively at some stage in the process of decision."[95] In his influential study of how pressure groups shaped federal legislation governing freight delivery charges, Earl Latham commended lobbying and backroom bargaining—the hobgoblins of "good government" reformers—as triumphs of American democracy. It was "impossible to witness the process," he thought, "without admiration" for the manner in which it allowed "a free people" to "refine[] and sift[]" a "fantastically complicated question of public policy."[96]

The pluralists were not in complete accord about the nature of groups. Latham, for example, thought groups served solely to promote the preexisting interests of their members; they were "devices" through which "the individual fulfills personal values and felt needs."[97] In contrast, Truman saw groups as not simply reflecting individual interests but helping to shape them. Groups molded attitudes and behavior; they were "the primary, though not the exclusive, means by which the individual knows, interprets, and reacts to the society in which he exists."[98] (Dahl seemed to side with Truman.)[99] But the pluralists all agreed that groups were "the basic political form"[100] and a key to the success of American democracy. And they agreed that group politics functioned not just outside government but also within it: between branches, between agencies, between bureaus and branch offices, and so on.[101] Official and unofficial groups were "inhabitants of one pluralistic world,"[102] and government bureaucracies were part of "the 'normal' American political process."[103]

The pluralists were optimistic about group politics in the United States for several related reasons. First, they thought America was particularly rich with groups. They liked Tocqueville's notion that in no other nation had "the principle of association been more successfully used or applied to a greater multitude of objects,"[104] and they thought the observation as sound in the mid-twentieth century as in the early nineteenth. Second, they believed groups were constantly forming and evolving in response to changing circumstances and changing interests. In Latham's words, the process was "dynamic, not static; fluid, not fixed"; society was "a moving multitude of human clusters," combining to "form coalitions and constellations of power in a flux of restless alterations."[105] Third, the pluralists thought that the nature of group politics in the United States worked to stabilize the system and to prevent any one group from gaining too much power. It was not just that there were so many groups, but also that the groups overlapped in complicated ways, that they focused on different but intersecting sets of issues, and that each group tended to enjoy its own distinctive array of political resources—some had time, some had money, some had expertise, some had social connections, and so on.[106]

The strength of the system lay in "complexity, or more to the point, multiplicity: multiplicity of issues, multiplicity of groups, multiplicity of memberships, multiplicity of influence resources, and multiplicity of access or check points."[107] Dahl called the pluralist political ideal "polyarchy."[108] All the multiplicity meant that American politics "worked essentially by bargaining."[109] In Dahl's memorable formulation, the United States had a system not of "government by a majority" nor of "government by a minority," but rather of "rule by *minorities*."[110] American democracy was "not a majestic march of great majorities united upon certain matters of basic policy"; instead it was "the steady appeasement of small groups."[111]

Pluralism and Consensus

All this bargaining—all this "flux of restless alterations"—held together only because of a powerful underlying consensus. After consumerism and group theory, the notion of consensus was the third social science fixture incorporated by the pluralists, and William Connolly may have been right to call it "the most important force sustaining political pluralism."[112] The pluralists thought that a successful democracy on the American model required two kinds of consensus.

The first was rough agreement about the range of reasonable policy alternatives. Dahl, in particular, stressed that unless the options on the table were somehow "winnowed down to those within [a] broad area of basic agreement," democracy "would not long survive the endless irritations and frustrations of elections and party competition." Consequently, democracy depended on an "underlying consensus on policy" among "a predominant portion of the politically active members" of society.[113] Second, and even more fundamental, there had to be broad agreement on underlying democratic norms—what Truman, echoing Schumpeter, called the "rules of the game."[114] The pluralists thought that "social training" in the "rules of the game" was critical to the success of a democracy.[115] The precise nature of these underlying norms was never completely clear, but their core seemed to be "respect for the dignity of man"[116] and dedication to the "rule of law."[117] Both of these commitments had important implications for the problem of democratic policing—implications we will take up in the next chapter.

The pluralists also agreed that the critical figures in forging consensus both on policies and on procedural norms were members of an elite "political stratum"[118]: "the politically active and articulate portion of the population."[119] Unlike Schumpeter's stable, class-based leadership stratum, the pluralist elite was in theory porous and heterogeneous.[120] It was for all that an elite, comprising not just government officials, but also, crucially, leaders of interest groups and shapers of public opinion. Members of the political stratum were apt to be better educated and more effectively trained in democratic values. They also tended to belong to more groups, and their leadership roles made them more worldly. The consensus at the heart of pluralism was thus an "elite consensus,"[121] a consensus formed through "the affiliations of the guardians."[122] As Michael Rogin put it, pluralism ultimately was "not the politics of group conflict but the politics of leadership conflict."[123]

Pluralism and Personality

The fourth and final social science concept relied upon by the pluralists was personality, in the Freudian sense of a complex, largely unconscious mental structure governing attitudes and behavior. The pluralists were particularly attracted to the notion that democratic and antidemocratic values were psychologically embedded, and that, in particular, there was something that could be called "the authoritarian personality."[124] The widely influential book first articulating this view described the authoritarian "character structure"[125] as including all of the following dispositions: "[r]igid adherence to conventional, middle-class values"; a "[s]ubmissive, uncritical attitude toward idealized moral authorities of the ingroup"; a "[t]endency to be on the lookout for, and to condemn, reject, and punish people who violate conventional values"; "[o]pposition to the subjective, the imaginative, and the tender-minded"; a "belief in mystical determinants of the individual's faith"; a "disposition to think in rigid categories"; a "[p]reoccupation" with "[p]ower and 'toughness'"; a "[g]eneralized hostility" and "vilification of the human"; a "disposition to believe that wild and dangerous things go on in the world"; a "projection outwards of unconscious emotional impulses"; and an "[e]xaggerated concern with sexual 'goings-on.'"[126]

This cluster of dispositions, the authoritarian personality, was thought to be especially prevalent among those with low to moderate levels of education, income, and political activity—that is to say, among people outside the political stratum.[127] Police officers, in particular, came to be seen as prime exemplars of the authoritarian personality; as we will see in the next chapter, that understanding had broad implications for the regulation of law enforcement. Beyond that, though, the role of personality in politics gave the pluralists another reason to leave the day-to-day functions of democracy to the elite. For reasons of individual psychology, broadening political participation was likely to mean bringing "the authoritarian-minded into the political arena."[128] Mass politics was authoritarian politics; democratic politics was, paradoxically, elite politics.

The notion of the authoritarian personality reinforced and in turn was strengthened by the pluralist emphasis on bargaining, for part of what distinguished "the authoritarian-minded" was precisely their extremism, their discomfort with compromise, their affinity for "total politics."[129] They cared too much; they were too reluctant to yield. They were overly attracted to the revolutionary aspirations that by the 1950s had come to seem like a "deep betrayal, treason not only to the narrow interests of the United States but to the basic values of Western civilization."[130] Democratic politics was thus elite politics in part because average citizens, if they became politically engaged, were likely to become engaged in the wrong way. They were apt to become "highly partisan" if not "rigidly fanatic."[131] Democracy depended on "an implicit division of political labor," in which the bulk of the work was left to those who could occupy the psychological middle ground between indifference and extremism.[132] What democracy required from most citizens was "occasional political participation . . . some of the time, and a moderate and dim perceptiveness—as if from the corner of the eye—the rest of the time. It could not function if politics and the state of social order were always on everyone's mind."[133]

The psychoanalytic orientation of the pluralists contributed to their mixed position on the subject of expertise. On the one hand, the pluralists shared Dewey's disdain for Platonic "philosopher kings," a disdain that by the 1950s had become intellectual orthodoxy.[134] And their attraction to Bentley's group theory of politics made them unsympathetic to "good government" managerialism of the kind associated with Herbert Hoover. They did not believe government was or should be a science. On the other hand, they did believe that government, and our views about government, should be *informed* by science, and by social science in particular. They saw themselves, after all, as bringing social science to bear on the practical problems of democracy.[135] They were empiricists—often in methodology, and always in disposition. An important part of their empiricism was rooted in Freud. They shared his faith in the analyst's ability to subjugate the irrational through detached inquiry, and they tended to see themselves as engaged in essentially the same project.[136] And, of course, they had little confidence in the ability of the average citizen to think rationally about public affairs, and a strong belief in the importance of delegating the main work of politics. All of this meant that respect for certain kinds of expertise—particularly scientific and professional expertise—suffused democratic pluralism.[137]

Summing Up

We finally are in a position to summarize the pluralist account of democracy. Consider in turn the four dimensions of democracy we identified earlier: purposes, processes, proximity, and particularity.

Purposes. The pluralists saw democracy not as end in itself, but as purely instrumental, a means of protection against violent upheavals and authoritarianism. Individuals were prior to politics. The purposes of democracy were to promote stability and to preserve a certain baseline of civil liberty.

Processes. The pluralists believed that democracy depended at bottom not on specific institutional arrangements, but rather on personality and culture.

They spoke of democratic *societies*, not democratic governments. The one institutional arrangement they did think critical was election of the officials with final say over government policy. But the true engines of politics were groups, both inside and outside government, and democratic politics required resolving group conflicts through competition, bargaining, and compromise. Those processes in turn required that politically active members of the community have democratic personalities, be trained in democratic norms, and share a rough consensus about the range of acceptable policies. These conditions, finally, were easier to secure when politics was largely the province of an elite, and the elite in turn made appropriate use of scientific and technical expertise.

Proximity. The pluralists thought that American democracy, while obviously imperfect, was on the whole fair, open, and remarkably successful. They therefore believed it far less important to improve the system than to recognize and to preserve its strengths. This orientation, in turn, reinforced and accentuated their concern with political stability.[138]

Particularity. Pluralism was very much a theory of *American* democracy. Partly because democracy was a property of a society rather than of a system of government, the pluralists did not assume that what worked here would work elsewhere.[139] American democracy was part and parcel of America's distinctive culture: daring, restive, and optimistic.[140] The pluralists, in short, were American exceptionalists, joining fully in the postwar "celebration of American deviation from Old World tradition."[141] In this respect, as in so many others, they were of their time. They lived and worked in a period when, as Edward Purcell has written, America seemed to many people "more and more a norm in itself, standing for practical democratic achievement and the fulfillment of that last, best hope."[142]

CHAPTER 2

"Where Officers Are Under the Law"

Pluralist Policing

By the end of the 1960s a commitment to democracy was broadly under-stood to carry with it a certain set of implications for policing. Those impli-cations reflected, in part, the distinctive theory of American democracy that held sway for most of the 1960s, the theory of democratic pluralism; but they also reflected a reform agenda that predated pluralism, the agenda of police professionalism. Democratic pluralism and police professionalism drew strength from each other, and the intersection of these two sets of ideas does much to explain the particular content given to the ideal of democratic policing from the late 1950s through the 1970s.

Democratic policing in this period meant, above all, bringing the police under the "rule of law": reining in the discretion of individual officers through rigid regulations and tight judicial supervision; zealously safeguard-ing the personal dignity of criminal suspects; and, in the process, reconcil-ing police agencies to the values and practical realities of modern urban life. These commitments did much to shape academic studies of the police in the 1950s, 1960s, and 1970s. They found expression, too, in the Supreme Court's "criminal procedure revolution"—the landmark series of restrictions imposed on law enforcement during the tenure of Chief Justice Earl Warren, and then largely preserved under his successor, Chief Justice Warren Burger.

The conception of democratic policing reflected in these rulings, and in the voluminous scholarship on the police produced during the Warren Court and Burger Court eras, still has many defenders, but it no longer can claim the status of orthodoxy. In the courts and in the academy, the "rule of law" approach to democratic policing—what we might call pluralist policing—is increasingly under attack. I will address the nature and significance of those attacks later in this book. In this chapter, I want to examine pluralist policing in its heyday, and to explore the ways in which it was tied to an underlying account of American politics—democratic pluralism—that itself has since fallen from favor. That investigation must start with a discussion of police professionalism, the older reform agenda that was reinvigorated and subtly reoriented by its encounter, in the 1950s and 1960s, with the then ascendant ideas of the democratic pluralists.

Police Professionalism, Before and After the Pluralists

Modern criminal procedure began, more or less, in the 1920s and 1930s. It was then that the Supreme Court, largely as a result of Prohibition, began to confront the kinds of search-and-seizure issues that have come to constitute such a large part of criminal procedure law—electronic surveillance,[1] automobile searches,[2] the use of informants,[3] and so on. More importantly, it was during the interwar period that the Supreme Court first applied the federal Constitution to overturn state criminal convictions—a pivotal move, because law enforcement in the United States was and remains chiefly a responsibility of state and local governments.[4] The seeds of Warren Court criminal procedure thus were planted long before the pluralists began to write.[5]

Unsurprisingly, though, the criminal procedure decisions of the 1920s and 1930s were rooted in concerns different in many respects from those that were later to occupy the pluralists. The Court's initial forays into state criminal procedure are best understood as responses to the worst excesses of Jim Crow: cases in which black defendants were sentenced to death with barely the facade of trial.[6] The Court confronted trials held in the midst of lynch mobs,[7] trials in which black defendants were denied anything resembling adequate counsel,[8] trials held before juries from which blacks were flatly excluded,[9] trials based on confessions obtained from black defendants by torture.[10] These were race cases, not democracy cases. More precisely, if they were democracy cases it was largely *because* they were race cases—and race was never central to the pluralist account of democracy. Here, for example, is Dahl: "[P]erhaps in no society have the conditions of polyarchy been so fully present as they were in the United States in the ante-bellum period (save, of course, for the position of Negroes)."[11] Pluralism was compatible with a certain measured egalitarianism, but on the whole the pluralists tended to think that groups could fend for themselves, even groups as historically disadvantaged as African Americans.[12]

Of the state criminal procedure cases the Court decided in the 1920s and 1930s, only *Brown v. Mississippi*, the confession-by-torture decision, involved the police. *Brown* became the basis for a series of coerced confession decisions in the 1940s, a line of cases that as it progressed had less and less to do with race and more and more to do with police brutality.[13] In is hard to find democratic pluralism in those decisions, but it is easy to see echoes of police professionalism, a reform movement reaching back to the last decade of the nineteenth century that was reinvigorated and reached new heights of influence in the middle of the twentieth century.

Police professionalism meant politically insulated police departments organized along hierarchical, quasi-military lines, with strong commitments to efficient operations, centralized command, technological sophistication, well-trained personnel, and high standards of integrity.[14] The roots of the movement lay in the "good government" managerialism of the Progressive Era and the interwar period.[15] Managerialism of this kind could hardly have been more antithetical to the thinking of a proto-pluralist like Arthur Bentley, but it permeated the work of the National Commission of Law Observance and Enforcement, appointed by President Herbert Hoover and chaired by George Wickersham.[16] The Wickersham Commission was sharply and famously critical of "the third degree," which it viewed as simply one, particularly egregious instance of the general problem of "lawlessness in law enforcement."[17] That criticism, so fully in accord with the "good government" approach to police reform, helped lay the groundwork for the coerced confession cases of the 1940s.

Although the roots of police professionalism thus lay in reform movements of the late nineteenth and early twentieth centuries, it entered a new phase in the 1950s. Early police reformers, drawn mainly from the ranks of civic and religious groups,[18] had aimed above all to get officers out of the hands of ward bosses and into the front lines in the fight against crime and, more particularly, vice. Their principal organizational strategies, shifting control from precincts to headquarters and adopting quasi-military lines of command, were adopted and expanded in the 1930s through the 1960s by a different set of reformers for a different set of ends. The historian Robert Fogelson calls this the "second wave" of American police reform.[19] It crested in the 1950s and early 1960s.

The second-wave reformers differed from their predecessors in several ways. They were police administrators, not civic or religious crusaders, and they tended to see police departments first and foremost as organizations, not all that different from military or industrial units.[20] They continued to insist on the political independence of the police, but their primary concerns were administrators' concerns: streamlining operations, strengthening lines of command, raising the quality of personnel, leveraging personnel with technology, clarifying the organizational mission, and building public support. Because they thought the mission of the police was crime control, they fought to rid the police of other, distracting responsibilities, like operating lockups or running youth programs.[21] And—like the pluralists—they viewed the public through the lens of consumerism, as a market that was and should be cultivated and directed.[22]

Chief William Parker of the Los Angeles Police Department, which in the 1950s emerged as the leading model of police professionalism,[23] was particularly clear about this last point. Like a private business, he argued, the police could not be successful without a market, and markets had to be created: "They seldom spring full-blown from the unshaped desires of the people. The vital elements of our civilized life, including our most sacred institutions, at one time or another have been laboriously *sold* to the people." The way to do this was to first to sell the police mission to "practical community leaders"; they would then help to sell it to the public. The key point was that public demands should be shaped to conform to the mission of the police department, and not the other way around. (Parker did not like the term "public relations," precisely because he thought it suggested too much responsiveness on the part of the police.)[24]

Much more than the first wave of reformers, the second wave took "professionalism" as their watchword.[25] By professionalism they emphatically did not mean that police officers should have substantial latitude to exercise trained judgment in matters of importance, nor did they mean that police officers should regulate themselves collectively in the manner of a guild. Rather, they had in mind enhanced prestige for the occupation of policing, high standards of integrity for officers, improved training, insulation from partisan politics, and the application of modern concepts of administration. It was a professionalism of *police forces*, not of *police officers*. It claimed autonomy "primarily for the institution of policing, and only secondarily, and then only in a severely limited sense, for its functionaries."[26]

In a variety of ways, police professionalism cohered well with democratic pluralism and the "rule of law" approach to democratic policing. We will explore several of these points of congruence later in this chapter, but two deserve mention now.

First, police professionalism, like pluralist policing, sought to give individual officers less leeway rather than more. The strong position of leading law enforcement administrators in favor of stricter standards for officers did much to create a climate hospitable to heightened judicial oversight of the police. In return, the judiciary proved highly receptive to the claims of quasi-scientific expertise made by police executives like William Parker.

When, for example, the Supreme Court promulgated the *Miranda* rules for police interrogations, it couched its decision as extending to state and local police certain longtime practices of the Federal Bureau of Investigation, practices which the Court suggested had not interfered with the FBI's "exemplary record of effective law enforcement."[27] Later the Court pursued an analogous strategy when it gave constitutional status to the emerging practice of metropolitan police departments to restrict the use of lethal force against fleeing felons.[28] Similarly, the Court carved out exceptions to the warrant and probable cause requirements for certain inventory searches conducted pursuant to internal regulations.[29] Writing in one of these case for a unanimous Court, Chief Justice Burger stressed that the justices were "hardly in a position to second-guess police departments as to what practical administrative method" was most appropriate for inventory searches.[30]

Second-guessing police *officers* was something else entirely. As we will see later in this chapter, the whole effort to rein in police discretion through judicial oversight—the lynchpin of the "rule of law" approach to democratic policing—amounted to institutionalized second-guessing of the police, and it was defended on precisely those grounds. But the judgments of forward-thinking police administrators were a different matter.

Second, police professionalism, like constitutional constraints on the police, offered a way to protect policing from mass politics while preserving, at least in form, the tradition of local control. That tradition was widely thought to guard against authoritarianism: it kept the police close to the communities they served, and it prevented the emergence of an American Fouché.[31]

Even J. Edgar Hoover—the closest this country ever came to a home-grown version of Napoleon's security chief—disavowed any interest in transforming the FBI into a national police force. Law enforcement, he agreed, should remain primarily a local responsibility, controlled by authorities attuned to "the pulse of the community"; centralized policing would pose "a distinct danger to democratic self-government."[32] Public opinion, as Justice Frankfurter wrote for the Supreme Court, could "far more effectively be exerted against oppressive conduct on the part of police directly responsible to the community itself" than against "remote authority pervasively exerted throughout the country."[33] But local politics seemed to offer fewer mechanisms for mediating group conflicts through elite consensus, and more opportunities for factions to seize control of the police for their own purposes.[34] That was the lesson of the police torture cases of the 1920s and 1930s. Police professionalism offered a solution: decentralization without true community control. By the 1970s this arrangement had begun to look to many people like a sham,[35] but in the 1950s and through most of the 1960s it seemed a logical response to the "political meddling . . . facilitated by local control of police forces."[36]

The Group Psychology of the Police

The distinctive outlook of democratic pluralism is absent, unsurprisingly, from the criminal procedure decisions of the early twentieth century— decisions that predated the pluralists by several decades. In contrast, democratic pluralism finds clear reflection in the criminal procedure decisions of the Warren and Burger Courts, and in the scholarship about policing that accompanied and informed those decisions. Democratic pluralism was not the only intellectual influence on criminal procedure in this period; it may not even have been the most important. But pluralism, particularly in combination with police professionalism, helps us make sense of several interrelated hallmarks of criminal procedure and police studies in the Warren and Burger Court eras: a deference, already noted, to the expertise of law enforcement executives; a focus on the group psychology of the police; a concern with police discretion and a reliance on judicial oversight; an emphasis on personal dignity; an embrace of modernity; a preoccupation with consensus; and a persistent disregard of institutional structure. Of these, the focus on the group psychology of the police was perhaps the most fundamental: it provided the motivation and the conceptual frame for the lion's share of police studies in the 1950s and 1960s, and a powerful subtext to an enduring system of criminal procedure rules crafted by the Warren Court. It also, as we will see, resonated strongly with the pluralists' concerns about the "authoritarian personality."

The year that Earl Warren became Chief Justice of the Supreme Court, 1953, also marked a turning point in scholarship about the police. The few prior studies of policing tended to be the work of journalists, of public figures like George Wickersham and his fellow commissioners, or of reform-minded police executives.[37] There was no tradition of independent, academic examination of American police. That changed with the publication in 1953 of two pioneering and highly influential articles, one by the sociologist William Westley and the other by the legal scholar Jerome Hall.[38] Westley's study, adapted from a doctoral dissertation later published in its entirety,[39] reported the results of firsthand observation of and interviews with working police officers. Hall's article was an "emergence study" of the modern law and practice of policing. Both authors focused on the ways in which the actual operations of police departments conflicted with "democratic ideals"[40] and "legal mandate";[41] both sought to understand the "basic causes" of those conflicts;[42] and both believed that the causes were to be found in social relations—relations among police officers, and relations between police officers and the wider society. In each of these respects, the work of Westley and Hall set the pattern for the many academic studies of the police published during the Warren and Burger Court eras.[43]

Westley, in particular, set the pattern in another respect as well. Drawing heavily on the group theory incorporated within democratic pluralism, Westley argued that the key to understanding the police was to analyze them "as a social and occupational group."[44] More precisely, the police were a "conflict group,"[45] united by the manner in which the job they shared isolated them from the community and threatened their collective sense of status. The police officer "felt himself to be a pariah"[46] and came to "regard the public as an enemy."[47] The collective alienation of police officers drove them to create a distinctive set of group norms, at war in important respects with "formalized social controls."[48] The norms of the police approved the selective use of illegal violence against suspects, for example, and they forbade officers to testify against each other. New recruits were systematically indoctrinated into both norms.

Westley thus thought that the key to understanding the police was to understand their shared mentality, and that the key to their shared mentality was the nature of their job, including the ways in which their job estranged them from the community and threatened their collective self-esteem. This set of premises—"the Policeman as Other"—became the central motif of police sociology in the 1960s and 1970s.[49] They link together, for example, the work of James Q. Wilson and Jerome Skolnick, two scholars whose perspectives are in other respects very different.[50]

Wilson and Skolnick shared another premise. Like other police scholars of the era, they believed that the psychology of the police was shaped not just by occupational role and outcast status, but also by a cluster of dispositions that officers brought with them to the job. Wilson speculated that the "working-class backgrounds" of police officers inclined them to view violence as legitimate and gave them "a preoccupation with maintaining self-respect, proving one's masculinity, 'not taking any crap,' and not being 'taken in.'"[51] Skolnick found it plain that "a Goldwater-type of conservatism was the dominant political and emotional persuasion of police."[52] The worldview of the police included a simplistic, acontextual understanding of criminality, an apprehensive traditionalism, an intolerance for nonconformity, and a hostility to permissive child rearing.[53] It sounded very much like the "authoritarian personality." Skolnick himself hesitated to call the police mentality "authoritarian," but others did not.[54] And even Skolnick's hesitation stemmed not from doubts about the accuracy or descriptive value of term,[55] but rather from a belief that the dispositions in question were shared with the "great mass of people."[56] That was what the pluralists thought, too.

The notion that the police have a distinctive mentality—rigid, insecure, inclined toward violence, hostile to anyone "different"—became widespread by the late 1960s, particularly on the Left and particularly after the 1968 Democratic Convention in Chicago.[57] It does not appear explicitly in the Warren and Burger Courts' criminal procedure decisions, but it is hard not to sense in some of those cases a degree of lurking wariness about the group psychology of the police. When insisting that searches and seizures be conducted pursuant to warrant, for example, the Court liked to quote Justice Jackson's famous warning in *United States v. Johnson* that the decision should not be entrusted to "the officer engaged in the often competitive enterprise of ferreting out crime."[58] So fond was the Court of this formulation that one begins to suspect it was, at least at times, a diplomatic way to address worries beyond an excess of zeal. Justice Jackson himself seemed concerned that the "point" of the Fourth Amendment was "often not grasped" by the police, even in their reflective moments,[59] and that concern was echoed in the Court's later opinions.[60] Herbert Packer, hardly unsympathetic to the direction the Warren Court took in criminal procedure, suggested in 1966 that "[t]o anywhere from five to nine members of the Court, depending on how hair-raising the facts of the particular case appear to be, the police are suspect." The judiciary in general, Packer explained, was "unconvinced that the police regard the rights of the accused as anything but a nuisance and an impediment."[61] Packer shared that skepticism, as did many if not most legal scholars writing in the 1960s and 1970s. Their concerns about the police mentality were only heightened by developments to which we will return later: the nature of police responses to rioting and political demonstrations in the late 1960s, and the campaigns that law enforcement administrators and police unions mounted against key Warren Court rulings and against emerging proposals for civilian review boards.

Ideas about social psychology are not necessarily ideas about democracy. But the two sets of ideas were closely related for the pluralists: their beliefs about the mentality of the masses heavily informed their notions about the importance of elites. So, too, we will see, underlying ideas about the group psychology of the police likely informed the views of many people in the 1960s and 1970s, perhaps including Supreme Court justices, about the proper ways to reconcile law enforcement and democracy. Tracing the paths of influence requires us to consider other pervasive themes of criminal procedure in the Warren and Burger Court eras. But two points merit passing mention here.

First, the conception of the police as a discrete and unified group, alienated from mainstream society, encouraged the notion that effective regulation of the police required strong oversight from a different group—if not politicians, then judges or some kind of civilian oversight board. It contributed to the great pessimism shown by scholars in the 1960s and later decades about the potential for police departments to regulate themselves, or even to cooperate with systems of outside review. The police were thought to be engaged "in a gigantic conspiracy against the outside world," a conspiracy so "deeply embedded in the norms and work routines of policemen" that "civilian review of police activities is bound to arouse frantic opposition by the police" and "even in-house investigatory agencies will usually fail to penetrate the protective wall that policemen have built around themselves."[62]

Second, a concern for the group mentality of the police may help to explain the lax standards the Warren and Burger Courts applied to searches by government agencies other than the police. Initially the Warren Court entirely exempted "administrative searches" from the warrant and probable-cause requirements imposed on searches conducted in the course of criminal investigations.[63] Later the Court held that an administrative search did require a warrant, but that the warrant could issue without the kind of probable cause that a criminal search would require—in fact, without any individualized suspicion at all.[64] In the early 1970s, the Court loosened the requirements again, holding that warrants often were not required for administrative searches of closely regulated businesses.[65] Subsequently, the administrative search doctrine was broadened into the "special needs" doctrine, applying relaxed standards to searches by public school teachers, government office managers, and so on.[66]

There always seemed something counterintuitive about giving the government more leeway to search when no crime is suspected.[67] The explanation could not be simply, as the Court said, that lower standards were necessary in order for the searches to go forward: a similar argument could just as easily have justified reduced standards for searches in criminal investigations.[68] Nor, despite the Court's suggestions, did the fact that no criminal case was contemplated seem to make a search any less invasive. If criminal searches felt more "hostile" to the Court,[69] perhaps that had less to do with the prospect of criminal charges than with the involvement of a specific group of government officials: the police. On occasion the Court applied the administrative search and "special needs" doctrines to searches carried out by police officers.[70] But those decisions were outliers, and they always seemed the least convincing applications of the doctrines.

That may be changing, in ways that illuminate the role that theories of democracy can play in shaping ideas about the police. In 2004, for example, the Court approved suspicionless stops of motorists when the police are looking for witnesses to a crime, rather than suspects, and the language of the ruling suggested the Court was now inclined to give the police fairly broad leeway in joining with "responsible citizens" to promote a cooperative goal like "public safety."[71] Two years later the Court upheld suspicionless searches of parolees as means of "reducing recidivism and thereby promoting reintegration and positive citizenship."[72] The Court's rhetoric in both of these cases resonated strongly with a view of the police as an arm of "the community"—a view different in important ways from the one that held sway from the 1950s through the early 1980s, and rooted in ideas about democracy very much at variance with those of the pluralists. We will explore these matters in later chapters. For now the important point is that the initial development of the administrative search and "special needs" doctrines, if not the current uses of those doctrines, may have reflected particular features of criminal procedure and police studies in the pluralist era: the preoccupation with the group psychology of the police, and the related agenda—to which we will now turn—of reining in police discretion through judicial oversight.

Bringing Police Under the Rule of Law

Jerome Hall's influential article of 1953 drew attention to the many circumstances in which the police operated without clear standards. He warned that the wide scope of police discretion opened the door to discrimination against minorities, and he argued that it violated a core component of democracy, the "rule of law."[73] The rule of law was also a key concept for many of the democratic pluralists. It was part of what David Truman meant by the "rules of the game": the whole system of interest-group competition made sense only if government involved something more than officials acting on their arbitrary whims.[74] Many of the social scientists who turned their attention to the police beginning in the 1950s shared the pluralists' view in this regard, and they agreed with Hall that police discretion represented a worrisome deviation from the rule of law—all the more worrisome given the characteristic mind-set of the police. Westley thought this way: he warned that the internal norms of the police threatened the "formalized controls" on which society increasingly depended.[75] Skolnick thought this way: that was why he titled his major work *Justice Without Trial*. And when legal scholarship on the police began to proliferate in the 1960s, much of it focused on the problem of police discretion.[76]

This was true, in particular, of a series of influential books and articles growing out of an unprecedented, large-scale survey of criminal justice institutions in the United States. The survey was undertaken in the mid-1950s as the first major project of the American Bar Foundation, an independent research institute established by the American Bar Association in 1952. Between 1955 and 1957 a team of researchers filed more than 2,000 field reports on the day-to-day operations of the police and the criminal justice system more broadly. The researchers were "overwhelmed by the pervasiveness of discretionary decision making," often accompanied by "lawlessness, racism, and casual unprofessional conduct."[77] When books and articles based on the ABF survey began appearing in the 1960s, they focused heavily on the problem of discretion.[78]

A scholarly consensus emerged not only on the nature of the problem but also on the principal solution: greater judicial oversight of the police. This was definitely what Hall had in mind. Stronger *executive* control of the police was too dangerous for democracy: "Certainly we do not want our police to be a Praetorian Guard available to some would-be Caesar."[79] Skolnick, reflecting the prevailing tone of criminal procedure scholarship in the 1960s, placed even more weight on the rule of law than Hall. As Jonathan Simon has noted, Skolnick saw identification with the rule of law to be both "the defining aspect of the police" and "a way to reconcile their fundamentally authoritarian character with the democratic society they were policing."[80] And the rule of law was applied to the police officer chiefly by the judge, both directly and through the intermediary of the prosecutor.[81]

Nor was this combination of diagnosis and prescription—the problem of police discretion, the solution of judicial oversight—restricted to scholars. It was perhaps the most characteristic feature of the Warren Court's approach to the police. Consider just the decisions that extended the Fourth Amendment exclusionary rule to state law enforcement,[82] conditioned investigatory stops and pat-downs on grounds sufficiently "articulable" to allow judicial review,[83] inserted defense attorneys as witnesses at interrogations and lineups,[84] constrained interrogations with bright-line requirements of prescribed warnings and automatic shutoffs,[85] required warrants for electronic surveillance,[86] required warrants for home searches following arrests,[87] and required warrants—after a fashion—for administrative inspections.[88]

Warrants, in fact, were the principal motif of the Warren Court's approach to the Fourth Amendment. The constitutional text does not explicitly require warrants; it requires only that searches and seizures be reasonable, and that warrants, when they do issue, be appropriately narrow and based on probable cause. The Court's efforts to harmonize these two commands were always erratic, but by the time Warren took the bench the Court seemed inclined to the general view that searches and seizures were constitutional if they were reasonable, regardless of whether they were pursuant to warrant.[89] The Warren Court emphatically rejected that position.[90] Again and again, the Court insisted that, with certain narrow exceptions, searches and seizures were reasonable only if the police obtained "advance judicial approval" in the form of a warrant.[91] The point was that judges should decide, not police officers. Adopting a position Justice Frankfurter had often expressed in dissent,[92] the Warren Court saw the Fourth Amendment as aimed above all at the evil of the arbitrary exercise of discretion, and it saw judicial pre-screening of searches and seizures as the Constitution's favored remedy. This view of the Fourth Amendment persisted into the Burger Court era, though its application grew more sporadic.[93]

As a prescription for the problem of police discretion, judicial oversight could draw strength from democratic pluralism in several ways. To begin with, of course, courts specialized in procedural regularity, so they seemed ideal bodies for applying the rule of law. More fundamentally, judges were *independent* of the police. They were a separate group, within the government, that could serve as a counterbalance against other governmental groups, including the police, in the classic manner described by the pluralists. Skolnick invoked this idea quite explicitly. Like "any agency," he explained, "the police would of course engage in activities promoting self-serving ends," unless other "regulators" intervened. It was precisely the inability of the police to "capture" their regulators—the judiciary—that kept our system from resembling a "police state."[94]

In addition to their independence and their association with procedural regularity, judges, unlike police officers, tended to belong to the political elite. They were among the educated, civically engaged people to whom pluralist theory gave the task of defending democratic values. Dahl made precisely this point in an influential essay on the Supreme Court: "it would appear, on political grounds, somewhat unrealistic to suppose that a Court whose members are recruited in the fashion of Supreme Court Justices would long hold to norms of Right or Justice substantially at odds with the rest of the political elite."[95]

Police officers, on the other hand, were manifestly *not* members of the political elite. They differed in this respect not only from judges, but also from top-level law enforcement executives, and from the white-collar bureaucrats who staffed and managed administrative agencies like the Interstate Commerce Commission, the Federal Trade Commission, the Federal Communications Commission, and so forth—the major institutional legacies of the New Deal. Pluralist ideas about American democracy may have encouraged the judiciary in the 1950s and early 1960s to leave these agencies alone: the regulatory process looked like the very model of interest-group competition moderated and brokered by political elites.[96] The same respect for leadership elites may have contributed to the respect that the Warren and Burger Courts occasionally showed for the judgments of law enforcement executives. But it provided no grounds for deference to the police rank and file.

Meanwhile, pluralism took the sting out of the most obvious objection to
placing police under the control of unelected judges: what Alexander Bickel
famously called the "countermajoritarian difficulty."[97] That objection
counted for little if, as the pluralists believed, there was no such thing as
majority rule to begin with. Dahl put it this way: "Few of the Court's policy
decisions can be interpreted sensibly in terms of a 'majority' versus a 'minority.' In this respect, the Court is no different from the rest of the political leadership."[98] Hall relied on the same notion in rejecting the argument
that police illegality might simply reflect what the public wanted. "[T]here
is no 'the public' in a democracy," he insisted, only various "groups and
organizations"—many of which surely wanted the police to obey the law.[99]

Return for a moment to Skolnick's use of the term "police state." This
was a familiar trope in criminal procedure and police studies by the time
Skolnick wrote in 1966, and yet another way in which these fields echoed
the ideas about American democracy associated with the pluralists. For
judges and criminal justice scholars as for political theorists, totalitarianism
had established itself as—to use, again, William Connolly's term—the chief
"contrast-model" for American institutions, including the machinery of
criminal justice.[100] The first point of comparison to surface in Supreme
Court opinions had pertained to the brutal interrogation practices of "dictatorial" regimes; oblique references to the atrocities of the Gestapo and the
NKVD helped the Court to underscore, in the 1930s and 1940s, its condemnation of police torture in the United States.[101] Jerome Hall drew the
same contrast, for the same purposes, more explicitly.[102]

Beginning in the late 1940s, references to totalitarianism in Supreme
Court opinions grew more pointed and more common. The term "police
state" began to be used. And the valence of the concept began to shift. Some
justices began to emphasize judicial control of the police, rather than civilized police practices, as the critical distinction between a democracy and a
"police state."[103] The closing lines of Justice Jackson's opinion for the Court
in *Johnson v. United States* were particularly influential in this regard. The
Fourth Amendment, he suggested, was "one of the most fundamental distinctions between our form of government, where officers are under the
law, and the police-state where they are the law."[104]

The specter of the police state became a fixture of criminal procedure rhetoric in the 1960s.[105] Invocation of the term functioned not just to invoke totalitarianism as the contrast-model for democracy, and not just to make the role of the police a defining difference between the two ideals, but also, and more specifically, to suggest that democracy depended in part on the systematic substitution of judicial judgment for police judgment.

Protecting Personal Dignity

If judicial control of police discretion was the primary *procedural* theme of Warren Court criminal procedure, the main *substantive* theme was the protection of personal dignity against the threat of an overpowering state. Thus, the coerced confession cases progressed from a focus on torture in the 1930s and 1940s to a focus on more subtle, psychological means of manipulation.[106] By time the Court decided *Miranda v. Arizona*, it saw the confession problem as essentially about defending "human dignity" against increasingly sophisticated efforts to "subjugate the individual to the will of his examiner."[107] The Fourth Amendment, similarly, came to be understood less as a protection of individual sovereignty and more as prophylactic against the prying eye of the government. No longer did the Fourth Amendment provide "an indefeasible right of personal security, personal liberty, and private property."[108] Now it safeguarded "reasonable expectations of privacy," which could be "defeated by electronic as well as physical invasion."[109]

Like the concern with police discretion, the Warren Court's emphasis of personal dignity drew support from the anti-authoritarianism strand of democratic pluralism. The overpowering, omnipresent state was not just a hypothetical hazard; it was modern democracy's very real rival. The "police state" trope thus advanced the substantive as well as the procedural theme of Warren Court criminal procedure.[110]

Just as it encouraged a judicial remedy for the problem of police discretion, democratic pluralism lent support to the notion that dignity should find its protection in the courts. Here as well, if there was no majority rule to begin with, there was no countermajoritarian difficulty. The value of dignity was part of the consensus the pluralists thought was a prerequisite for democracy. It was often thought to be the core of that consensus. David Truman, for example, thought it obvious that "the system rests at bottom on a respect for the dignity of man. This much is imperative; this much is indispensable."[111]

In giving content to that commitment, it made no sense under the pluralist view to rely on popular votes. Elections were useful for resolving conflicts between groups and for concentrating the minds of government officials. But democratic norms were not up for grabs; they were the "rules of the game." They needed to be a matter of social consensus—not among everyone but among the elite. Judges, again, were parts of that elite. So were legislators and party leaders, but their jobs naturally focused them less on preserving norms and more on balancing group interests. So it made sense to entrust judges with responsibility for articulating and enforcing the core democratic value of dignity. (Robert Dahl argued, in fact, that the Supreme Court's highest function was precisely "to confer legitimacy, not simply on the particular and parochial policies of the dominant political alliance, but upon the basic patterns of behavior required for the operation of a democracy.")[112]

Embracing Modernity

Not the least of the appeals of police professionalism in the 1950s and 1960s was that it seemed *modern*—new, scientific, and bold. The attraction of the Warren and Burger Courts to police professionalism thus reflected, in part, the pluralists' broader embrace of modernity. That broader embrace had at least two other manifestations in criminal procedure law and scholarship.

The first of these was the virtual disappearance of original intent as a guide to interpreting constitutional restrictions on the police. This development was particularly striking in search-and-seizure law, where the Supreme Court had long relied on eighteenth-century history to clarify the vague commands of the Fourth Amendment. The Warren Court abandoned that tradition and refocused Fourth Amendment law on the realities of modern life—particularly modern *urban* life.[113] Electronic surveillance of a telephone booth, for example, was a "search" within the meaning of the Constitution, and therefore required a warrant, not because of the language or history of the Fourth Amendment, but simply because of "the vital role that the public telephone has come to play in private communication."[114] The coverage of the Fourth Amendment depended not on text or original intent but on "reasonable expectations of privacy" *in today's world.*[115] Similarly, the constitutional restrictions on street confrontations between police officers and suspects were set not by eighteenth-century understandings but rather by the reasonableness of particular intrusions in light of modern urban circumstances.[116] In interpreting the Fourth Amendment, the justices and most scholars were in agreement: "Its language is no help and neither is its history."[117]

Warren Court and early Burger Court criminal procedure reflected the pluralist embrace of modernity in another respect as well. The idea that democracy resided in an open, flexible, diverse, freewheeling culture—the notion, in short, of twentieth-century democracy as distinctively urban[118]— contributed to the relatively low priority the Court gave to the values of order, decorum, and safety. In striking down vagrancy statutes as unconstitutionally vague, for example, the Court was only partly concerned with the risk of arbitrary or discriminatory enforcement. It saw vagrancy laws as archaic constraints on "independence," "creativity," "self-confidence," and "high spirits"—the "unwritten amenities" at the heart of modern, democratic ways of life.[119] These were the very "amenities" against which the "authoritarian personality" found itself in conflict, so placing a premium on them meant, among other things, having even more reason to worry about the mind-set of the police.

It also inclined the Court and its academic commentators toward a certain resignation about the risk of victimization. Crime was among the hazards of modern life, like industrial accidents and traffic fatalities. To some extent this attitude reflected the historically low crime rates of the 1950s and early 1960s.[120] But crime rates were only part of the story. Homicide rates, for example, are now at the same levels they were in the mid-1960s. At their peaks in the late 1970s through the early 1990s, moreover, they were roughly twice the levels of the 1950s and early 1960s—hardly a change in order of magnitude.[121] And people in the 1950s and 1960s did not think that crime rates were low. When they thought about crime rates at all, the rates seemed high to them. But there was relatively little alarm about crime—a fact about which police executives regularly complained, and which their "marketing" efforts attempted to change.[122] Even among law enforcement professionals, the goal was "crime control"; no one spoke yet of "zero tolerance."[123] And outside law enforcement, and particularly among scholars, there was widespread sympathy for the view that the chief task of criminal procedure was to protect individuals against the state, because "[i]t inflicts no tangible harm on anyone when a criminal evades punishment."[124] That view was rendered more plausible by the rise during the 1960s of "labeling theory" as an approach to the sociology of crime: the rise, that is to say, of the views that designating someone a criminal or a delinquent was likely to be self-fulfilling, and that the initial designation often said as much as about society as about the individual in question.[125]

All these intellectual currents echoed the pluralist enthusiasm for the spontaneity and freedom of modern urban life. The enthusiasm grew less evident in the opinions of the Supreme Court during the Burger Court era. That development that was very much an intended consequence of Richard Nixon's election in 1968; it also reflected, in part, changes in urban life itself, and particularly changes in patterns of urban crime. Unlike national homicide rates, big-city homicide rates really did begin to skyrocket in the late 1960s.[126] Nixon's "law and order" campaign was a reaction to the dramatic increase in urban crime, but it was also a backlash against protests and disturbances that themselves reflected, in ways we will explore, attacks on the pluralist understanding of democracy. It was a testament, in a way, to pluralism's continuing purchase that both sides in the late 1960s found things to hate about it.

Securing Consensus

We have already seen two ways in which criminal procedure law and police scholarship, as they developed in the 1960s, reflected the emphasis the pluralists placed on consensus. The reliance on judicial oversight, and the embrace of "second-wave" police professionalism, both can be understood in part as efforts to regulate the police through consensus, and specifically through consensus developed and defended by elites. The emphasis on consensus cut still deeper, though, in Warren Court and Burger Court criminal procedure. It was not just a strategy for controlling the police; it was a way in which the criminal justice system served the larger goal of social stability. Broad agreement on the legitimacy of the criminal justice system thus became not just a *sign* that the system was operating effectively; it became part of what it *meant* for the system to operate effectively.

This made imagery greatly important, and it further underscored the critical significance of personal dignity. The core elements of Warren Court criminal procedure—the exclusionary rule, the *Miranda* doctrine, the *Terry* rules for stops and frisks—have all been criticized, particularly in retrospect, as more about symbolism than about substance. The exclusionary rule keeps the courtroom clean but does little to stop police illegality.[127] *Miranda* dresses up interrogations without altering their fundamental dynamics.[128] *Terry* purports to regulate the police but actually gives them wide berth.[129] These criticisms were raised when the cases were decided, too, but the criticisms then seemed in some ways beside the point. The point was, at least in part, to sustain the consensus without which, it was thought, American society would fly apart. Social stability preserved democracy, and consensus preserved social stability. As the 1960s wore on, social stability grew to seem more precarious, and consensus became, correspondingly, all the more imperative.

In seeking stability through consensus, criminal justice jurisprudence in the 1960s and early 1970s paralleled and built upon the work performed by the series of blue-ribbon commissions appointed in this period to investigate the causes of urban riots and campus unrest. The most important of these were the Governor's Commission on the Los Angeles Riots (commonly known as the McCone Commission), the National Advisory Commission on Civil Disorders (commonly known as the Kerner Commission), the National Commission on the Causes and Prevention of Violence, and the President's Commission on Campus Unrest.[130] Each of these task forces visibly embodied the pluralist ideal of elite consensus: a cross section of group leaders, informed by experts, hammering out and lending credence to a middle-of-the-road response to threats to social stability.[131] It does not take away from the real contributions made by some of these bodies, particularly the Kerner Commission, to recognize that they were, to a large extent, exercises in pluralist political theater. There was an element of that, too, in criminal procedure law: the elite endorsement of a moderate path of reform that redeemed and legitimized the underlying system, in part by safeguarding and valorizing its cherished symbols and its core commitment to dignity.

Disregarding Institutional Structure

The pluralist emphasis on psychology and sociology encouraged people interested in the police to train their sights on the behavior of individual officers and the police mentality. It discouraged attention to the structure of decision making within police departments. Even without pluralism, the reliance on judges to regulate the police probably would have directed criminal procedure away from questions of systemic design; those are not the kinds of questions judges are thought well positioned to address. But the psychosocial framework of pluralism made this selective competence of courts seem like a happy fortuity, and all the more reason to lean heavily on the judiciary in approaching the problems of the police. The problems that courts were ill equipped to tackle were not the important ones, anyway.

Scholars, too, paid less attention to institutional structure than to police psychology and sociology. In part this reflected the ability of the Supreme Court to set the intellectual agenda of legal scholars, and the unremarkable tendency of sociologists to focus on sociology. But political scientists studying the police also tended to neglect questions of organizational design, and here the influence of pluralism is particularly easy to trace. James Q. Wilson, the only student of the police to rival Skolnick for influence in the 1960s, was in many ways a thoroughgoing pluralist. He took group theory and consumerism as givens: " 'the people' do not govern—organizations, parties, factions, politicians, and groups govern. The people choose among competing leaders and thereby constrain them."[132] He shared, too, the pluralists' overriding concern with social stability, their strong aversion to mass politics, their focus on group psychology, and—most fundamentally—their conviction that institutional structures were epiphenomenal, that the real action took place at the level of cultural norms. Wilson therefore sought to explain police policies as expressions of the local "political culture."[133]

The political culture created a police culture within each department. Initially Wilson suggested that police cultures came in two versions: a rule-bound, "good government" professionalism and a patronage-based network of relationships and reciprocity. He called the first "the code of profession-alism" and linked it to what Richard Hofstadter had characterized as the "'Yankee-Protestant' style" of politics; he called the second "the code of the system" and linked it to Hofstadter's "immigrant" style.[134] Because Wilson saw police cultures as outgrowths of the broader political cultures of partic-ular municipalities, he was pessimistic about efforts to graft police profes-sionalism onto the political systems of inner-city areas traditionally run in the "immigrant" style: "the law of the Yankee" was not made for "the condi-tions of the jungle."[135]

Later, in a comparative study of eight American police departments, Wilson identified three "styles" of law enforcement: the "watchman style," which corresponded roughly to the "code of the system"; the "legalistic style," which was more or less the "code of professionalism"; and the "ser-vice style," which was the form of policing Wilson found in the affluent New York suburbs of Brighton and Nassau County.[136] Once again, he at-tributed the styles of particular police departments to the local political cul-tures in which they operated. He was therefore dismissive of most efforts at police reform, particularly those involving structural innovations.[137] It was all pie in the sky. "The 'problems of the police,'" Wilson thought, were "longstanding and inherent in the nature of their function." The reform proposals of the late 1960s revealed simply that "our definition of those problems has changed and, by changing, has misled or unsettled us."[138]

By 1969, when Wilson offered that counsel of quietism, pluralism and the police were both under attack. The attacks were related, in ways we will explore. For now, though, the important point is the way in which pluralism shaped Wilson's response to attacks on the police. Not only did it give him an almost Burkean suspicion of institutional engineering; it made him par-ticularly unsympathetic to calls for greater community control of urban policing—calls that he correctly understood to reflect widening interest in "participatory democracy."[139] Wilson warned that the "service style" could work in homogeneous communities of the well off and well educated, but not in the inner city. Group conflicts there were too acute, and norms of co-operation too weak. "Community control" would therefore mean "putting the police at the mercy of the rawest emotions, the most demagogic spokes-men, and the most provincial concerns."[140] The end result could well be authoritarianism rather than democracy; Wilson compared proposals for neighborhood control of policing to the Soviet Union's system of "People's Patrols."[141]

Wilson had little more sympathy for the growing calls among police officers themselves for greater participation in departmental decision making; he dismissed police unions as a form of "criminal justice syndicalism."[142] In this respect he found himself once again in accord with Skolnick. Skolnick's wariness about police unions had much to do with the circumstances of the late 1960s. Police unionism surged in that period, and it was a highly politicized form of unionism: the rallying cry was as likely to be opposition to civilian review boards or reform-oriented chiefs as support for better benefits or enhanced job security.[143] Skolnick therefore saw police activism as a threat to the rule of law: like judges or soldiers, police officers should be apolitical.[144]

Even without pluralism, the direction taken by police unions in the late 1960s would have soured many people on the prospects for bringing true participatory democracy to policing: there was always the nettlesome difficulty of participation by the police themselves. The point I wish to emphasize here, though, is that pluralism made this reaction more likely in two different ways. First, it made many people, such as James Q. Wilson, suspicious of any calls for broadening political participation, including by the police. Second, it led many people, including Skolnick, to see police unionism first and foremost as a social movement, and not as a set of institutional possibilities. It would have been difficult in any event in the late 1960s to think past the immediate political context and to imagine what collective bargaining or arbitration might mean once police unions had become "normalized." Normalization of anything was not on the horizon in 1968. But the strong emphasis that pluralism placed on social psychology made it even harder to think in terms of institutional structure. Structure seemed superficial.

This is not to say that the institutional structure of policing was wholly ignored in the 1960s and 1970s. Police administrators spent time thinking about the structure of their institutions, but with few exceptions they focused on efficiency, not democracy. Outside reformers *did* think about restructuring police departments to make them more democratic, but their energies were overwhelmingly devoted to a particular, relatively modest form of restructuring: adding a layer of civilian review to particular categories of police decision making.[145] Building on the model of judicial review, this innovation found support in the pluralist emphasis on group politics, while also appealing, if only symbolically, to emerging notions of participatory democracy. What was missing in this period was sustained, systematic attention to the ways in which organizational design in law enforcement might advance democracy. For reasons to be explored below, it is still missing today.

Summing Up

We have not exhausted the ways in which pluralist ideas about democracy influenced criminal procedure and police scholarship in the 1960s and beyond. The American exceptionalism incorporated within pluralism, for example, may well have contributed to relative disinterest that judges and scholars showed in police procedures abroad. But I hope the discussion so far has established three important points.

First, ideas about democracy are tied up with ideas about the police. Just as the pluralist conception of democracy was defined in opposition to the specter of the "police state," pluralism—particularly in conjunction with police professionalism, which proved so congenial with many of the pluralists' central ideas—helps to explain some of the hallmarks of criminal procedure and police studies from the late 1960s through the early 1980s: the focus on the group psychology of the police, the concern with police discretion and the reliance on judicial oversight, the emphasis on personal dignity, the embrace of modern urban life by the Warren Court and its commentators, the centrality of consensus, and the tendency both of the Court and of many scholars throughout this period to disregard institutional structure. These were not minor features of Warren and Burger Court criminal procedure. They were some of its most conspicuous features. They are also features that from today's vantage point can seem particularly mysterious and hard to justify.

It bears reiterating that pluralism and police professionalism were not the only influence on criminal procedure law in the 1960s and 1970s. The widely recognized theme of racial equality in Warren Court criminal procedure, in particular, is hard to trace to the pluralists, or to the advocates of police professionalism.[146] Pluralism may well have played a role, though, in keeping that theme "domesticated" and almost entirely subtextual.[147] I will have more to say in later chapters about the relationship between democracy and equality—or, more precisely, between democracy and opposition to entrenched systems of *in*equality. For now, the important point is that pluralism downplayed this relationship: first, through its emphasis on leadership elites, and second, through its assumption that the complexity of the American political system prevented any particular group from achieving undue dominance. Pluralism thus does little to explain the egalitarianism of criminal procedure in the Warren Court era, but it may help to explain why that egalitarianism never became more thoroughgoing, more explicit, or more lasting.

Second, in order to trace the influences of ideas about democracy on ideas about the police, we need to pay attention to the complexity of ideas about democracy. Pluralism, for example, is sometimes counterposed with faith in expertise.[148] There is truth in that formulation: the pluralists were eager to distance themselves from people like Walter Lippman, and they stressed the role of group competition in sustaining American democracy. But the real pluralists were not ideal types; their theory of democracy was richer and more complicated than a simple analogy of politics to markets. Their tempered their distaste for philosopher kings with an appreciation of scientific and technical know-how, and they matched their emphasis on competition with a heavy reliance on consensus. It was this actual set of beliefs, held by flesh-and-blood people, that influenced ideas about policing in the 1960s, the 1970s, and into the 1980s. Oversimplifying pluralism hides its influence.

Third, and more particularly, pluralism must be understood within the context of the social science paradigm from which it emerged. Ignoring that paradigm makes the central tenets of pluralism harder to identify, and it makes pluralism's largest impacts on criminal procedure and police studies all but invisible. It also, as we will see, obscures an important point of continuity between pluralism and the theories that emerged as its chief rivals, participatory democracy and deliberative democracy.

The continuity is important, because it explains two of the most persistent themes in our thinking about the police: the conception of the police as a breed apart, and the sense that culture matters more than structure in regulating the police. There are good grounds to take both these views. The social science paradigm triumphed for a reason. But democratic pluralism triumphed for a reason, too. Its explanatory power was no illusion. The problem with pluralism, as its critics pointed out, was not so much what it said but what it left out.[149] Over the past decade or so, some of what pluralism left out—participation, deliberation—has worked its way back into our thinking about policing. What the social science paradigm leaves out, on the other hand, still remains muted in criminal procedure.

In a larger sense, for reasons we will explore in the following chapters, democracy itself has become muted in criminal procedure. Theories of participatory democracy and deliberative democracy have never achieved the combination of comprehensive explanatory power and broad, almost unquestioned acceptance that pluralism enjoyed in its heyday. Pluralism itself retains adherents, although it survives largely in forms that sacrifice clarity and rigor for ecumenicalism. Even pluralists now endorse participation. Our ideas about democracy are broader today than they were in the 1950s and early 1960s, but they are also less coherent. That may be one reason why democracy tends to enter into discussions of policing today in ways that are hesitant, weak, and confused.

CHAPTER 3

Losing Faith in Sergeant Friday

Pluralism's Fall

If pluralist policing had a fictional paragon, it may have been Sergeant Joe Friday, the no-nonsense, by-the-books protagonist of the 1950s radio and television drama *Dragnet.* Jack Webb, who produced the show and performed the role of Friday, greatly admired the professionalism of the Los Angeles Police Department under Chief William Parker. Friday embodied that professionalism: well trained, fervently dedicated to his work, unquestioning in his devotion to the rule of law, unshakable in his rectitude, proud of the department that employed him, and fully committed to its methods and procedures. Friday was an organization man, and the true hero of the series was Parker's LAPD.

Dragnet aired on radio from 1949 through 1957 and on television from 1951 through 1959. Both versions were hits.[1] Webb made the cover of *Time* in 1954; the story called Friday "one of the most famous fictional detectives of all time," and it credited *Dragnet* with giving the nation "a new appreciation" of the police and "its first rudimentary understanding of real-life law enforcement."[2] Among the greatest fans of the series was the LAPD, which—particularly under Parker—was keenly attentive to its public image. In exchange for being portrayed so favorably (and for sizeable donations from Webb's production company), the LAPD gave Webb unprecedented access and support. Not only the true hero of the series, the LAPD also became a kind of unofficial co-producer.[3]

Webb revived *Dragnet* in 1967, and the new version of the show ran on television until 1970. The new *Dragnet* had the same format as its earlier incarnations, and the character of Joe Friday—once again acted by Webb—was little changed. The ratings, again, were strong. But the times were different, and the appeal of the show had altered and narrowed. In the 1950s, *Dragnet* had been admired across the political spectrum for its gritty realism. In the late 1960s, it rallied one side of a cultural civil war. Webb said he hoped the new *Dragnet* could "help restore respect for the law" and "constituted authority."[4] Even more than during the 1950s the show functioned as weekly propaganda for the LAPD, with the department's full cooperation. Half of the audience for *Dragnet* in the late 1960s welcomed the strong stand it took for decency; the other half saw the show as camp.[5]

Part of what had changed, of course, was that law enforcement was under siege—particularly the aloof style of "professional" policing epitomized by the LAPD. Chapter 4 of this book will examine the downfall of police professionalism in some detail. But *Dragnet* was "not merely a hit"; it was an "ideology"[6]—and the ideology included more than police professionalism. Each episode began with a video montage of Los Angeles: busy freeways, bustling streets, miles of homes and businesses, crowded parks and beaches. "This is the city," Webb's voice-over would begin.[7] The Los Angeles of *Dragnet* was sprawling, kaleidoscopic, and in constant motion. It was held together, and kept from anarchy, only by an underlying consensus on basic social mores, chief among them obedience to the law, and a police force that itself played by the rules. It was the modern, pluralist metropolis. The civic ideals of *Dragnet* were, to a great extent, the ideals of democratic pluralism—albeit tempered with a strong dose of law-and-order conservatism, and pointedly unsympathetic to judicial second-guessing of the police.[8] And by the late 1960s democratic pluralism in any version—much like police professionalism—was beginning to show its age.

A "Democracy of Participation"

The disastrous course of the Vietnam War, followed by the revelations of Watergate, would have placed great strain on any theory of democracy that relied as heavily as pluralism did on leadership elites—whether in black robes or with badges. But pluralism's decline began long before Watergate, and before Americans took up arms against the Vietcong. A signal event came in 1960, when the philosopher Arnold Kaufman coined the term "participatory democracy" in the course of an argument that insisted on what the pluralists above all else denied: the importance of widespread political involvement.[9] The phrase "participatory democracy" had an extraordinary career over the next decade and a half. It became the slogan of the New Left, and then, remarkably, it went mainstream. The story of that progression is, to a great extent, the story of pluralism's downfall.

Kaufman's essay did not contest the utility of representative government for promoting social stability and safeguarding individual liberty. But he thought those arrangements could and should be supplemented with "institutional forms" that facilitated a "democracy of participation." The chief purpose of these other arrangements was not to promote good policy, but to assist "the development of human powers of thought, feeling, and action." Participation was "an essential condition of the good society and the good life."[10] These were old ideas, of course, and Kaufman's essay was self-consciously an effort at recovery. In this respect it continued a small counter-tradition in political theory that had been slowly gathering steam for half a decade.[11] But Kaufman's essay was also a direct and pointed attack on the consumerism the pluralists had inherited from Schumpeter—the notion that political "outputs" were all that mattered, and that the complexity of modern life made widespread participation impractical.

Kaufman's argument, and even more so his phrasing, proved enormously influential, largely by virtue of their incorporation into the manifesto adopted by Students for a Democratic Society at the organization's June 1962 conference in Port Huron, Michigan. The principal drafter of the manifesto, Tom Hayden, was a student of Kaufman's, and Kaufman himself attended the conference as an informal adviser. "Participatory democracy" was the rhetorical centerpiece of the Port Huron Statement.[12] The document called for "a democracy of participation governed by two central aims:

that the individual share in those social decisions determining the quality and direction of his life; that society be organized to encourage interdependence in men and provide the media for their common participation."[13] The Port Huron Statement became possibly "the most widely distributed document of the American left in the sixties,"[14] and—somewhat to Kaufman's dismay—it helped make participatory democracy the catchphrase of the New Left, the slogan that "defined what was *new* about this left."[15]

Participatory democracy in the 1960s was not first and foremost a theory of scholars; it was a theory of activists. (For all their influence, Arnold Kaufman and C. Wright Mills may have mattered less to the student radicals at Port Huron than the model set by the Student Nonviolent Coordinating Committee.)[16] Partly as a result, participatory democracy was never as coherent and consistent as democratic pluralism. It also changed over time. There was quite a distance, for example, from the committed pacifism of the Port Huron Statement—"we find violence to be abhorrent"[17]—to the glorification of street crime at the decade's end.[18] The ambiguities and contradictions in the rhetoric of the New Left are by now well known; we will return to them shortly. But they should not be overstated. For all their differences, people who invoked the concept of participatory democracy in the 1960s tended to agree on several key points.

First, they shared Kaufman's discomfort with the consumerism that led the pluralists to see democracy as solely a mechanism for delivering good policies. They thus disagreed with the pluralists about the *purposes* of democracy. Advocates of participatory democracy thought much of the value of democracy lay in the way it facilitated individual development and enriched social interaction. In the words of the Port Huron Statement, politics in a participatory democracy served "the function of bringing people out of isolation and into community, thus being a necessary, though not sufficient, means of finding meaning in personal life."[19] Nor was it simply a matter of personal satisfaction. Political consumerism, like economic consumerism, stunted society as well as its members. By making people alienated, helpless, and stupefied, it blocked critical thinking and prevented the emergence of alternative forms of collective life.[20]

In this respect the rhetoric of participatory democracy drew heavily on a broader attack in the 1960s on consumerism. That attack, characteristically couched as a call to replace "conformity" with "authenticity," was embraced with special fervor by the counterculture, but its presence was felt more widely. It reflected a growing discomfort, particularly among intellectuals, with the power of modern advertising, and a growing sense that middle-class life in America had become too passive, too comfortable, too manipulated, and too shallow.[21]

Second, believers in participatory democracy disagreed with the pluralists about the *processes* of democracy. The pluralists had distrusted mass politics and had placed their faith in leaders, guided by scientific and technical experts. That strategy obviously made no sense if political participation was essential for individual development. But the pluralists' emphasis on leadership and expertise ran into trouble in the 1960s on its own terms as well. The Vietnam War shook confidence not just in the technical competence of experts and elites but, more importantly, in precisely those features of the political system on which pluralists relied to make leadership democratic: the commitment of elites to core democratic norms, the disciplining function of electoral competition, and the accommodation of interests facilitated by group competition. The secrecy and deception practiced by "the best and the brightest" made the whole notion of "rules of the game" seem almost farcical. As two social scientists asked in the early 1970s, "[i]f the Kennedys and McNamaras and Rostows and Johnsons can conceive, plan, and initiate a 'secret war,' how are we to remain confident that the principles of representative democracy rest secure in the inward convictions of the elite?"[22] That same pattern of opacity, combined with the turbulence and violence of the 1960s, made elections seem to many people, particularly on the Left, increasingly beside the point,[23] and eroded confidence in the ability of interest-group politics to accommodate peacefully the concerns of ordinary people.

With regard to this last point—the disenchantment with interest-group politics—the New Left could draw on escalating skepticism about pluralism within mainstream social science. The belief that organized groups could be relied upon to represent all interests, no matter how diffuse, came under particularly heavy attack. The influential political scientist E. E. Schattschneider spoke in 1960 for a growing group of critics: "The flaw in the pluralist heaven is that the heavenly chorus sings with a strong upper-class accent. Probably about 90 percent of the people cannot get into the pressure system. . . . The system is skewed, loaded and unbalanced in favor of a fraction of a minority."[24] The notion that interest-group politics had a built-in bias received a particularly strong boost in 1965, when Mancur Olson published *The Logic of Collective Action*. Olson pointed out that the pluralist optimism about group politics rested on an unsubstantiated assumption that whenever existing groups failed to take sufficient account of an important interest, a new group would organize to represent that interest. Not only was this idea unsubstantiated, Olson argued; it was almost certainly false. Microeconomic analysis confirmed what politicians and journalists had always known: small "special interest" groups found it easier than larger groups to organize and therefore to wield political power. Narrow, "vested interests" therefore could defeat the broader public interests, "which are normally supposed to prevail in a democracy."[25]

Third, and as consequence of the foregoing, advocates of participatory democracy in the 1960s tended to differ strongly with the pluralists on the question of *proximity*—that is, the issue of how close America actually was to achieving the democratic ideal. (Partly for this reason, they were also less impressed with the *particularity* of American democracy.) For most of the 1960s, the rhetoric of participatory democracy was both a rhetoric of critique and a strategy of attack. As rhetoric, it took aim at "complacency" and "contentment"[26] by identifying what was missing in American democracy. As strategy, it endorsed political involvement as a means of developing, among other things, the individual's powers of critical thought.

Fourth, and notwithstanding the preceding points of contrast, supporters of participatory democracy tended to agree with the pluralists that democracy had more to do with culture than with institutions. They shared what I have been calling the social science paradigm. They rejected the reliance the pluralists had placed on two fixtures of that paradigm, consumerism and group theory. But believers in participatory democracy tended to talk about consensus as much as the pluralists. It was a different kind of consensus: a consensus reached through face-to-face discussions rather than through overlapping elites and "social training." And advocates of participatory democracy, unlike the pluralists, tended to see the formation of a framing consensus as a key *part* of democratic politics, rather than a *precondition* for it. Again, Schattschneider put it well: "Political conflict is not like an intercollegiate debate in which the opponents agree in advance on a definition of the issues. . . . [T]he definition of the alternatives is the choice of conflicts, and the choice of conflicts allocates power."[27] Still, the consensus reached in participatory democracy appealed, like the pluralist consensus, to the post-Lockean ideal of "an ever-widening identification of self and world, individual and society."[28] Not for nothing did the conferees at Port Huron call themselves Students for a Democratic *Society.* Writing in 1967, the sociologist Richard Flacks—who had himself been one of those conferees—identified "community" and "anti-institutionalism" as two of "the main value themes which characterize the student movement."[29]

Nor did participatory democracy as developed in the 1960s reject the emphasis the pluralists had placed on personality. If anything, participatory democracy gave psychology a new, heightened importance, by stressing the role of politics in personal growth.[30] Political participation did not just deepen the individual's critical faculties; it also assisted the growth of a democratic personality: self-confident, public-minded, civically engaged, and "authentic." Authenticity, in particular, figured prominently in New Left thinking. The concept of authenticity was notoriously hard to pin down, but it drew heavily on the "humanistic psychology" of Abraham Maslow and his followers, a psychology that departed from Freudianism by stressing the universal human drives for meaning and "self-actualization."[31]

There obviously was some tension between the notion of an "authentic" personality and the idea that personality was shaped by politics. This tension was merely one aspect of larger divide in the rhetoric of participatory democracy. One strand of this rhetoric emphasized community, consensus, and rational deliberation. Another strand—the authenticity strand—stressed a kind of romantic existentialism, "the re-assertion of the personal" in politics.[32] In his perceptive history of the New Left, James Miller describes participatory democracy as combining "two distinct political visions": the "face-to-face community of friends sharing interests in common," and the "experimental collective, embarked on a high-risk effort to test the limits of democracy in modern life."[33] Miller calls the two visions "contradictory."[34] That may exaggerate the conflict: there can be plenty of daring in efforts toward community. But he is surely right that reconciling the two images proved difficult: "The will to act can easily be sapped by endless debate. And thoughtful discussion is rarely advanced through heroics."[35] All of this is to say that although participatory democracy shared the emphasis pluralism had placed on both consensus and personality, it never combined those two emphases as seamlessly as pluralism had.

The Apologetic Turn

In the 1970s and 1980s, when participatory democracy moved back from the world of manifestos to the world of scholarship, the "consensus" strand and the "experimental" strands began to separate. The first strand figured in the revival of civic republicanism, in some versions of communitarianism, and more recently in the escalating academic enthusiasm for deliberative democracy. The second strand has been less prominent and harder to categorize, beyond saying that it has tended to focus on strategies of popular "empowerment."[36]

Both strands have continued to view democracy as more a matter of culture rather than of institutions. Communitarianism and civic republicanism followed Tocqueville in stressing public spirit and the norms of community involvement.[37] Deliberative democracy has been less a comprehensive account of American politics than a philosophical argument for a particular democratic ideal, an ideal characterized chiefly by the nature of political discussion rather than by structural arrangements. The core idea is that we should arrive at political decisions through sincere public debate, based on arguments that "appeal to reasons that are shared or could come to be shared by our fellow citizens."[38] As for the "experimental" strand of participatory democracy, scholars writing in this tradition have focused their attention on building movements rather than institutions. Participatory democracy has meant for them not any specific set of structural arrangements but instead a process of progressive liberation, an "ideal under which the possibilities of joint social life are collected."[39]

Alongside these descendents of New Left ideology emerged a third form of participatory democracy, what might be called the status quo version. Robert Dahl predicted in 1970 that participatory democracy would soon prove "only a youthful fashion of the sixties, which the youth of the seventies will disdain as the foolish ideas of their elders."[40] It never quite worked out that way. Instead something stranger happened: participatory democracy became a lasting fixture of mainstream political rhetoric, but as a strategy of stability rather than an avenue of critique. Richard Nixon, for example, promised in his 1968 campaign "an expanded democracy" in which "the people can participate, they can be involved, their voices can be heard and heeded."[41] As president, he called for giving "all Americans . . . full and effective participation in the decisions that affect their lives."[42] Arnold Kaufman pointed out the obvious: the appeal of participation for a politician like Nixon lay less in its transformative potential than in its power to "allay discontent."[43] Participation was "a double-edged political instrument"; instead of promoting "radical change" it could easily result in "the disappearance of outside critics—those who possess the cool detachment and ability to calculate consequences that come with having little identification with the organization, no axe to grind, no piece of the action."[44] What Kaufman did not foresee was that participation would become not just "an instrument of co-optation"[45] but a rhetoric of apology, that the very *possibility* of involvement would be used to defend existing arrangements as democratic.

Before explaining how that has happened, I should say a bit more about deliberative democracy. The growing body of political philosophy that invokes that label varies in its claims (and in its clarity), but some generalizations seem safe. Like participatory democracy, deliberative democracy is a reaction against aspects of democratic pluralism, including the notion that politics is and should be largely a matter of aggregating and balancing preexisting interests. Unlike participatory democracy, though, deliberative democracy does not stress the effects of political involvement on human development, either at the level of the individual or at the level the community.[46] Instead, deliberative democracy is primarily a theory of "democratic legitimacy"[47]—that is to say, of the "normative essence of democracy," what makes democracy morally appealing.[48] Advocates of deliberative democracy find that essence in the idea of collective self-determination. They further argue that collective self-determination requires that political decisions be made through sincere public debate, in which "we offer considerations that others (whose conduct will be governed by the decisions) can accept," instead of simply "count[ing] those interests in deciding what to do, while keeping our fingers crossed that those interests are outweighed."[49]

Although justified first and foremost on grounds of political morality, public debate of this kind is said to have two practical benefits, as well. The first is that decisions made in this matter are likely to be smarter and better informed.[50] This part of the argument for deliberative democracy harks back to John Dewey's championing of face-to-face dialog as a means of "securing diffused and seminal intelligence," a notion that appealed greatly to C. Wright Mills and, through his influence, found its way into the Port

Huron Statement.[51] The second practical benefit of sincere public debate is that it is likely to make the losers more willing to accept the outcome. Dewey noted this benefit as well,[52] but he downplayed it, for reasons that are easy to understand. Mollification always serves the interest of stability, but stability—depending on the circumstances—may or may not serve the cause of justice, or even the cause of overall material welfare. This is why Kaufman worried about the potential of participatory democracy to allay discontent. And it is presumably for this reason that modern advocates of deliberative democracy echo Dewey in downplaying the pacifying advantages of sincere public debate. Pluralism had lost favor, after all, in part because of its "preoccupation with the stability of the political system"[53] and its relative inattention to "whether or not the situation to be stabilized is itself desirable."[54]

Nonetheless, concerns about actual, objective "legitimacy" prove hard to separate from concerns about *perceived* legitimacy. Certainly this happens often in arguments for deliberative democracy. The "value of self-determination" slides over into the imperative "to instill a *sense* of self-determination."[55] Considerations of moral "acceptability" slide into questions of *practical* acceptability.[56] Most advocates of deliberative democracy stress that they are describing an ideal: deliberation among "free and equal citizens . . . motivated by justice or the common good."[57] And the practical acceptability of decisions *in that kind of society* might be thought an especially good indication of their moral acceptability. But most advocates of deliberative democracy also insist that they are not simply constructing a thought experiment, along the lines of John Rawls's "original position." It is "actual deliberation" that matters,[58] and they tend to recommend doing as much as possible to facilitate deliberation even in our imperfect society.[59] Their reform proposals tend to focus on mechanisms for changing attitudes toward public debate rather than on changing economic and political structures. Amy Guttmann and Dennis Thompson, for example, stress, in their influential account, the need for schools "to develop their students' capacities to understand different perspectives, communicate their understandings to other people, and engage in the give-and-take of moral engagement with a view to making mutually acceptable decisions."[60]

There are two points to be made here. The first is that deliberative democracy, perhaps even more than 1960s-style participatory democracy, tends to focus attention on the cultural underpinnings of democracy at the expense of the institutional structures of decision making. The second is that the rhetoric of deliberative democracy has something of a conservative tilt. It emphasizes the importance of people understanding each other, respecting each other's positions, and accepting political decisions with which they disagree. It directs attention away from the possibilities that some arguments are incoherent, that some political positions are unworthy of respect, and that some systems should be overthrown.

There is nothing intrinsically conservative about the *theory* of deliberative democracy: even if true democracy depends on public-spirited deliberation among free and equal citizens, deliberation in the real world of today might do nothing to promote legitimacy. The first task might be to strengthen freedom and equality, not to promote deliberation. But advocates of deliberative democracy tend to urge more deliberation in the here and now, alongside incremental efforts to improve the conditions of deliberation.[61] The point is not just that deliberation in the real world can be the enemy of action.[62] The point is that even describing real-world political debate as a form of "deliberation" tends to suggest that the outcomes of that process are worthy of respect.

The same is true of "participation." Like deliberation, participation in government can be pacifying; this is the point Kaufman stressed at the end of the 1960s. Equally important, though, the mere *possibility* of participation can be invoked to legitimize decisions as democratic. Used in this way, participatory democracy becomes a rhetoric of apology.

Justice Breyer, for example, sees "participatory democratic self-government" as a core constitutional value, and he urges judges to pay it more attention.[63] But the kind of participation he has in mind is what we already have. In public lectures he has stressed that "today's citizen does participate in the democratic self-governing process."[64] Here is how he has described that process:

> Serious complex changes in law are often made in the context of a national conversation involving, among others, scientists, engineers, businessmen and women, and the media, along with legislators, judges, and many ordinary citizens. . . . That conversation takes place through many meetings, symposia, and discussions, through journal articles and media reports,

through legislative hearings and court cases. Lawyers participate fully in this discussion, translating specialized knowledge into ordinary English, defining issues, creating consensus. Typically, administrators and legislators then make decisions, with courts later resolving any constitutional issues that those decisions raise. This "conversation" is the participatory democratic process itself.[65]

There is good reason for the quotation marks around "conversation." Breyer's "participatory democratic process" is far from the face-to-face deliberation that Dewey had in mind, and even further from the romantic existentialism of "the experimental collective." It is far from anything we ordinarily think of as a "conversation." It is not really a "conversation" at all; the term functions here as an apologetic metaphor. It suggests that our system is democratic, and its decisions therefore entitled to respect, because it is "*open* to participation," and participation of a relatively attenuated sort.[66] As we will see, it is this apologetic, status quo "form of participatory democracy"[67] that has wound up having the greatest impact on criminal procedure law and scholarship.

The Allure of the Past

There is an additional way in which the rhetoric of participatory democracy has become more conservative. This has to do with the waning attraction of modernity.

The student radicals who popularized "participatory democracy" in the 1960s had conflicting attitudes about industrialization and urbanization. The ideal of the "experimental collective," associated with the "authenticity" strand of their thinking, drew heavily on the values of modern urban life: "spontaneity, imagination, passion, playfulness, *movement*—the sensation of being on the edge, at the limits of freedom."[68] The Port Huron Statement took notice of "the growing complex of 'city' problems," but it attributed those problems not to urbanization but to "the present system of economic priorities and a lack of public planning." The solution was not a retreat from modernity but the forward-looking creation of a new "*model city.*"[69] Like Jane Jacobs, who published her influential attack on traditional city planning the year before Port Huron, the student radicals of the early 1960s linked together "city diversity, freedom and life."[70] In this respect they were no different from the pluralists.

On the other hand, though, the "consensus" strand of participatory democracy, the strand inherited from Arnold Kaufman and C. Wright Mills, was conceived from the outset as an exercise in intellectual recovery, an effort to restore pride of place to ideas and forms of social interaction that modernity had pushed aside. There was a mild touch of nostalgia to the enterprise, stronger and more calculated in the case of Mills than in the case of Kaufman.[71] The element of nostalgia in New Left rhetoric grew more pronounced as the decade progressed. It resonated with a key theme of the counterculture: the desire to return to simpler, more honest ways of living. And it fed and in turn drew strength from the romantic portrayal of the Vietnamese Communists as pure-hearted practitioners of "'rice-roots' democracy."[72]

There was rarely anything that sentimental in the academic defenses of participatory democracy that began to emerge in the 1970s. But the theme of intellectual recovery remained pronounced, particularly in work associated with the "consensus" strand of participatory democracy.[73] In this way the academic literature on participatory democracy differed strikingly from the work of the pluralists, who saw themselves as developing a new, more sophisticated account of democracy. The backward-looking posture of the "consensus" strand of participatory democracy grew even noticeable in the "republican revival" of the 1980s, and it can be found as well in some of the recent calls for deliberative democracy.

The chief function of intellectual recovery in the literature on participatory democracy and deliberative democracy has been as a tool of critique. But the backward-looking posture of much of that literature has also helped to give it an anti-modern spin. Coupled with the rhetoric of consensus, deliberation, and reason, the turn to the past has helped to make theories of participatory democracy and deliberative democracy compatible, in ways pluralism never was, with the values of order, decorum, and public safety. Those values are in strong tension with the experimental, "authenticity" strand of 1960s-style participatory democracy, and they are downplayed in academic discussions of participatory democracy that draw on that strand. But the theme of authenticity finds no place in the dominant tradition of scholarship on participatory democracy, the tradition that includes civic republicanism and deliberative democracy. Nor is it part of the mainstream, apologetic version of participatory democracy.

In most of its current forms, therefore, participatory democracy tends to highlight the importance of order and public safety. It lacks the enthusiasm the pluralists had for the spontaneity and freedom of modern urban life. Some of that enthusiasm, of course, was in fact a casualty of the radical experimentalism of the late 1960s, or more precisely of the backlash it elicited: the backlash that fueled Nixon's 1968 "law and order" campaign, that convinced Jack Webb to take *Dragnet* out of mothballs, and that made *The Andy Griffith Show* the best-rated television series of 1967–68.[74]

Summing Up

We are now in a position to summarize what the various theories of participatory democracy and deliberative democracy have to say about the *purposes, processes, proximity,* and *particularity* of democracy. We will start with *processes,* because this is the area in which these theories are most in accord. Even here, the answers provided by post-pluralist democratic theory are far less unified and consistent than the answers provided by pluralism. Once we get to the other elements of democratic theory, the range of disagreement becomes even broader.

Processes. Theories of participatory democracy and deliberative democracy reject the pluralists' reliance on leadership elites, group competition, and periodic elections. They insist on the centrality of what pluralism scorned, widespread political participation. They tend to share the pluralists' assumption that democracy is more a matter of culture than of institutions. But the cultural patterns they emphasize are different: instead of bargaining and adherence to "rules of the game," we have public spiritedness, political engagement, authenticity (in the case of 1960s-style participatory democracy), empowerment (in the case of scholarship drawing on the "authenticity" strand), and/or a commitment to reason and civility (in the cases of civic republicanism, deliberative democracy, and the "consensus" strand of 1960s-style participatory democracy).

Purposes. Theories of participatory democracy and deliberative democracy largely reject the assumption of democratic pluralism that democracy is simply a procedural tool for avoiding instability and authoritarianism. But the newer theories disagree regarding the purposes to be substituted for those of the pluralists. The radical version of participatory democracy championed in the 1960s followed Arnold Kaufman in emphasizing the importance of politics in human development. The more recent, mainstream version of participatory democracy stresses the role played by participation in making people feel connected to and satisfied with their government. And deliberative democracy sees democracy first and foremost as a prerequisite for political legitimacy.

Proximity. Participatory democracy in the 1960s was a form of critique; it stressed the distance between true democracy and the current state of American politics. The more mainstream version of participatory democracy that began emerging in the 1970s turned participatory democracy into a rhetoric of apology. The key difference between this new version of participatory democracy and the older, 1960s version was that the new version was much less demanding; the "participation" it envisioned was much closer to what already existed. Deliberative democracy, for its part, is first and foremost a theory of the democratic ideal, with no necessary implications for the question of proximity. Advocates of deliberative democracy often seem to assume, however, that we are sufficiently close to the ideal that the problem of the second best can be overlooked.

Particularity. Participatory democracy and deliberative democracy have sometimes been developed in ways that suggest the American experience is in fact sufficiently unique so that foreign comparisons are unlikely to be helpful. (This has been particularly true of some of the scholarship on civic republicanism.) But the new theories do not share the strong, consistent theme of American exceptionalism found in democratic pluralism.

CHAPTER 4

Public Safety as Community Empowerment

Participation and the Police

William Bratton, who made the cover of *Time* forty years after Jack Webb, was for the 1990s what Sergeant Friday was for the 1950s: the public face of American policing. Bratton ran the New York Police Department from 1994 to 1996. During that time serious crime in New York dropped almost forty percent and the homicide rate was cut in half. Bratton was not shy in claiming credit, or in taking on the mantle of "America's top cop."[1] He left the NYPD in 1998, but returned to law enforcement in 2002 as Chief of Police in Los Angeles—William Parker's old job. Bratton shares Parker's flair for publicity, his anti-crime evangelism, and his devotion to high standards within law enforcement. But Bratton's arrival in Los Angeles was welcomed in part because he seemed to reject so much else that Parker stood for and that the LAPD had come to stand for: the whole aloof, technologically intensive, reactive style of law enforcement "professionalism." *Time* called Bratton "a leading advocate of community policing." "The role of police power in a democracy," Bratton has written, "should be the expression of social consensus."[2]

Bratton's appointment to Parker's old job nicely symbolized the replacement of an old orthodoxy of police reform with a new one: out with *Dragnet*-style "professionalism"; in with "community policing."

This shift in orthodoxies—the downfall of police professionalism and the triumph of community policing—is part of a broader set of developments in our thinking about the police since the 1960s, developments that are starting to make themselves felt in criminal procedure doctrine and scholarship. This broader set of developments includes a waning concern with police discretion, a renewed faith in majoritarian politics, a growing discomfort with judicial review, a new emphasis on transparency, a preoccupation with trust and legitimacy, and a nostalgic appreciation for order and decorum. These developments are the subject of this chapter. They are connected, we will see, with changes during the same period in prevailing ideas about American democracy—specifically, the slow shift away from democratic pluralism and toward theories of participatory democracy and deliberative democracy.

The course of influence here was not as smooth as in the case of pluralism; it was punctuated and redirected in important ways by the extraordinary politics of the late 1960s. Before examining the ways in which ideas about the police today reflect the turn away from pluralism, I need to discuss some false starts and lost opportunities: the neighborhood policing movement of the late 1960s and early 1970s and the efforts around the same time to bring a measure of workplace democracy to policing. The fate of those initiatives is bound up with the history of the New Left, with the nature of police activism in the late 1960s and early 1970s, and with the emergence, in the 1980s, of community policing as the new *lingua franca* of law enforcement.

The Police and the Sixties

To a degree that now appears remarkable, the police figured hardly at all in the early thinking of student radicals in the 1960s. The Port Huron Statement, rarely faulted for brevity or narrow focus, says not a word about the police. By the end of the decade, of course, police—often in riot gear—had become a fixture of New Left iconography.[3] In retrospect this seems a predictable manifestation of themes present in New Left thinking from the outset: the rebelliousness, the suspicion of authority, the "anti-institutionalism."[4] But it also reflected the course of protest politics in the 1960s, a sequence of events only partly determined by the ideology of student activists.

To begin with, the escalating war in Vietnam pushed the student movement beyond tactics of lawful protest and into increasing conflict with the police, confrontations that culminated in the debacle outside the 1968 Democratic Convention in Chicago and, two years later, in the shootings at Kent State. During this same period, black protest grew more militant, and urban rioting became widespread. The police response to all of these events was often disproportionate, unsophisticated, emotional, and inflammatory.

The urban rioting itself was typically sparked by some instance of police activity and fueled in significant part by accumulated resentment of law enforcement in the inner city. Among the causes of that resentment were some of the central achievements of police professionalism: the insulation of police departments from local political control, the militaristic training of officers, the replacement of precinct stations and foot patrols with centrally dispatched patrol cars, the aggressive employment of the "stop and frisk," and personnel policies—including standardized entry examinations and the elimination of residency requirements—that severely limited the hiring of minority officers.[5] In combination, these practices alienated the police from inner-city residents, contributed to widespread racism among the police, and sharpened the sense in which the police officer in the ghetto seemed, in James Baldwin's resonant words, "like an occupying soldier in a bitterly hostile country."[6]

But the police were controversial in the late 1960s for reasons that went beyond their operational practices. The police themselves entered the political fray, vocally and visibly. They complained bitterly about their public image, they attacked the restrictions imposed on them by the Supreme Court, they spoke out against left-wing groups ranging from the Communist Party to the Black Muslims and the ACLU, and they organized against efforts to insert civilians into police disciplinary procedures. All of this occurred not just at the level of police executives but also at the level of the rank and file.

Law enforcement unionism, long crippled by the public backlash against a failed strike by Boston police officers in 1919, began to surge in the late 1960s and early 1970s, and in a strongly politicized form. As we saw in Chapter 2, the rallying issues included not only working conditions and compensation but also, crucially, opposition to civilian review boards and related efforts at police reform. And these were some of the tamer forms of police politics in the late 1960s. The less tame forms included active participation in reactionary organizations, organized brutality against political protesters, open defiance of civilian authorities, and vigilante attacks on black militants.[7]

By the end of the 1970s, when policing was among the most heavily organized of all public occupations, police unions had joined "the mainstream of American trade unionism," devoting the bulk of their attention to working conditions, job security, and the "bread-and-butter . . . issues that have been near and dear to the hearts of U.S. trade unionists for decades."[8] But the politically charged nature of police organizing in the late 1960s and early 1970s left two lasting impacts on efforts to bring participatory democracy to policing. The first had to do with community supervision of police departments, and the second had to do with efforts to give police officers themselves a degree of democratic control over the nature of their work.

The first set of effects was more obvious. Rank-and-file police organizations actually succeeded in killing off civilian review boards by the end of the 1960s, suing to invalidate Philadelphia's Police Advisory Board, launching a successful ballot referendum to abolish New York City's Civilian Complaint Review Board, and fighting off efforts to create similar panels in other cities.[9] The victory proved transitory, though. Civilian oversight boards began to reappear in the 1970s, especially after Watergate, and have continued to spread. Today Samuel Walker counts roughly one hundred police agencies across the country subject to some form of citizen oversight, including eighty percent of the departments in the fifty largest cities. Citizen oversight, he concludes, is now "firmly established as an important feature of American policing."[10] Still, the strong resistance that police unions initially displayed to civilian review boards (and, in many cases, have continued to display),[11] succeeded in making panels of this kind the central battleground of police reform throughout the 1970s and well into the 1980s. It drew attention away from more far-reaching proposals for reasserting public control over policing. If the relatively mild notion of civilian review of disciplinary decisions was controversial, anything more radical seemed off the table.

There was another reason, also associated with the politics of the late 1960s, that proposals for strong community control of police departments never gained traction. The proposals became tainted by their association with militant forms of left-wing radicalism. An important case in point was the 1971 ballot measure in Berkeley that would have reorganized the city's police into three neighborhood-based departments, each governed by a separate, elected council of civilians. The proposal lost by a two-to-one vote.[12] Even some liberals sympathetic to police reform had doubts about the plan,[13] but the real cause of the lopsided defeat may have been the ballot measure's association with the Black Panthers (who provided the impetus for the proposal) and certain other radical groups (who conspicuously supported it). Jerome Skolnick, who thought the proposal flawed but deserving of serious consideration, complained at the time that a favorable vote had been "made to appear a vote for the kind of people who go around screaming 'Off the Pigs.'"[14]

The defeat of the ballot measure drew nationwide notice. If efforts to bring the police under neighborhood control failed even in Berkeley, the prospects for success elsewhere seemed dim. And, in fact, similar proposals, also tainted by association with left-wing militants, were easily defeated in Chicago and Washington, D.C. By the middle of the 1970s the movement for neighborhood control of policing seemed dead.[15] "Community policing," which came into vogue in the 1980s and has stayed in vogue ever since, shares some of the rhetoric of the earlier movement; but, as we will see, it abandons its commitment to giving neighborhoods true control over the police.[16]

Police Departments as Workplaces

If police activism in the late 1960s helped to take proposals for strong community control of policing permanently off the table, it ironically had a similar effect on proposals to bring participatory democracy *inside* police departments, efforts to give police officers themselves significant control over the nature of their work. Much of the thinking about participatory democracy in the late 1960s and early 1970s, particularly the "consensus" strand of that thinking, focused on the workplace as the ideal locus for collective self-determination. Workplaces were small enough for true face-to-face discussions, and important enough to make participation manifestly worthwhile.[17] For a brief moment at the end of the 1960s, it looked as though workplace democracy might become a theme of efforts at police reform. William Westley, when his doctoral dissertation was finally published in 1970, suggested that the alienated and repressive mentality of the police could be remedied in part by encouraging police unionization and "involving as many policemen as possible in decision making on all aspects of the department's job."[18] He was echoing George Berkley, who had argued a year earlier that strong, democratic police unions and widespread participation by officers in departmental decision making would help train the police in the "rules and values" of democracy.[19]

The police scholar John Angell carried the argument even further in 1971. The "basic hope for correcting the dysfunctional trends of American police organizations," he suggested, was to bring policing in line with the participatory, "humanistic democratic values of the United States," especially as reflected in "the trend toward employee involvement in decision-making process." That required, among other things, abolishing the chain of command.[20] Angell's ideas attracted a good deal of attention from police executives in the early 1970s. But the notion of eliminating middle management proved too radical even for reform-minded departments,[21] and the frightening form taken by police activism in the late 1960s soon dulled the appetite of virtually all scholars and police reformers for bringing even weaker versions of workplace democracy to law enforcement.

Still, support lingered throughout the 1970s for giving police officers a certain kind of voice in the management of their work. Calls for thoroughgoing democracy within police departments, along the lines suggested by Berkley and Westley, quickly went out of fashion. But several departments experimented in the 1970s with "team policing": a loosely defined idea that generally involved a designated group of officers working cooperatively and with a degree of collective operational autonomy to address the problem of a particular neighborhood.[22] Those experiments drew support, in part, from an emerging interest among social scientists in the 1970s in the notion that rank-and-file police officers could and should contribute intellectually to the improvement of police tactics and procedures. The general theme of this scholarship was that police work, and particularly the commonplace tasks of peacekeeping, required far greater skill and understanding than had previously been acknowledged, and that getting officers to think explicitly and systematically about their jobs would make them more effective and less alienated.

The first of these advantages—greater effectiveness—was stressed most famously by Egon Bittner, who argued that policing needed to become a true profession, with its own traditions of scholarship and research-based academic programs. Bittner thought it was for "scholarly policemen," not law professors or social scientists, to "develop an intellectually credible version of what police work should be like." He had no illusions that academic training, even in the hands of "scholarly policemen," could teach aspiring officers everything they needed to know. But he thought it could give them what it gave, say, lawyers: a set of "generalized methods and approaches to facts and problem solving," an inquisitive and studious frame of mind, and habits of methodical, dispassionate reasoning.[23]

William Muir echoed and expanded some of these themes in a widely praised study published in 1977.[24] Muir did not call for academic schools of policing staffed by officers-turned-scholars. But he did think it crucial for police officers to engage in ongoing and collective reflection about the nature of their work. He thought this was how officers became mature, fair-minded, and wise—how they became, in short, people who could be trusted with power. Muir was highly impressed with the efforts that Chief Charles Gain made to infuse the work of the Oakland Police Department with "dignity and moral meaning" by satisfying officers' "appetite for understanding."[25] Gain ran the department from 1967 to 1973. He ruled with a heavy hand and was never popular with the rank and file; in 1971 the Oakland Police Officers' Association voted no confidence in his administration. But he was a dedicated reformer, and his vision of reform included encouraging many of the same qualities of mind that Bittner thought police officers needed: inquisitiveness, methodical reasoning, and self-reflection. To that end he overhauled the department's training program, "inviting participation, discussion, argument, and questioning in every class,"[26] and he welcomed outside researchers interested in police reform.

Three of those researchers themselves mimicked Gain's approach, asking a specially recruited group of rank-and-file officers to come up with ways to reduce violence between officers and citizens. With the outside scholars serving largely as consultants, the officers set their own agenda, carried out their own research, and devised their own proposals. One of those proposals, a "Peer Review Panel" for counseling and assisting officers with a history of violent encounters, appeared to prove effective. The scholars came away impressed with the ability of rank-and-file officers to serve as "agents of change," not only in the day-to-day operation of the Peer Review Panel, but also in coming up with the idea for the panel, and in carrying out the research on which it was based.[27]

The thrust of all this work—Bittner's, Muir's, the Oakland violence study, and to a lesser extent the "team policing" movement—was to embrace police discretion and to find ways to make its exercise more informed, methodical, and collectively self-reflective, rather than to control discretion from above (the strategy of "second-wave" police professionalism) or from outside (the idea behind judicial oversight and civilian review boards).[28] The idea harked back, in a way, to a distinction the sociologist Reinhard Bendix had drawn in the late 1950s between totalitarian and nontotalitarian responses to the "strategies of independence" adopted by employees in a bureaucracy—responses, that is to say, to employees' "tacit evasion of rules and norms" through the application of individual judgment. Bendix suggested that totalitarian regimes sought systematically to suppress independent judgment by employees, while nontotalitarian regimes sought to capitalize on it, through "managerial appeals . . . addressed to the good faith of subordinates."[29] Skolnick drew explicitly on Bendix's distinction and saw clearly the tension it created with efforts to rein in police discretion. The "dilemma of the police in democratic society," Skolnick suggested, "arises out of the conflict between the extent of initiative contemplated by nontotalitarian norms of work and restraints upon police demanded by the rule of law."[30] Skolnick found "forceful normative claims" on each side of this conflict, but ultimately his primary allegiance was to "the ideal of legality," which he took to be the "highest stated commitment" of "democratic society."[31] Scholars like Bittner and Muir struck the balance the other way. Skolnick's position, as we have seen, was consistent in important ways with democratic pluralism; Bittner's and Muir's was consistent with increased sympathy in the 1970s for notions of participatory democracy.[32]

During the 1980s, though, views like Bittner's and Muir's grew marginalized, and, except among line police officers themselves, the taste for bringing even a mild form of workplace democracy to policing all but disappeared.[33] Team policing remained a "buzz phrase in police circles," but it lost its earlier connotation of participatory management.[34] The diminished enthusiasm for giving police officers greater control over the nature of their work likely had several causes: lingering concerns with the disturbing character of police organizing in the late 1960s; escalating budgetary constraints and a correspondingly heightened emphasis on public sector managerialism; diminishing aversion to military-style hierarchy as the Vietnam War receded; and—a matter to which we return momentarily—monopolization of the police reform agenda by community policing. Possibly, too, the growing power of police unions made it more difficult for departments to explore new strategies of collaborative decision making that circumvented seniority systems or bypassed the union hierarchy.[35] By the 1990s, in any event, the idea of employee participation had largely dropped off the screen of police reform. The theme is entirely absent, for example, from a recent, otherwise balanced encyclopedia article on police and democracy by the sociologist Gary Marx, despite the fact that both Berkley and Muir appear in the bibliography.[36]

The New Ideal

And so we come to community policing. Writing in 1977, Robert Fogelson noted that critics of 1950s-style police professionalism, while proliferating, as yet lacked "anything like a military analogy or a professional model that might draw them together."[37] By the late 1980s, though, the new model had emerged—or at least the new, unifying rhetoric. Community policing was by then what it remains today: the new, "preferred ideal" of police reformers and law enforcement executives alike.[38] It is an ideal notorious for meaning different things to different people, but at its core is a rejection of the form of police professionalism that came to be epitomized by the Los Angeles Police Department under William Parker and valorized in *Dragnet*: arrogant, heavy-handed, technologically driven, and aloof.[39]

Much of the spirit of the community policing movement was anticipated in the criticism that began to be leveled at the LAPD in the 1960s. Paul Jacobs's 1966 critique in *Atlantic* is illustrative. Published the same year that *Dragnet* returned to television, the article condemned Parker's repressive tactics, particularly in minority areas of Los Angeles, but made clear that "[t]he overwhelming majority of the people living in the ghettos of Los Angeles are not seeking to rid their communities of the police."[40] Rather, they wanted a different kind of police. They wanted the police to take time to learn about the people they patrolled, to shift their emphasis away from arrests, and "to act as the lady from Watts remembered they once did, to 'come to the house and talk to the kids if they did something bad.' "[41]

The notion that the police should work *with* communities, rather than against them, became the heart of the community policing movement. The theme is community *partnership*, not community *control*: with minor exceptions, community policing programs are implemented unilaterally by the police.[42] Still, from the outset the movement has appealed in part to the sense that community policing is "*more democratic* than conventional policing," because it improves "the public's capacity to influence policing."[43] Underlying this appeal have been ideas about democracy far more congruent with participatory democracy than with democratic pluralism.

We will return repeatedly to the linkages between participatory democracy and community policing in the pages that follow, but a few of the connections are worth noting now. First, and most obviously, the rhetoric of community policing drew heavily on the emphasis that participatory democracy placed on the involvement of ordinary citizens, precisely the political mechanism the pluralists had spurned above others. Of equal importance, the new rhetoric typically assumed the existence of a unitary, easily defined "community" or "public"—also an assumption the pluralists had rejected, and an assumption for which the community policing movement has frequently been faulted.[44] Finally, the community policing movement has included from the get-go an element of nostalgia for a friendlier and more orderly past, the past recalled by "the lady from Watts." The very phrase "community policing" summons forth images of clean, safe sidewalks walked by "beat cops (usually with brogues) giving homespun and salubrious advice."[45] The nostalgia wrapped up in the term—out of keeping with pluralism's embrace of modernity but fully in step with certain versions of participatory democracy—contributed significantly to its ambiguity: the

1950s represented both the apogee of the policing practices the new movement purported to reject, and the golden age of orderliness it sought to
recover. Aggressive "stop and frisk" campaigns, for example, might be a hall-
mark of heavy-handed police professionalism, but they also could be (and
were) justified as efforts to "work with communities" in restoring a sense of
safety and order.[46]

Anti-pluralism in Contemporary Criminal Procedure

The emergence of community policing as the new common language of police reform coincided with the end of the Burger Court and the beginning
of the Rehnquist Court. William Rehnquist was elevated to Chief Justice
in 1986, the same year that Antonin Scalia was appointed to the Supreme
Court. By the early 1990s, the Rehnquist Court was beginning to chart a
distinctive course in criminal procedure, often with Scalia's prodding. During this same period the academic field of criminal procedure changed, too.
There is widespread agreement about that, if not on the precise nature of
the change or even its general direction. What seems clear is that the generation of legal scholars who began writing about criminal procedure in the
late 1980s and early 1990s approached the subject in different ways than
their predecessors, whose careers and outlooks had been shaped so strongly
by the controversies surrounding the Warren Court and its legacy.

Criminal procedure scholars now are a diverse lot, and many, perhaps
most, of them are sharply critical of the directions in which the Supreme
Court has taken criminal procedure law. Nor has the Supreme Court's
approach to criminal procedure under Chief Justice Rehnquist, and now
Chief Justice Roberts, been entirely consistent. Nonetheless, I want to suggest there are some themes held in common both by some of the most important criminal procedure scholarship of the past decade and a half and by
some of the most interesting things the Supreme Court has had to say on
the subject. The themes include an enthusiasm for community participation, a premium placed on transparency, a distrust of elites and expertise, a
preoccupation with legitimacy, and a retreat from modernity. Each of these
themes, I will suggest, is consistent with the shift away from pluralism as the
dominant understanding of American democracy and toward theories of

participatory democracy and deliberative democracy. Three other features of criminal procedure jurisprudence and scholarship today—the continued treatment of the police as a breed apart, the persistent de-emphasis of institutional structure, and the comparative neglect of inequality—reflect important points of continuity between pluralism and the theories which have supplanted it.

In defending these claims I will make no effort to survey contemporary criminal procedure scholarship comprehensively. Nor will I try to identify global motifs of criminal procedure jurisprudence under the Rehnquist and Roberts Courts. In each case the field is too diverse. Both at the level of jurisprudence and at the level of scholarship, criminal procedure is less unified and coherent than it was in the Warren and Burger Court eras—just as democratic theory today is less unified and coherent than it was when pluralism was the reigning orthodoxy. So the discussion here necessarily will be selective. I will highlight certain, particularly noteworthy developments in criminal procedure jurisprudence and scholarship, developments that seem to reflect assumptions about American democracy different from the assumptions that animated criminal procedure in the years of the Warren and Burger Courts.

On the scholarship side, I will focus chiefly on the work of three law professors: Akhil Amar, Dan Kahan, and Tracey Meares. I should say a word or two about why—particularly since, although Kahan and Meares have been frequent collaborators, grouping them with Amar may seem odd. Amar is famously textualist; his chief goal has been to wring sense from the words of the Constitution. Kahan and Meares, in contrast, are concerned above all with contemporary problems of social control, and Meares, in particular, is a committed empiricist.[47] But the work of all three scholars merits special attention here, and for similar reasons. First, in each case it is exceptionally thoughtful work, cutting across traditional debates in criminal procedure. Whatever their faults, neither Amar nor Kahan nor Meares has followed the pattern that people like Robert Weisberg already found tiresome more than a decade and a half ago: attacking or defending the criminal procedure legacy of the Warren Court largely in the terms set by the Warren Court itself.[48] All three scholars have been creative, sophisticated, and quite self-conscious in urging a break with criminal procedure scholarship of the Warren and Burger Court eras. Second, the work of all three scholars has clearly touched nerves. Often (but not always) the ensuing debate has taken the form of an intergenerational dispute—adding to the impression that we are dealing here with something new. And, in each case, there has been a widespread sense that the something new is somehow representative: these are scholars who seem to "captured the moment."[49] Third, more than many other criminal procedure scholars, Amar, Kahan, and Meares have explicitly incorporated the theme of collective self-government into their work. All three scholars have taken democracy seriously. Fourth and finally, the very differences between Amar on the one hand and Kahan and Meares on the other will prove useful for a certain kind of analytic triangulation: their shared points of departure from traditional approaches to criminal procedure are less likely to be idiosyncratic, and more likely to reflect broader intellectual trends.

The Enthusiasm for Community Participation

The rhetoric of community policing, as we have seen, appeals strongly to notions of popular participation in government, and more specifically to the notions of *community* participation—notions, that is to say, that communities exist, that they have coherent views and interests, and that law enforcement, and the criminal justice system more generally, can and should reflect those interests. These same notions are reflected in some of the most influential criminal procedure scholarship of the last decade or so; they are an important part of what makes that scholarship novel and important.

Take, for example, Amar's widely discussed call for renewed reliance on civil juries to set appropriate bounds on law enforcement.[50] Amar shares Tocqueville's famous enthusiasm for the jury as the preeminent instrument of participatory democracy. Like Tocqueville, Amar praises the jury both as a school of democratic virtue and as a site of popular sovereignty. Tocqueville thought the first function was the most important: he was unsure whether the jury was "useful to those who have lawsuits," but he was certain it instilled "practical judgment and political good sense" in the jurors themselves.[51] Amar, on the other hand, is much more taken with the jury as a vehicle for community control of the criminal justice system. He praises the educative role of the jury, but his argument here feels slight. First and foremost, the jury represents for Amar "the common sense of the common people."[52]

Or, closer to home, consider the enthusiasm that Kahan and Meares show for local communities taking law enforcement into their own hands.[53] That enthusiasm extends not just to the direct involvement of private citizens in policing, through volunteer patrols, campaigns of unofficial "shaming," and collaborations with law enforcement by churches and civic organizations. It also includes efforts by local governments to strike their own balances between liberty and security. If a particular community believes it needs, say, an aggressive anti-loitering policy to combat street gangs, or blanket inspection of homes for evidence of drug trafficking, Kahan and Meares think courts should look askance on claims that the policy violates civil liberties.[54] Now that racial minorities "are no longer excluded from the nation's political life," courts by and large should honor the outcome of the local democratic process.[55]

Like Amar, Kahan and Meares share none of the discomfort the pluralists showed with widespread political participation. Also like Amar, they rest their argument on an assumption the pluralists found utterly untenable: that there exists, in any particular polity, an identifiable "public" or "community" position on controversial policy questions, embraced by ordinary citizens as well as political leaders, and rising above the narrow interests of particular groups.[56] That assumption in turn rests on other beliefs, also rejected by the pluralists: that ordinary people are rational and well informed about matters of public concern, and that politics can and does proceed through reasoned discussion. Inner-city residents, in particular, "are reasonable people,"[57] and if left to their own devices will decide questions of criminal procedure through a process of collective deliberation.[58]

Now, Kahan and Meares do not write chiefly about democracy. As coauthors they are concerned first and foremost with the informal social mechanisms—the "norms"—of crime control. Nor is Amar writing mainly about democracy. The vision of democracy one encounters in the work of these scholars is largely implicit. For all that, the vision is recognizably rooted in the anti-pluralist tradition of participatory democracy and deliberative democracy. Here, for example, are Kahan and Meares:

> [T]he worst consequence of the ongoing commitment to the 1960s
> conception of rights may be its *disempowering* effect on inner-city
> communities. Criminologists have long recognized that crime both creates
> and is sustained by atomization and distrust, which in turn make it harder
> for individuals to engage in the cooperative self-policing characteristic of

crime-free communities. A healthy democratic political life can help repair these conditions. That is precisely what residents of the inner city enjoy when they are free to decide for themselves whether to adopt building searches, gang-loitering ordinances, curfews and the like. Thus, in addition to standing in the way of potentially effective law-enforcement policies, the 1960s conception of rights pre-empts deliberative experiences that reduce crime through their effect on public dispositions and habits.[59]

It is all there: the concern with "atomization" and "disempowerment," the emphasis on cooperation and deliberation, the focus on habits of partic-ipation, the metaphor of social "health."[60] The vision of participatory democracy invoked by Kahan and Meares is far from worked out. They are vague, for example, regarding the contours of the inner-city "community," what it means for members of that community to decide matters "for them-selves," and what the preconditions for "deliberative experiences" might be, other than the withdrawal of judicial oversight. Their vagueness on these matters is noteworthy, and we will return to it later. For now, though, the important points are these. First, Kahan and Meares, like Amar, draw on a vision of democracy. Second, that vision of democracy, although thinly ar-ticulated, parts with pluralism in placing great weight on notions of com-munity participation. Third and finally, the kind of participation that Kahan and Meares have in mind is, essentially, the kind of participation we already have today: the only structural change they propose is a relaxation of judi-cial review. Their argument is consistent with what I have called the status quo version of participatory democracy.

An enthusiasm for community participation, even in its status quo ver-sion, is difficult to reconcile with the thrust of current criminal procedure doctrine, most of which was constructed during the Warren and Burger Court eras and, as we have seen, echoes democratic pluralism both in stress-ing the protection of individual dignity and in giving little weight to majori-tarianism. This is precisely the reason Kahan and Meares think that criminal procedure faces a "coming crisis."[61] The Supreme Court has yet to modify criminal procedure doctrine to place greater weight on local participatory politics. But there are scattered signs that it may be moving in that direc-tion. Community participation still plays no formal role in criminal proce-dure doctrine, but it has begun to be part of the rhetorical atmosphere of some of the Court's decisions.

The change may be most striking in the Court's treatment of searches in public schools. The Burger Court had treated searches of students by school personnel the way it treated other searches by government agencies other than the police: subject to lesser restraints than police searches, but still requiring a "balance" between government objectives (here, "the need to maintain an environment in which learning can take place") and individual dignity ("the schoolchild's reasonable expectations of privacy").[62] For the Burger Court, the notion that school teachers should be seen as agents of their students' parents—the old doctrine of *in loco parentis*—flew in the face of "contemporary reality."[63] Teachers and school administrators were not parents; they were "representatives of the State."[64] In contrast, when the Rehnquist Court upheld a school district policy mandating drug testing for student athletes, Justice Scalia's opinion for the majority explicitly embraced the doctrine of *in loco parentis* and stressed, furthermore, that before adopting the policy the district had solicited the views of parents at a public meeting, and that the parents in attendance all favored the proposed rule.[65] Several years later, when the Court upheld a policy by a different school district requiring drug tests not just for athletes but for all students engaged in extracurricular activities, Justice Breyer took occasion to show the practical implications of his views about "participatory democratic self-government." Concurring in the Court's decision, Breyer emphasized that the local school board had held "public meetings designed to give the entire community 'the opportunity to be able to participate' in developing the drug policy." Since the ultimate question of constitutional interpretation raised in the case seemed "close," Breyer thought it "important" that the school board had used a "democratic, participatory process to uncover and to resolve differences."[66]

Scalia and Breyer are not generally seen as kindred spirits. They have staked out starkly adverse positions, for example, on the appropriate methods of constitutional adjudication.[67] When they are both drawn to emphasize community participation in thinking about student drug testing, despite the fact that current Fourth Amendment doctrine makes this factor irrelevant, something is afoot.

The student drug testing cases are not, strictly speaking, cases about the police, even though the threat of police involvement always hovers in the background. But notions of community participation have also begun to seep into the rhetoric of cases addressing police practices, if only, so far, in the dissents. Take *Chicago v. Morales*,[68] which addressed the constitutionality of a Chicago ordinance that criminalized loitering by gang members—an ordinance that Kahan and Meares repeatedly identify as the kind of "innovative community policing measures" that inner-city residents wanted and should be allowed to adopt.[69] The Illinois courts struck the measure down on vagueness grounds, and the Supreme Court affirmed. For a majority of the justices, the case was not about community self-determination; it was about unconstrained police discretion.[70] But the dissents, by Justice Scalia and Justice Thomas, saw the case roughly the same way as Kahan and Meares. Justice Thomas, in particular, pointed out that the ordinance was the product of a "democratic process" that included "extensive hearings" at which "[o]rdinary citizens" came forward to testify about gangs in their neighborhoods.[71]

The dissenters touched relatively lightly on this theme; their chief concern was not community participation but the need to allow police officers some discretion in order to maintain "a safe and orderly society."[72] We will return to that concern below. For now, though, the most important point about the Supreme Court's decision in *Morales* is that democracy entered into the discussion *only* through the limited use that the dissenters made of the rhetoric of community participation and self-determination. The majority never tied its concerns about police discretion to any recognizable notion of democracy. There was no discussion of police states, no coded references to authoritarian mentalities.[73] As a result the focus on police discretion felt a little rootless and insubstantial. Even two of the justices who joined in the judgment felt obliged to agree with Justice Thomas that "some degree of police discretion is necessary to allow the police 'to perform their peacekeeping responsibilities satisfactorily.' "[74]

The Premium on Transparency

The enthusiasm for community involvement in contemporary criminal procedure scholarship is accompanied by, and often overlaps with, an emphasis on the public exposure of policing strategies. This theme is muted in the work of Amar (although congenial to his focus on popular sovereignty), and it is largely absent from the work of Kahan and Meares. It is front and center, though, in legal scholar Eric Luna's recent argument that democracy

requires "transparent policing," by which he means visibility of what the police do and how they decide to do it.[75] And Luna has good company. Jerome
Skolnick, for example, has recently called openness "a master ideal of democratic policing," and Chief Bratton has stressed the need for police agencies
to open themselves up to "scrutiny and public exposure."[76]

Pluralism, with its emphasis on elites, made widespread dissemination of
information about the government seem relatively unimportant—perhaps
even counterproductive. Partly for this reason, public visibility of policing
never became a central part of criminal procedure law or scholarship in
the Warren and Burger Court eras. True, certain key rulings of the Warren
Court were motivated by a concern about police secrecy. One thinks particularly of the rulings giving criminal defendants the right to counsel at cus-
todial interrogations and post-indictment lineups; in each case the Court
made clear that part of its objective was to give defense counsel the information they would later need to challenge the admissibility of evidence obtained improperly.[77] The point, though, was to get information *to the defense*,
in order to improve the fairness of the adversarial process, not to expose the
police to general public scrutiny.

Theories of participatory democracy and deliberative democracy, on the
other hand, make the broad visibility of government decision making much
more important.[78] This may be particularly true of a status quo theory of
participatory democracy like the one Justice Breyer has defended: a theory
that ties the legitimacy of our current system of government to the meta-
phorical "conversation" that takes place in the media, at public hearings, at
professional meetings, and so on. Without disclosure, this conversation cannot take place; with disclosure, legitimacy becomes almost automatic. It
is therefore not surprising that Luna draws heavily on rhetoric similar to
Breyer's, stressing the role of transparency in "[e]mpowering citizens," "giving them a voice in the decisionmaking process," and "establishing a basis
for trust in otherwise distrusting communities."[79]

The Distrust of Elites and Expertise

The enthusiasm for community involvement, and the premium placed on
public discussion, are only two of the contemporary trends in criminal

procedure that reflect a shift from democratic pluralism to theories of participatory democracy and deliberative democracy. Another is the strain of anti-elitism. This often takes the form, both in scholarship and in jurisprudence, of hostility to claims of professional expertise, and pronounced distrust of the "political stratum" in which the pluralists placed so much confidence—particularly judges, administrators, and "civil libertarians."

The problem of police discretion, such a central preoccupation of Warren Court criminal procedure, exercises the current generation of criminal procedure scholars much less. Kahan and Meares are hardly alone in calling for a relaxation of "discretion suspicion."[80] But the remedy of judicial oversight, which made so much sense from the perspective of democratic pluralism, worries scholars today—including Amar, Kahan, and Meares—a good deal more. Because they understand democracy in vaguely Rousseauian terms, as the collective formation of a community will, judicial review does not strike them as exercise in the mediation of intergroup conflicts. Rather, it appears to them as it always appeared to the Warren Court's critics: as the abrupt imposition of a decision from above. It looks like the polar opposite of democracy. This is an increasingly common theme of the Supreme Court's criminal procedure jurisprudence as well, particularly the opinions of Justice Scalia and Justice Thomas.

The notion is hardly new that judicial oversight of policing frustrates democracy. Again, this was always part of the case against the Warren Court. But the argument has clearly gained ground over the past couple of decades. One reason for that—although certainly not the only reason—is that background ideas about democracy have changed. Democratic pluralism has lost its hold, and the theories of participatory democracy and deliberative democracy that have supplanted it make judicial oversight harder to defend.

They make other forms of elite governance harder to defend, as well, including the reliance on expertise of varying kinds—judicial, administrative, and clinical—in the formation and execution of criminal justice policy. Jonathan Simon and other legal scholars seem right, for example, to link the recent popularity of mandatory sentences and "zero-tolerance" policies to disenchantment with the kind of "individualized justice" previously dispensed by "expert judges, and supported by a panoply of normalizing professionals (psychologists, social workers, probation officers, and so on)."[81]

Like many of today's criminal procedure scholars, Meares is an empiricist. So is Kahan, to a lesser extent. This creates for them a problem similar to the one that confronted the pluralists: in principle they believe that claims of expertise should bow to politics, but they also think that social science has important lessons to teach about current problems and their solutions. Meares, in fact, has called repeatedly for greater reliance on social science research in criminal procedure.[82] As we saw in Chapter 1, the pluralists' respect for social science led them to a broader respect for professional and technical expertise. But for scholars like Meares and Kahan, anti-elitism appears to trump scientism. (It is hard to tell for sure, because Meares and Kahan see no conflict between what social science has to say about policing and what inner-city residents already know.)[83] Although Meares argues that *judges* should pay more attention to recent work in criminology, she never makes a similar claim about local politicians or community activists. With Kahan, she respects the unmediated "local knowledge" of "average citizens," and presumes that community leaders speak on behalf of their constituents.[84]

The Preoccupation with Legitimacy

The status quo version of participatory democracy shares with deliberative democracy, in its most common forms, an overriding emphasis on legitimacy, both actual and perceived. Deliberative democracy, as we have seen, is first and foremost a theory *about* legitimacy: that is to say, about what makes democracy both worthy of respect (actual legitimacy) and likely to achieve respect (perceived legitimacy). Likewise, the status quo version of participatory democracy—the version reflected in the criminal procedure work of scholars like Amar, Kahan, and Meares, and the version that has begun to make itself felt in criminal procedure jurisprudence—stresses the value of participation in making governmental decisions more acceptable to those affected by them.

In the last decade and a half the theme of legitimacy has become increasingly prominent in criminal procedure jurisprudence and scholarship. One way this has happened is through renewed attention in criminal procedure to the "countermajoritarian difficulty," a development that also reflects, as we have seen, a strain of anti-elitism. Amar, along with other scholars, sees the jury as in large part a device for giving "legitimacy" to the criminal justice system.[85] Amar argues for textualism in similar terms: "A Constitution that speaks in the name of the people and that draws its legitimacy from ratification by the people—ordinary citizens—should be presumed to use words in their ordinary sense, absent a strong countervailing argument."[86] And legitimacy looms large for Kahan and Meares, as well. It figures not only in their arguments for increasing community participation in policing,[87] but also in their enthusiasm for law enforcement strategies and penal policies that rely less on deterrence than on the moral authority of the law,[88] and on the trust that police departments build in the communities they patrol.[89]

Trust and moral authority were important to the pluralists, too, but in different ways. As we saw in Chapter 1, the pluralists thought that a successful democracy required widespread commitment, particularly among elites, to a set of core values. Most of these—the "rules of the game"—had to do with the peaceful resolution of intergroup conflicts. In the 1960s and 1970s, therefore, the perceived legitimacy of the criminal justice system tended to be valued not as a goal in and of itself, nor even as a way to make the system more effective in controlling crime, but rather as a way to protect social stability by building nationwide consensus. And the chief strategy for bolstering that legitimacy was not widespread participation in policing, or in government more generally; it was instead the visible commitment by political elites, including the Supreme Court, to substantive values thought to transcend group politics, particularly human dignity.

The Retreat from Modernity

As we have seen, criminal procedure doctrine and scholarship in the 1960s and 1970s echoed the pluralist embrace of modernity in three ways: in an enthusiasm for the new, quasi-scientific, technology-intensive methods of "second-wave" police professionalism; in the abandonment of original intent as a guide to interpreting the criminal procedure provisions of the Constitution; and in the relatively low priority given to values of order, decorum, and safety. Criminal procedure today, both in the courts and in the academy, is marked by the opposite tendencies: a disenchantment with police professionalism; a return to original intent; and a renewed appreciation for order, decorum, and safety. In each of these respects, contemporary criminal procedure reflects the backward-looking posture characteristic of much (although certainly not all) of the rhetoric associated with participatory democracy and deliberative democracy.

We have already touched on the disenchantment with the technologically intensive form of police professionalism epitomized in the 1950s and early 1960s by William Parker's Los Angeles Police Department. The roots of the community policing movement lay in that disenchantment. Even today, the manifold strategies grouped together under the umbrella of community policing probably share, above all else, a rejection of Parker-style police professionalism. (That may be one reason why the LAPD has found it particularly difficult to align itself credibly with the new orthodoxy.)[90] Criminal procedure scholars overwhelmingly join in that rejection, and in the embrace of community policing. Kahan and Meares have been particularly vocal champions of community policing, but their enthusiasm is widely shared.

Amar's efforts to return criminal procedure to "first principles" through a renewed attention to original intent have been more controversial. But they have drawn so much criticism in part because, in many quarters, they have been so well received. Even some of Amar's critics now fight on the ground of original intent.[91] In sharp contrast to the situation in the 1960s and 1970s, when both the Supreme Court and its critics seemed in broad agreement that neither the language nor the history of the Fourth Amendment were of any help, many if not most criminal procedure scholars now view history as "crucial to an understanding of the Fourth Amendment"— and, for that matter, of the Fifth and Sixth Amendments as well.[92]

Today's Supreme Court is of a similar mind. Led by Justice Scalia and Justice Thomas, the Court in recent years has started paying much more attention to history in criminal procedure. The trend is particularly striking in Fourth Amendment law, where a solid majority of the Court has made the primary criterion for identifying constitutional violations "whether a particular governmental action . . . was regarded as an unlawful search or seizure under the common law when the Amendment was framed."[93]

Amar's work exemplifies not only the return to history in constitutional criminal procedure but also the heightened appreciation for orderliness. The orderliness that most concerns Amar is jurisprudential: he has a pronounced aversion to doctrinal "mess,"[94] and a strong attraction to interpretations that are "snug," "well-fitted," and "aesthetically pleasing."[95] Complaints about the untidiness of Fourth Amendment law are hardly new,[96] but Amar makes those complaints with special insistence. The heavy emphasis he places on doctrinal coherence and consistency is mirrored by a more general appreciation for the virtues of order, decorum, and safety. Among the central themes of his work has been the importance of factual accuracy in criminal procedure: the importance of avoiding not only the conviction of the innocent, but also the acquittal of the guilty. In interpreting the Fourth Amendment, for example, he urges us to keep in mind that "the people are *more* 'secure in their persons, houses, papers, and effects'" when "rapists, burglars, and murderers are convicted."[97]

In this respect he is representative. It is hard today to find scholars who think the "basic purpose" of criminal procedure is solely to protect the individual from the state, or that "[i]t inflicts no tangible harm on anyone when a criminal evades punishment"—views that remained common well into the early 1980s.[98] Resignation about the risks of criminal victimization has become much less common. In part this reflects the successful, and long overdue, effort by feminist scholars over the past twenty years to draw greater attention to the gendered tilt of private violence, and to the systems of subordination it enforces.[99] But it also reflects a renewed emphasis on order and safety more broadly, and a diminished willingness to accept a certain level of crime as the price of freedom, spontaneity, and the related attractions of modern urban life.

The freedom and spontaneity of modern urban life—the "exuberant diversity" Jane Jacobs celebrated in the early 1960s—have, in fact, lost much of their luster.[100] The "broken windows," or "order maintenance," approach to policing pioneered by James Q. Wilson in collaboration with George Kelling—an approach sometimes taken as the essence of community policing—views street-level urban disorder as the seedbed of crime, and treats it accordingly. Kahan and Meares have been especially taken with the broken windows theory,[101] but in this respect they have hardly been outliers among criminal procedure scholars. On the contrary, this is another respect in which their work has seemed to have captured the moment.[102] Dissenting voices are starting to be heard, and even Kahan's enthusiasm has grown more qualified.[103] But broken windows policing, and the "aesthetic of orderliness"[104] to which it appeals, continue to enjoy broad support. Some of that support may reflect the way in which the image of clean, orderly neighborhoods resonates with the nostalgia often associated with participatory democracy and deliberative democracy.

Many of the criticisms of order maintenance policing have themselves appealed to notions of democracy—including, in particular, notions of popular participation and public deliberation. In different ways, Bernard Harcourt and Jonathan Simon have both suggested that the aggressive patrol tactics associated with broken windows policing can corrode the sense of shared fate and collective agency required for meaningful self-government.[105] The fact that both champions and critics of order maintenance policing draw on the rhetoric of participation and deliberation is a sign of the degree to which pluralism has been supplanted as the dominant theory of American democracy. But it also reflects the malleability of the new rhetoric, and it underscores the need for greater rigor in discussions of the relationship between democracy and policing.

The Continued Treatment of the Police as a Breed Apart

One way in which theories of participatory democracy and deliberative democracy have *not* influenced contemporary thinking about the police is by altering the long-standing conception of the police as a breed apart. The notion of an "authoritarian personality" has fallen into disfavor, but scholars today still show little affinity for any vision of democracy that includes political participation by, or deliberation among, police officers themselves. The experiments during the 1970s with bringing participatory management and rank-and-file intellectual engagement to policing have not been renewed. The rhetoric of community policing, meanwhile, calls for the police to be *partners* of the community, not part of the community itself. In reality, the relationship falls far short of true partnership: community policing as actually practiced rarely intrudes much on the operational autonomy of the police.[106] But community policing does even less to make the police a genuine part of the community. Almost always, a police department engaged in community policing remains, in every significant respect, "a force of outsiders."[107]

It is telling in this regard that the reinstatement of residency requirements for police officers has never become part of the community policing agenda. Even James Q. Wilson—no fan of community control of the police—had some sympathy in the late 1960s for the view that officers should live in the neighborhoods they patrol.[108] A few departments in fact brought back residency requirements in the early 1970s, but police unions strongly opposed the idea, and in most cases the opposition was successful.[109] Since the 1970s the number of departments imposing a residency requirement appears to have declined.[110] The notion that police officers should be fully "integrated with the community"—the notion that appealed so strongly to George Berkley and William Westley at the end of the 1960s—has been all but discarded.[111] So too has the related notion, also shared by Berkley and Westley, that the internal operations of police forces should conform as closely as possible to the democratic "norms and values" of the larger society.[112]

Democratic pluralism did not lead to calls for greater participation by police officers in the internal operation of police departments or in the political life of the broader community, because pluralism de-emphasized political participation as a *general* matter, particularly among people, like police officers, who might be expected to have authoritarian personalities. Pluralism inclined scholars to think of the police as a breed apart, moreover, because pluralism suggested that *all* groups were essentially breeds apart, and that only the political elite could be counted on to share democratic values. Theories of participatory democracy and deliberative democracy might be thought to be more amenable to the idea that the police, along with everyone else, should participate as much as possible in collective self-governance. And for a few years in the early 1970s that idea was in fact sympathetically received. The dictates of democracy for people in general were thought fully applicable to the police. For a variety of reasons, though, primarily having to do with the specific politics of the late 1960s and early 1970s, that notion has been all but abandoned; thus, this first point of continuity with pluralist-influenced thinking about police.

The Persistent De-emphasis of Institutional Structure

As we have seen, the theories of participatory democracy and deliberative democracy that have gained favor in the last few decades share with democratic pluralism an emphasis on culture rather than on institutions. Like pluralism, that is to say, the new theories are grounded in what I have called the social science paradigm: the inclination of American intellectuals since the late nineteenth century to take psychology and sociology, rather than political economy, as the keys to understanding politics and society. The continuing hold of this approach has meant that today, as in the 1950s and 1960s, most thinking about reconciling police with democracy focuses heavily on issues of culture and tends to neglect questions of institutional structure: both the internal decision-making structures of police departments and the external processes of political control. This is the second point of continuity with the ideas about the police developed during the Warren and Burger Court eras.

Discussions of the inner workings of police departments persist in stressing the group psychology of the police and in treating formal structures of decision making as largely irrelevant. In the words of one police scholar, "[r]esearchers have generally neglected studying police organizations in favor of studying police work—including situations, encounters, strategies, and occupational characteristics, and police officers—their attitudes, feelings, beliefs, behaviors, and interactions."[113] A recent overview finds that theories about the causes of police misconduct, for example, fall into three categories: "*sociological* theories which focus on situational factors such as the conduct of suspects, the context of suspect–police encounters and such factors as gender, race, and socioeconomic status; *psychological* theories, which emphasize officer attitudes and personality traits; and *organizational* theories, which explore the role of organizational culture."[114] Sociology, psychology, and organizational culture: *structures* of decision making are not in the picture. Similarly, the blue-ribbon commissions appointed after each police scandal inevitably underscore the importance of changing the culture and mind-set of the department at issue.[115] The emphasis that scholars like Kahan and Meares have placed on extralegal norms has, if anything, only increased the interest of scholars and policymakers in the "milieu" of policing, and drawn attention even further away from institutional structure.[116] The questions that rarely get asked about policing today are the ones that would have seemed most obvious to, say, the authors of *The Federalist Papers*, had they foreseen the emergence of modern police departments: How should law enforcement be organized to best assure that the powers given to police officers are used wisely and fairly? What departmental structures will best harness and counterbalance the ambitions of police officers, aligning their collective objectives with public purposes?

Criminal procedure scholars rarely ask structural questions about external political control of police departments, either. In fact, the declining influence of democratic pluralism may have pushed scholars further away from these questions. Kahan and Meares again are illustrative. They argue that a range of strategies they associate with "the new community policing"—specifically, loitering laws, curfews, and blanket searches of housing projects—deserve judicial deference because they reflect the considered judgments of the affected inner-city communities about how best to "balance liberty and order."[117] But they give little attention to the structures through which these communities actually make decisions, in large part because they see this matter as unproblematic: inner-city communities deliberate, reach collective agreements, and then have those agreements carried out by their political representatives. In the 1960s, it is true, "law enforcement officials were accountable only to representatives of the white majority."[118] But voting rights legislation fixed that problem. So today courts should get out of the way and allow inner-city residents "to decide for themselves whether to adopt building search, gang-loitering ordinances, curfews and like policies."[119] Chicago's gang-loitering law deserved particular deference, because it "was to be enforced only after consultation with 'local leaders' and 'community organizations'—the representatives of the average citizen."[120]

The heavy emphasis the pluralists placed on interest groups forced them to pay a certain minimal amount of attention to institutional structure: elections had to keep government officials in check, and decision making needed to be sufficiently decentralized to allow multiple points of access. But where the pluralists saw interest groups competing with each other, Kahan and Meares see a unified community.[121] They vacillate about whose views they are describing—sometimes it is "inner-city residents," sometimes "inner-city minorities," sometimes "African Americans." But the views ascribed to the community in question, however it is defined, are clear and coherent: a desire for more law enforcement; fervent support for "the new community policing"; a "strong sense of 'linked fate' with inner-city law-breakers, with whom they are intimately bound by social and familial ties"; "an intense commitment to individual liberty"; sensitivity to "the risks associated with excessive discretion" and to "the political dynamics that surround law enforcement"; and, ultimately, a "judgment that in today's political and social context, the continued victimization of minorities at hands of criminals poses a much more significant threat to the well-being of minorities than does the risk of arbitrary mistreatment at the hands of the police."[122]

This faith in a coherent, unified public will—the same faith that has Amar praising the ability of juries to "represent the people"[123]—is part of what leads Kahan and Meares to disregard questions about the structure of democratic decision making. They applaud, for example, the "strategic alliance[s]" that police in Boston and Chicago have formed with black church leaders; they see these alliances, which have included police-sponsored prayer vigils and arrangements giving selected church authorities "a say in the disposition of potential offenders," as promising examples of "the New Community Policing."[124] Kahan and Meares are hardly alone here, and the arrangements in question may in fact deserve praise. But they raise some fairly obvious questions about evenhandedness and democratic control—leaving aside the problem of religious establishment. Those questions all but disappear when Kahan and Meares discuss police–church collaboration, because church leaders and everyone else in the inner city are assumed to share the same interests.[125] For similar reasons, the threats to democratic control posed by privatized policing more generally vanish from Kahan's perspective. Even unofficial campaigns of sustained harassment—"private shaming"—strike Kahan as unqualified blessings.[126] From his perspective, in fact, this is community policing at its best. Because these campaigns are conducted not by the police but by that imagined collective, "the citizens themselves," Kahan sees little reason to fear abuse.[127]

The institutional mechanisms traditionally relied upon for democratic control of the police—city councils, mayors' offices, and, more recently, civilian oversight agencies—continue to receive relatively little attention from criminal procedure scholars.[128] The matter of civilian oversight deserves special comment. Agencies of this kind continue to proliferate: there are now perhaps a hundred across the country. The vast majority of big-city police departments are now subject to some form of civilian oversight.[129] The institutional structure of that oversight varies widely. There are boards of part-time volunteers and offices of full-time professionals. Some oversight agencies have independent investigative authority; some do not. Some agencies review citizen complaints; others advise the police on matters of policy. Some consist only of civilians; others include some police officers.[130] Very little scholarly attention has been paid to how well these agencies operate, or to whether certain variations have been more successful than others in making the police, in one sense or another, more democratic. In particular, an unusual coalition of police administrators and liberal-minded police reformers have warned for decades that certain common forms of civilian review can actually *undermine* democratic control of police forces by diffusing responsibility and undermining the chain of command.[131] We know less than we should about whether they have been proved right.

We know even less about the internal affairs divisions that virtually every American police agency of any significant size now uses to investigate allegations of wrongdoing by officers.[132] Here the focus on culture at the expense of institutions intersects with the continuing tendency to see the police as a breed apart. Internal affairs divisions vary widely in their functional organization, lines of reporting, operational protocols, and staffing policies. Police officers do not view internal affairs investigations lightly, nor should they: on average internal affairs divisions sustain allegations against officers at significantly higher rates than civilian oversight boards. No one thinks internal affairs departments can take sole responsibility for improving the quality of policing: wholly aside from conflicts of interest, internal affairs investigations tend by their nature to be punitive rather than forward-looking, and to focus on specific incidents rather than systemic failures. But some internal affairs divisions clearly work better than others, and a few even depart from a pure incident-by-incident focus.[133] Very few scholars, though, have spent any time studying internal affairs departments and assessing what features of institutional design seem to make them to work best. Police reformers tend to neglect internal affairs divisions, too. Seeing the shared mentality and culture of the police as the root problem, they tend to write off disciplinary institutions run by police officers as exercises in futility.

The Comparative Neglect of Inequality

The emphasis that both pluralism and its rivals have placed on culture at the expense of structure is related to another point of continuity: the tendency to downplay what the political theorist Ian Shapiro recently has called "the oppositional traditions of democratic politics"[134]—those dimensions of democracy, that is to say, that have to do less with collective self-government than with ongoing resistance to "arbitrary hierarchy and domination."[135] Shapiro points out that, both historically and in our time, "[t]hose who fight for democracy often define their goals reactively"; they are driven less by a utopian vision than by the conviction that certain existing and unjustified forms of domination should be abolished.[136] There is a long history of viewing this leveling impulse as the core of democracy. Tocqueville, for example, thought the democracy he found exemplified in America was first and foremost a matter of "equality of conditions"—and, more precisely, a matter of sweeping aside the powers and privileges of monarchs and aristocrats.[137] Lincoln famously drew on the same idea when he tied democracy to ending slavery: "As I would not be a *slave*, so I would not be a *master*. This expresses my idea of democracy. Whatever differs from this, to the extent of the difference, is no democracy."[138] And when W. B. Gallie identified democracy a half century ago as an "essentially contested concept," he argued that what held the concept together was "a long tradition (perhaps a number of historically independent but sufficiently similar traditions) of demands, aspirations, revolts and reforms of a common *anti-in*egalitarian character."[139] The core use of the term "democracy," Gallie suggested, was to invoke "certain political aspirations which have been embodied in countless slave, peasant, national and middle-class revolts and revolutions, as well as in scores of national constitutions and party records and programs"—aspirations that were "centered in a demand for increased equality" and were advanced against regimes committed to prolonging "gross forms of *in*equality."[140]

As Shapiro points out, this understanding of democracy, which subjects all patterns of social hierarchy to "presumptive, but rebuttable, suspicion," has been pushed to the sidelines since the rise of pluralism in the 1950s.[141] The faith the pluralists put in leadership elites, the emphasis they placed on stability, the confidence they had in the complex balance of cross-cutting interest groups—all these factors led the pluralists to downplay concerns of continuing inequality, and gave them little enthusiasm for the notion of democracy as a tradition of opposition. Political equality has played a larger role in theories of participatory democracy and deliberative democracy. These theories, as we have seen, were crafted largely in response to pluralism's perceived defects, not the least of which was its elitism. But in the mainstream version of participatory democracy, the version that has had the most influence on criminal procedure, the element of egalitarianism has lost most of its bite. Like the pluralists, people who invoke the mainstream version of participatory democracy tend to start with the assumption that, in pertinent respects, the United States is *already* egalitarian. (Kahan and Meares are good examples; so is Justice Breyer.) That assumption—particularly when combined with the apologetic cast of mainstream participatory democracy, and the emphasis it shares with deliberative democracy on "getting along"—minimizes the ongoing significance of "demands, aspirations, revolts and reforms."[142]

Despite the half-century tendency of democratic theory to neglect the "anti-inegalitarian" dimension of democracy, criminal procedure in the Warren Court era was famously preoccupied with issues of illegitimate inequality, particularly those associated with race. Pluralism had little to do with this preoccupation, but it may, as I have already suggested, have contributed to the Supreme Court's reluctance to tackle the problem of criminal justice racism explicitly, and its tendency to treat instances of inequity as aberrational rather than systemic. The gingerly, subtextual manner in which the Warren Court pursued racial equality in criminal justice eventually made it much easier for its successors to drop the pursuit altogether.[143] It would not have been so easy, perhaps, if the accounts of democracy that have largely supplanted pluralism underscored the importance of continuing opposition to entrenched systems of unjustified hierarchy—if, that is to say, the most influential theories of participatory democracy and deliberative democracy incorporated the "spirit of democratic oppositionalism."[144] But they did not.

The spirit of democratic oppositionalism is missing not just from current criminal procedure jurisprudence, but also, as I have suggested parenthetically, from the work of scholars like Kahan and Meares. The most troubling assumption of that work—the assumption of a unified, coherent, and easily identified community will—diverts attention not only from questions of institutional structure but also, and more fundamentally, from the ongoing power dynamics of inner-city politics. It tends to obscure, too, the ways in which local police practices can reinforce (or alleviate) regional and nationwide patterns of domination, matters to which I will return below.

Summing Up

It bears reiterating that the work of Kahan and Meares, like the work of Amar, is neither a microcosm of criminal procedure scholarship today nor a reliable reflection of the state of criminal procedure jurisprudence. On the whole, for example, criminal procedure scholars cannot be faulted for ignoring the relationship between police practices and racial inequality, although they rarely view that relationship through the lens of "anti-inegalitarianism." Still, the manner in which Amar, Kahan, and Meares draw on theories of participatory democracy and deliberative democracy is instructive. It demonstrates again that ideas about democracy influence ideas about policing. It helps explain why criminal procedure scholarship and jurisprudence from the 1960s and 1970s, written under the sway of democratic pluralism, can seem incomprehensible or silly to scholars and judges writing today, with different notions about democracy. It warns us about issues that criminal procedure scholarship more broadly continues to slight. And it underscores the need for more careful thinking about the relationship between democracy and policing.

It is not just that pluralism remains, in many ways, an attractive account of democracy. It is also that theories of participatory democracy and deliberative democracy have never been as coherent and consistent as pluralism, so that precision is particularly important when invoking them. Democratic pluralism is democratic pluralism, but the participatory democracy of Arnold Kaufman is not the participatory democracy of Richard Nixon.

The first step in thinking more carefully about the relationship between policing and democracy is to understand the dilemmas, contradictions, and choices presented by democratic theory, and to see how those difficulties have manifested themselves in discussions about the police. That has been the chief task of the first part of this book. The second and concluding part of the book, in contrast, will look forward rather than back.

CHAPTER 5

Deepening the "Democratic" in Democratic Policing

The first part of this book has explored the connections between the dramatic transformation in ideas about the policing in the United States over the past half century and the equally dramatic ways in which ideas about American democracy have changed during roughly the same period. Democratic pluralism has been supplanted by theories of participatory democracy and deliberative democracy, but democracy continues to be understood more in terms of culture, personality, and social norms than in terms of institutions. Police professionalism has given way to community policing as the shared orthodoxy of law enforcement executives and police reformers, but there are continuing tendencies, in discussions about the police, to treat officers as a breed apart, to de-emphasize institutional design, and to downplay issues of inequality. These two stories, the transformation in democratic theory and the transformation in policing, are rarely set side by side, but in fact they are strongly linked.

This book so far has been descriptive and analytic. The remaining chapters will be more prescriptive, drawing lessons from the first half of the book, for criminal procedure scholars, police reformers, and other people concerned about law enforcement in the United States.

Three of those lessons—probably the three most important—are relatively straightforward. The first of these is to take democracy seriously. Ideas about democracy have long influenced ideas about the police. Conceivably they should not. But I hope it is clear by now that anyone taking that view has a heavy burden of tradition to discredit, and much of that tradition cannot be understood—let alone challenged—without an appreciation of the manifold ways in which criminal procedure and policing studies have reflected and incorporated distinct theories of democracy.

The second lesson, which by now should be almost as obvious, is not to oversimplify. Ideas about democracy have come in complicated clusters. Those clusters have generally included suppositions about four different things: the basic *purposes* of democracy, the distinctive *processes* of democracy, the *proximity* of current arrangements to the democratic ideal, and the cultural and geographic *particularity* of what democracy means. The answers given to each of these four questions over the past half century have varied. The main purposes of democracy have sometimes been thought to be social stability and the avoidance of authoritarian repression; sometimes the facilitation of human development; and sometimes the "legitimacy" of government, both actual and perceived. The bedrock processes of democracy have sometimes been found in elections, group politics, and leadership elites; sometimes in mass participation; and sometimes in respectful deliberation. Sometimes the participation or deliberation thought central to democracy has been roughly the same kind of participation or deliberation we already have; sometimes it has been a good deal more. Sometimes American democracy has been seen as idiosyncratic; at other times it has not. All of these permutations have had implications for the meaning of "democratic policing."

The third and final lesson, which builds on the other two, is to watch for blind spots. Every theory of democracy highlights certain parts of our experience and directs attention away from other parts. It therefore helps to keep in mind the realities and possibilities that current ways of thinking about democracy tend to mask.

Today that means, first and foremost, taking into account democratic pluralism, because the principal unifying thread of democratic theory over the past few decades has been the reaction *against* pluralism. There was a lot to react against. The pluralists' own blind spots were legion. But if pluralism never deserved the uncritical acceptance it won in the 1950s, even its toughest critics acknowledged that the theory triumphed in part because it incorporated some genuine insights. Those insights included, I believe, the usefulness of group theory as a way of understanding American politics and the corresponding dangers of assuming a unified public; the grounds for skepticism about the feasibility, necessity, and desirability of universal political engagement; the limited but real ability of elections to keep government in check; and the democratic attractions of modernity. In the context of policing, keeping these insights in mind can help to guard against several kinds of mistakes: a romanticized picture of local politics; an overoptimistic expectation of community involvement in questions about policing; a neglect of the dangers of placing police powers in private hands; and a sentimental nostalgia for a clean and orderly past.

If appreciating pluralism can help guard against some of the blind spots of current thinking about democratic policing, so can appreciating the ambitious varieties of participatory democracy that gained currency in the 1960s and 1970s. The gulf between those theories and the watered-down, status quo version of participatory democracy that has grown so familiar can be hidden by their common vocabulary. So it helps to keep in mind what seemed like live options not so long ago. In the context of law enforcement, this means considering the possibilities of greatly strengthening neighborhood control of police departments, and of involving rank-and-file officers, intellectually if not politically, in shaping the nature of their work. It also means, necessarily, grappling with the tension between these two agendas. Any theory of democratic policing that valorizes the participation of ordinary citizens in the decisions that affect their lives needs to address police officers themselves as well as the communities they patrol.

Along with pluralism and thoroughgoing participatory democracy, there is a third perspective, even more foreign, that it is helpful to hold in mind: eighteenth-century political economy. The great insights of that perspective are that institutions matter, that the rational pursuit of individual objectives matters, and that the former should take account of the latter. In the context of policing, this means that an appreciation for the role of culture in policing—the role of norms and personality and discourse—should not blind us to the role of institutional structure—chains of command and routes of advancement within police departments; occupational opportunities and rewards; systems established for internal review; mechanisms of civilian oversight; and external political checks. Of course culture matters. But structure matters, too.

Last but emphatically not least, efforts to think systematically about the relationship between policing and democracy should strive to incorporate the perspective from which democracy is less about a stable system of collective self-government than about opposition to entrenched patterns of unjustified inequality. This view of democracy, what Ian Shapiro calls the spirit of democratic oppositionalism, seems a particularly promising vantage point for discussions of law enforcement because it makes apparent, in ways that pluralism and its most visible rivals have not, precisely why police practices matter so much for democracy. Why are law enforcement policies more important for democracy than, say, trash-collection policies? Why should democracy have more implications for police departments than for sanitation departments? Pluralism offers no answer, beyond suggesting that the occupational psychology of police officers may be particularly worrisome. Participatory democracy and deliberative democracy provide no real answer, either. But once democracy is understood to involve ongoing opposition to patterns of unjustifiable hierarchy, the special salience of the police immediately becomes clear: the police are both a uniquely powerful weapon against private systems of domination and a uniquely frightening tool of official domination.

From this perspective, making policing more democratic entails making it as effective as possible in combating unjustified patterns of private domination and unthreatening as possible as a tool of official domination. Reconciling these goals is of course quite difficult, and so is balancing them against other things we want the police to do (e.g., protecting us against crime even when it has at most a tenuous connection with patterns of dominance) and other things we want the police to avoid (e.g., spending money that could better be spent elsewhere). But we knew all along that policing requires trade-offs. The virtue of the "anti-inegalitarian" view of democracy is that it makes clear certain important aspects of those trade-offs, including the fact that democracy is, as it were, on both sides of the balance.

Ian Shapiro has usefully identified three basic tactics for pursuing an agenda of anti-inegalitarian democracy, one substantive and two procedural. The substantive tactic was mentioned in Chapter 4: "presumptive, but rebuttable suspicion" of all systems of hierarchy. The notion is not that hierarchies should be eliminated, even were that possible. The idea, rather, is that patterns of inequality can easily "atrophy into systems of domination which impose on people unnecessarily"[1] and, worse, with a false appearance of benignity: "escapable hierarchies masquerade as inescapable ones, involuntary subordination is shrouded in the language of agreement, unnecessary hierarchies are held to be essential to the pursuit of common goals, and fixed hierarchies are cloaked in myths about their fluidity."[2] The procedural tactics are, first, to make mechanisms of collective decision as inclusive as possible and second, to clear space, institutionally, for opposition and dissent.[3] Both of these procedural principles are, in part, efforts to accommodate and to capitalize on disagreement and conflict. They reflect a view of dissensus as not just a sign of a well-functioning democracy but a precondition for it, a view that "one person's consensus is often another's hegemony."[4]

The remaining chapters of this book will explore how the meaning of "democratic policing" might be deepened by remedying these various blind spots in our understanding of democracy—by recovering the tradition of democratic oppositionalism, and by remembering the core insights of democratic pluralism, 1960s-style participatory democracy, and eighteenth-century political economy. To answer this question we need a provisional account of democracy, one purposely intended to be eclectic and rounded. Since our goal here is to suggest new possibilities and to highlight neglected avenues of inquiry, we are less concerned with theoretical purity than with avoiding unjustified narrowness. We can assemble this kind of rounded theory of democracy by considering in turn the four elements we discussed earlier in connection with pluralism and its rivals: *purposes, processes, proximity,* and *particularity.* Element by element, we can construct a provisional account of democracy, taking care to avoid the blind spots we have identified.

First, *purposes.* From an eclectic perspective, democracy is a set of practices engaged in by different people for different but overlapping purposes. Certainly democracy is widely valued as a protection against oppression and a means of social stability. It is also valued, although certainly not by everyone, as a way to achieve personal development, build community, and add meaning to life. (Ian Shapiro shares the pluralists' view that "essential as democracy is to a tolerable existence, expecting much in the way of spiritual enrichment or edification from it is wrongheaded."[5] But the categorical denial that democracy can serve these purposes *for anyone* seems at odds with a point Shapiro himself stresses elsewhere: that democracy can mean, among other things, refraining as far as possible from imposing any theory of value on people as objectively correct.[6] And whether or not democracy itself requires this kind of openness to the multiplicity of human purposes, a commitment to catholicity in our understanding of democracy certainly does.) Democracy is valued by some people for the way it which it lends government legitimacy, both perceived and deserved. And, finally, democracy is prized as means of resisting and attacking entrenched forms of illegitimate domination.

Second, *processes*. If democracy is a set of practices engaged in by different people for different but overlapping purposes—what are those practices? Elections, certainly. But in an age of bureaucracy, democracy has to mean more than elections. The pluralists and their critics have been right to agree about that. They have been right, too, to stress the role of culture in sustaining democracy—but wrong to neglect so badly the role of institutional design. So our rounded theory of democracy will need to include attention to the concerns at the heart of eighteenth-century political economy: concerns about structuring institutions to capitalize on, and to shape productively, individual ambition and self-interest. We will want to keep an open mind about the merits of widespread political participation, steering a middle course between the excessive elitism of the pluralists and the naïve faith some of their successors have had in universal political engagement. And we will want to remain attentive to democratic attractions of modernity, guarding forms of sentimental nostalgia.

With regard to *proximity*, we will want to guard against the complacent assumption that our current political arrangements are about as good as can they can get. Perhaps more important, we will want to keep in mind the ways in which democracy is a journey rather than a destination: a tradition of ongoing resistance to patterns of unjustified hierarchy and domination that themselves shift over the course of time. We will want to supplement our interest in democratic governance with an interest in democratic oppositionalism.

Finally, with regard to *particularity*, we will want to remain open to lessons about democracy from other places and other times. But if democracy is as much a journey as a destination, then the way to pursue it necessarily depends a good deal on context. As Ian Shapiro writes, "[w]e are born into ongoing complexes of institutions and practices. The task is to democratize them as we reproduce them, not to design them anew."[7] This means that democratic policing in the United States today may mean something significantly different from democratic policing in Iraq, or Russia, or Brazil, or South Africa. There will be important points of overlap, but also points of divergence—ways in which the particular challenges each society faces in the ongoing pursuit of democracy will shape the kind of policing it should want and can reasonably expect.

The following chapters will apply this provisional, purposely eclectic set of ideas about democracy to a range of issues currently associated with American law enforcement, seeking in the process to develop a richer set of meanings for "democratic policing" at a particular place and time—the United States today.

Chapter 6 will begin this exercise by examining the relationship between law enforcement agencies and the communities they serve. The first part of Chapter 6 will reassess of community policing, in all its common guises. The second part will revisit the "neighborhood policing" agenda of the late 1960s and early 1970s and ask whether any part of the agenda deserves to be revived. The last part of the chapter will address the challenges and opportunities presented for democracy, and more specifically for community control of policing, by the recent, explosive growth in the private provision of order maintenance.

Chapter 7 will take up the issue of equality in policing—both its "external" and "internal" dimensions. The external dimensions of equality in policing have to do with the racial and ethnic profiling and the broader problem of inequitable treatment of suspects, victims, and other people who come into contact with law enforcement officers. The internal dimensions concern the dramatic but still incomplete diversification of police workforces themselves by minority officers, female officers, and openly gay and lesbian officers. That transformation, I will argue, has far broader consequence than is typically appreciated.

Chapter 8 will focus on the role of participation in policing—not the participation of community members, but the participation of rank-and-file police officers themselves in the shaping of their work. It will reexamine calls made decades ago for giving police officers themselves a degree of collective, democratic control over the nature of their work. Those calls were rejected in part because the rigidly homogeneous, politically reactionary police forces of thirty or forty years ago seemed exceptionally unsafe places for experiments in workplace democracy. We will want to ask whether, in the intervening time, police departments have changed enough to warrant revisiting that judgment.

CHAPTER 6

Police and Community

It makes sense to begin our efforts at deepening the "democratic" in democratic policing with a discussion of police and community, if only because the police reform agenda since the late 1980s has been so heavily focused on the wide variety of programs marching under the banner of "community policing." Federal funding is targeted at "community policing," local leaders ask the police to pursue "community policing," police professional organizations preach "community policing." So police managers wind up applying that label to most of what they do, and to virtually every specialized program they develop. Community policing has become "the ubiquitous common terminology for describing the current era in policing"[1]—much as police professionalism served, a generation ago, as a "catchall concept" for "'practically any effort . . . aimed at improving law enforcement.'"[2]

Community policing is linked, rhetorically if not causally, with another large-scale change in policing over the past few decades: the dramatic growth in the proportion of policing carried out by the private sector. In the heyday of democratic pluralism and police professionalism—the 1950s and 1960s—Pinkerton guards, private eyes, and the whole, old-fashioned apparatus of private peacekeeping and criminal apprehension seemed on their way out. A careful study in 1971 concluded that public law enforcement already employed more people than private security, and predicted that by mid-decade the disparity would be nearly two-to-one.[3] Instead, the private security industry exploded, and growth in public law enforcement slackened. Private guards now greatly outnumber sworn law enforcement officers throughout the United States, and the discrepancy continues to widen.[4]

Private security firms have been eager to share the mantle of community policing,[5] and the same claims of "accountability" and "empowerment" often made for community policing are made for private policing, as well.[6] Community policing, in turn, has sometimes been described as "police treating a neighborhood the way a security guard treats a client property."[7] In part because of this rhetorical convergence, public and private police managers increasingly see themselves as partners, "with similar goals but different approaches and spheres of influence."[8]

To understand what a deepened sense of democratic policing might mean for community policing and police privatization, we need to take the two trends in turn. How much they have in common turns out to depend, in part, on what we want from them—what we mean, for example, by "accountability" or "empowerment." We will start with community policing—what it is, what it leaves out, and how it should be assessed. We will turn to the burgeoning business of private policing and the challenges it poses for the agenda of democratic policing. Along the way, we also revisit the proposals made in the late 1960s and early 1970s for placing police departments under much stronger neighborhood control.

Community Policing

Not only are the programs lumped together as community policing highly varied, but some of them claim justification for reasons related only tangentially to any theory of democracy. Even the most sophisticated understanding of democracy therefore cannot tell us, by itself, which of these programs deserve support. But it can warn us away from certain mistakes in trying to answer that question, and it can flag certain issues that deserve close attention.

First and foremost, the rounded, eclectic view of democracy outlined in Chapter 5 makes clear why community policing, no matter how it is defined, should not be understood or defended as a way to make the police more answerable to "the public." This way of thinking ignores what the pluralists rightly stressed: the heterogeneity of interests in any community—particularly in a modern, urban community. Ignoring that heterogeneity means ignoring the ways in which law enforcement tactics can reflect and reinforce patterns of social hierarchy. The interests of shopkeepers are not necessarily the interests of the homeless, the interests of African Americans in the inner city may differ from those of Latinos, and so on. No single set of interests should be valorized as belonging to "the community."[9]

This does not mean that community policing cannot be justified as an exercise in promoting democracy. It simply means that the justification, to be plausible, cannot rely on the notion that there is a unified community with desires that are clear, coherent, and consistent. A promising account that carefully avoids that fallacy has been provided by the police scholar David Thacher. He describes community policing as an effort to reduce the "institutional segregation" of police departments by opening new channels of communication and cooperation with a variety of outside groups, both governmental and nongovernmental.[10] These groups are inevitably "more localized than 'the general public,'" and Thacher warns against reducing community policing to "an apple-pie issue of 'getting closer to the community.'"[11] But he points out that the very existence of fundamental disagreement within the community can make community policing valuable, for two related reasons. The first is that different kinds of channels give voice to different groups, and can even elicit different sentiments from the same group.[12] The second reason, which flows from the first, is that creating multiple channels for public communication with the police makes it more likely the police will be forced to confront conflicts between values. That process of confrontation makes space within police decision making for the articulation of "dissident values," and it also helps officers to develop precisely the kind of professional maturity that William Muir, studying the Oakland police, praised thirty years ago.[13]

Institutional segregation has its advantages, of course. Asking a single organization like a police department to reconcile conflicting objectives, like keeping the peace while seeking justice and maximizing liberty, can be a recipe for paralysis—or for giving some goals little more than lip service. As Thacher himself points out, sometimes the best strategy is to allow each organization to pursue its own, narrow mission, with values balanced through interagency competition.[14] This was more or less the strategy of democratic pluralism: police pursue crime control, courts pursue the rule of law, prosecutors pursue justice, and they all keep each other in check. It was a more successful strategy than we sometimes acknowledge. But there is no doubt that the extreme degree of institutional segregation achieved by big-city police departments in the 1950s and 1960s made some problems associated with the police much worse, and too often made the police instruments for the reinforcement of social hierarchy rather than tools for empowering the disempowered. So Thacher seems right that community policing, understood as a program for opening up new channels of communication with the police, can be an attractive way to democratize law enforcement.

Whether community policing serves that purpose, though, will depend on the kinds of channels that it opens up—whether it gives voice to disempowered groups and marginalized perspectives or simply grants another avenue of access to people and viewpoints already well served by the political process. More avenues of the latter sort may be beneficial—but not because they promote democracy. And in some circumstances they may be harmful, precisely because they may exacerbate the risk that the police will become instruments for reinforcing unjustifiable forms of hierarchy. For community policing to be democratizing in the way Thacher identifies, it should help lend influence to groups and interests to whom the police otherwise unlikely to be adequately attentive.

On this score, some structural strategies for community participation are more promising than others. In Chicago, for example, a city-wide program of "beat meetings," strongly supported by the police department and accompanied by energetic efforts at outreach, appears to have drawn disproportionately heavy participation from black residents of economically depressed, high-crime neighborhoods—not a group traditionally well represented in the formulation of law enforcement policy. The degree to which the beat meetings have actually affected policing practices remains unclear, and rates of participation among Latinos have been disappointing. But the levels of attendance in poor black neighborhoods have been impressive, and the meetings appear to be genuine exercises in two-way communication.[15] (Even aside from their democratizing effects, moreover, Chicago's beat meetings probably have other important benefits. By getting residents to work together on neighborhood problems, the meetings appear to build the kind of "collective efficacy"—i.e., the "social cohesion" and community spirit—that recent, influential research suggests may reduce violent crime.)[16]

In contrast, Chicago's system of district advisory committees—groups of community leaders who meet with their local police commander—have been far less successful, partly because the committee members have been selected by the police and tend, by definition, to come from what the pluralists called "the political stratum." The team of researchers led by the crime scholar Wesley Skogan, who have generally been quite impressed by community policing in Chicago, report that the district advisory committees tend not to represent residents' views, but instead pursue an agenda set largely by the police department, and "receive more advice than they give."[17] Moreover, the committees often "are dominated by long-established leaders with an insular view of their functions," who "fail to reach out to new members of their community."[18] As a result, the committees "noticeably under-represent Latinos, even in heavily Latino areas,"[19] and entirely exclude "smaller but rapidly growing immigrant groups (particularly Asians)."[20]

Some of the success of the beat meetings, and some of the failure of the district advisory committees, may have to do with factors unique to Chicago. The important point is not that "town hall" exercises like Chicago's beat meetings are likely to do better than police-appointed committees of worthies in introducing new voices into police policy making. That is probably is true, at least when the "town hall" exercises are executed as well as they have been in Chicago, and—a matter to which we will return later in this chapter—receive the kind of institutional support they have enjoyed there.[21] The important point, though, is simply that different programs of community participation in policing can be expected to have different levels of success in exposing the police to "dissident values," and that those differences deserve attention if we truly want community policing to make policing more democratic.

A rounded view of democracy—in particular, a view that incorporates a degree of presumptive discomfort with entrenched social hierarchies and, relatedly, an appreciation for the benefits of dissensus—has another implication for the broad array of programs lumped together under the title of community policing. It gives reason to be wary of a certain subset of those programs, the segment associated with the "broken windows" or "order maintenance" strategy of controlling crime by suppressing street-level disorder. The pluralists were right to see democratic value in the freedom and fluidity of modern urban life, just as Tocqueville was right to praise the "tumult" and "confusion" he found in nineteenth-century America. Disorder loosens things up; it clears space for dissent and makes patterns of dominance easier to attack. It can also be its own worst enemy: taken too far, it can make self-government impossible and clear the way for new, more malignant forms of dominance. But once democracy is understood as, at least in large part, a matter of anti-inegalitarianism, there are strong grounds to think that it benefits from a strong dose of disorder. That is why people like Bernard Harcourt and Jonathan Simon have cause to worry that broken windows policing, with its heavy emphasis on orderliness, may undermine democracy.

That does not mean broken windows policing should be abandoned. In some circumstances, it may do more to help democracy than to hurt it. If, for example, street-level disorder really does breed serious crime—a matter that is far from certain—then allowing that disorder to continue may create worse patterns of dominance than the ones it helps to alleviate. Even if street-level disorder has little to do with serious crime, it may threaten democracy in other, more direct ways. It might chill grassroots political participation, for example, by making people afraid of their neighbors and dispirited about the prospects for community improvement. And even if a particular level of disorder is, on balance, good for democracy, that benefit may not be worth the costs. Democracy is not the only thing we care about.[22] Still, a rounded view of democracy gives reason to be concerned about the "aesthetic of orderliness, cleanliness, and sobriety"[23] that accompanies and motivates broken windows policing. This is not the only consideration weighing against the broken windows approach, and it may not be a dispositive one. But it deserves more attention than it has received.

Neighborhood Policing Revisited

A rounded account of democracy can do more than help us to distinguish between different versions of community policing and to assess their comparative strengths and weaknesses. It should also draw our attention to what
community policing, in all its myriad variations, almost never does. It almost
never gives communities a strong degree of control over police departments—
the kind of thing sought by the "neighborhood policing" movement of the
late 1960s and early 1970s. That movement reflected the downfall of democratic pluralism, and more particularly the reaction against pluralism's strong
faith in leadership elites and aversion to mass politics. The backers of neighborhood policing saw the defects of pluralism but lost sight of its genuine insights, including the grounds for skepticism about the feasibility and necessity
of universal political engagement. This is one of the reasons that neighborhood policing never got off the ground, one of the reasons that, by the 1970s,
its ambitious program was supplanted by the more limited agenda of civilian
oversight of police disciplinary procedures. Herman Goldstein, though sympathetic to calls for greater community control of policing, concluded in 1977
that "enthusiasm to compensate for the insulation of the past" had led police
reformers "to misjudge both the feasibility of achieving greater citizen involvement and the contribution that can be realized." The lessons Goldstein
drew from years of experience observing police advisory groups was "that it
is often difficult to achieve a consensus, that interest soon fades, and persons
representing special interests, such as the business community, become the
strongest voices through the default of others."[24]

Part of the problem with the advisory groups Goldstein was describing
was precisely that they had such little power. "The results might differ," he
pointed out, "if citizens had formally established roles and were vested with
specific authority to determine certain policies."[25] But it was not idle for James
Q. Wilson to worry that even a truly empowered neighborhood police board
could be taken over by "a small, self-serving minority."[26] It was even less idle
for Jerome Skolnick to predict that neighborhood police boards might wind
up controlled by "precisely the sort of people who now control the City
Council"—and, he might have added, the school board. Skolnick faulted the
backers of neighborhood policing for assuming "that people, especially poor

people, have all kinds of free time and public interest."[27] He faulted them, in other words, for forgetting that the pluralists had a point.

None of this is to say that a broad agenda of neighborhood policing deserves to stay buried. In some ways, in fact, public control over police management has grown more important over the past two decades, as law enforcement strategies have changed. (Put aside for the moment whether the most appropriate locus for that control is the "neighborhood"—we'll return to that question in the next chapter.) The model of law enforcement professionalism that held sway in the middle decades of the twentieth century insulated police departments from outside politics and embraced strategies of patrol and rapid response that at least nominally treated all parts of department's jurisdiction equally. Police resources were distributed daily and hourly, in response to the emergency calls the police received. A degree of democratic leveling was built into the system: anyone could call the police, and the police went where they were called.[28]

The insulation of police departments from outside politics never made much sense, in part because the promise of equal treatment never came close to being fully honored. But it makes even less sense now, given recent developments in police strategies, which depart radically from the old goal of making law enforcement resources uniformly available through a central dispatch system. Two developments are particularly noteworthy in this regard: "hot spots" policing, and "problem-oriented" policing.

Hot spots policing, which has become "a core strategy in American policing agencies,"[29] calls for concentrating resources on locations responsible for a disproportionate share of criminal activity. The original inspiration for the trend was a series of studies suggesting that crime tends to clump geographically—that there are, in fact, hot spots of offending.[30] Hot spots policing has been the subject of an unusually rich set of randomized evaluations.[31] Those studies have suggested that concentrating police resources on hot spots does in fact reduce crime in those locations, at least in the short run, and—encouragingly—does so without displacing crime to adjoining areas.[32]

Problem-oriented policing (or "problem-solving policing") is now often treated as just a synonym for, or a "facet" of, community policing.[33] But as originally conceived in the late 1970s and the 1980s—initially, as it happens, by Herman Goldstein—problem-oriented policing was better defined than community policing and had a different "distinctive thrust."[34] Problem-oriented policing emphasizes flexible, decentralized, "tailor-made" responses to specific problems the police are asked to solve.[35] Sometimes the solutions make use of police–community partnerships—neighborhood watch groups and so forth—but sometimes not. Sometimes the solutions make use of the kind of intensive patrolling associated with hot spots policing—but, again, sometimes not.[36]

Hot spots policing and problem-oriented policing both require that resources be targeted where they will do the most good. But there is no objective or uncontroversial way to decide where resources will do "the most good." The determination unavoidably pits the concerns of one neighborhood against the (typically different) concerns of another neighborhood: drug dealing in a housing project, say, versus a rash of burglaries in a middle-class neighborhood.

The geographic focusing employed in hot spots policing and problem-oriented policing thus heightens the distributional stakes in police decision making. (The community–police partnerships valorized by the community policing movement heighten those stakes, too, albeit less directly. Communities are not monolithic, so consulting with "the community" means, in practice, consulting with certain individuals and groups within the community—clergy, say, or merchants, or homeowners, or established ethnic groups—and giving those individuals and groups a greater voice than they used to have. The problem is that other groups—the irreligious, say, or unemployed teenagers, or the homeless, or new immigrants—may be left out.)[37] We have grown accustomed to thinking that policing and democracy operate in hydraulic opposition: the more resources and leeway we give to the police, the more democracy is imperiled. This way of thinking is among the lasting legacies of democratic pluralism; it follows naturally from the assumption that the chief rival to democracy is authoritarianism, and more specifically the "police state." But sensitivity to the tradition of democratic oppositionalism should remind us that policing is, among other things, "a form of redistribution."[38] It redistributes resources in the same way as other government-funded services, from fire protection to social security, and—going beyond those other programs—it uses the redistributed resources to reallocate power, by curbing the private use of coercive force. The most basic questions of police management—questions about how and where to deploy police resources—are questions about who gets government protection, and what kind of protection they get. This is why new police strategies, which focus law enforcement resources geographically, make public control over police management even more important than it used to be.

The trick is to facilitate democratic participation that is both broad and meaningful, recognizing the practical difficulties identified by the pluralists and addressing them as best we can. One promising approach to this challenge is what the political scientist Archon Fung calls "empowered participation"—not just providing opportunities for participation, but encouraging the exercise of those opportunities, structuring the process of participation to maximize deliberation, and making sure that the outcomes count.[39] Fung points to the community policing in Chicago—particularly the system of beat meetings—as an example of empowered participation.[40] In fact, the extent to which the beat meetings have actually altered police policy is unclear, but in some ways this makes the apparent success of the meetings all the more striking. It suggests that even broader participation may be achieved by processes with a stronger degree of influence over police decision making.

Two other ways of broadening public participation in policing decisions deserve mention. One is to change the selection rules for the civilian review boards that over the past thirty years have become a fixture of big-city policing in the United States, making those boards more broadly representative of the diverse communities served by the police departments they oversee.[41] Another is to empower nongovernmental community groups by giving them the information they need to make full use of existing levers of political control over law enforcement agencies—the electoral accountability of sheriffs and the accountability of appointed police chiefs to mayors and other elected officials. In calling for "transparent policing"—greatly heightened visibility of what the police do and how they decide what to do—the legal scholar Eric Luna has stressed the manner in which trust in the police depends on the police operating under rules and practices adopted openly, with ample opportunity for public input.[42] This is an argument rooted in what I have called the status quo version of participatory democracy. But transparency in policing can also assist participatory democracy in its old, 1960s sense, by placing tools in the hands of activists and community groups. And the case for transparent policing can draw further strength from the tradition of democratic oppositionalism. Criticism and dissensus are greatly facilitated by the free flow of information; it is hard to dissent from policies and practices that no one knows about. For example, effective criticism of racial profiling of minority motorists—a problem discussed in the next chapter—arose only when statistical studies by journalists and social scientists demonstrated its widespread prevalence.

There is a further issue associated with broadened public participation in police decision making that deserves mention now, although we will postpone full consideration of it, as well, until the next chapter. Widespread participation in police matters may at times conflict with other democratic values, including the oppositional agenda of "anti-inegalitarianism." What happens when the public wants the police to carry out their business in ways that worsen inequalities? There are no easy solutions to this dilemma; it arises out the complexity of our underlying democratic ideals. Fortunately, it is hardly unique to policing. Reconciling democratic aspirations of self-government with democratic aspirations of minimally decent treatment to all citizens is the central task of modern democratic constitutionalism. There are two standard approaches to this task that could be applied to policing, and in fact already have been—constraining majoritarianism with judicially enforced rights, and structuring the processes of decision making to promote bargaining and compromise. Both of these strategies have been employed to guard against overzealous policing. Neither has been used in any systematic way to ensure a fair allocation of police resources—but they could be. We will discuss how in the next chapter, when we turn our focus to the complex relationship between policing and equality.

Private Policing

We have been talking as though police protection is a service provided solely by the government. In fact, though, the past several decades have seen a dramatic shift of policing responsibilities from public agencies to the private sector. Increasingly, private security firms patrol not only industrial facilities and commercial establishments but also office buildings, transportation facilities, recreational complexes, and entire shopping districts and residential neighborhoods. Many Americans—particularly wealthier Americans—are more likely to encounter a private security guard than a police officer on any given day. In the words of one industry executive, "[t]he plain truth is that today much of the protection of our people, their property and their businesses, has been turned over to private security."[43]

Whether this is a good or bad thing has been widely debated, but the debate has largely overlooked the implications of police privatization for democracy. In a recent, perceptive review of the literature, Elizabeth Joh identifies five persistent themes: the historical pedigree of private policing, the relationship between police privatization and privatization more broadly, the functional characteristics of private policing, the division of labor between public law enforcement agencies and private police, and the exemption of private police from the constitutional rules imposed on public law enforcement.[44] One can quarrel with some of the details, but not with the most conspicuous absence from this list: the ramifications of privatized policing for American democracy. That issue has been doubly marginalized—largely ignored even in the small body of work that focuses on private policing.[45]

The oversight is understandable. The push for police professionalism in the 1950s and 1960s succeeded so well at insulating police departments from political interference that even today, after nearly two decades of "community policing" reforms, police departments often seem to operate outside the normal processes of local government, accountable to no one. In fact, as we have seen, community policing rarely reduces the operational autonomy of the police. Community policing is about partnership, and sometimes about consultation; it is rarely if ever about control. Against this backdrop, there has sometimes not seemed much democracy to lose when policing is privatized. In fact, private policing is regularly praised for *increasing* accountability, because market pressures at least keep private firms attentive to their paying customers.[46]

But praise like this obviously begs some important questions: accountability to whom, and for what? Even the most autonomous police departments are subject to *some* political oversight—more public supervision, almost certainly, than virtually any private security firm. The Los Angeles Police Department, for example, enjoys a notorious degree of independence under the city charter, because the civilian commissioners who nominally run the department serve part-time with only modest staff support. Virtually the only real leverage the commissioners can exercise is to fire the police chief, but that leverage has turned out to be significant—as the last two chiefs of the department, both ousted by the commission, can testify. Public police agencies, moreover, understand their *charge* as protecting everyone within their jurisdiction. Their day-to-day practices and priorities may often fall far short of that ideal, but at least the ideal remains in view. And structures of local government, including those pertaining to the police, can be reconfigured. If we want police departments that are less insulated from politics, we can get them. We had them, after all, before the 1950s.

To some degree, private policing can be reconfigured, too. If we want private security forces to behave in particular ways—complying with constitutional restrictions on the police, say, or paying attention to the concerns of people other than their customers—there are legal mechanisms at our disposal. Statutes can be passed; regulations can be promulgated; administrative oversight can be imposed; tort duties can be created.[47] In the not uncommon situation where government itself is the purchaser of private security services,[48] "public norms" can be imposed by contract.[49]

To fashion a regulatory regime of this kind, though—and to assess its limits—we need to determine exactly what "public norms" we care about in the context of policing. We need, that is to say, a theory of democratic policing. We need, as well, to understand the functional relationship between private policing and public policing.

Start with the first requirement. The rounded, eclectic theory of democracy we developed in Chapter 5 cannot tell us, by itself, whether the growth of private policing is a boon, a bane, or both. But it can help us to see more clearly some of the issues that private policing poses for democracy, and some of the choices and assumptions underlying much discussion of private policing. For example, people committed to the watered-down version of participatory democracy most commonly encountered today—what I have earlier called the status quo version—can easily defend private policing as "empowerment at its best": business owners who band together to hire private guards, for example, "take on the responsibility that comes with being truly empowered."[50] But if we mean something more radical by participatory democracy—if we mean something like the Port Huron Statement's call for allowing every individual to "share in those social decisions determining the quality and direction of his life" and organizing society "to encourage interdependence," bring people "out of isolation and into community," and give them the "means of finding meaning in personal life"[51]—well, then the notion of private patrols as "empowerment at its best" begins to sound like a weak joke.

Similarly, our thinking about private police can benefit from sensitivity to the tradition of democratic oppositionalism. That tradition suggests that "democratic policing" should mean, in large part, making the police as effective as possible in combating unjustified patterns of private domination and unthreatening as possible as a tool of official domination. Private police forces complicate this agenda. They may weaken the threat of official domination—or then again they may not, depending on the nature of the relationship between the private police and their public counterparts. And they may exacerbate or ameliorate illegitimate patterns of private domination—depending in part, again, on how they change the role and effectiveness of the public police.

This takes us to the second question I raised a moment ago: what is the functional relationship between private and public policing? Three different relationships are possible, which I will call *augmentation*, *displacement*, and *transformation*. It is likely that all three exist, but in different places, at different times, and to different degrees.

Augmentation is the relationship that the private security industry has traditionally claimed to have with public law enforcement. Industry executives long have sought to mollify concerns over the expansion of private security by arguing that their employees just provide another layer of protection on top of public policing: "an additional set of eyes and ears."[52] The public police are left as they were before, but with some new allies.

If private policing serves merely to augment public policing, the implications it raises for democracy are largely limited to the danger that, by abusing their power (perhaps with the government's explicit or tacit encouragement), private police will threaten the "democratic values" of due process and human dignity. Of all the possible implications of private policing for democracy, this is the danger raised most frequently. Part of the reason for this focus is that critics of private police, like the industry's boosters, have tended to assume that the functional relationship between private and public policing is largely additive.

But there is good reason to question that assumption. In the short run, of course, private policing usually *does* augment public law enforcement. It may even assist neighborhoods too poor to afford private security services by freeing up public law enforcement resources in areas that *can* afford private security. Over the long term, though, private policing can wind up *displacing* public law enforcement rather than simply augmenting it. Why should Bel Air residents vote for higher taxes to pay for policing throughout Los Angeles, when they can—and do—hire private patrols for their own neighborhood? Private policing easily can become part of what Robert Reich has memorably called the "secession of the successful."[53] There is evidence, in fact, that the widespread reliance on private security in wealthier areas of Los Angeles has already dampened support for increased city-wide expenditures on public policing.[54]

Here, as elsewhere, we need to keep an eye on the redistributive dimensions of policing. Murray Kempton once described the supplanting of the Pinkerton Detective Agency by the FBI as "the only episode in our social history to realize Marx's prescription for the transformation of capitalist private property into social property."[55] But the episode is better understood as part of the broader socialization of law enforcement in the late nineteenth and early twentieth centuries.[56] The displacement of public policing with private security puts that redistributive process into reverse.

That does not mean that private policing is always a bad thing. There are aspects of democracy other than anti-inegalitarianism, and there are things that we care about other than democracy. In some cases, moreover, market-supplied policing may redistribute power downward in ways that public law enforcement has failed to do. Private patrols hired by a business improvement district, for example, may make the streets safer and more welcoming for the physically frail. But the interests of merchants depart in predictable ways from the interests of their poorest neighbors, at least in anything but the very long term, and private security firms focus, understandably, on the interests of the people who hire them.

Leave aside the ugliest ways in which that kind of accountability can manifest itself—harassment of deviants, physical assaults of the homeless, etc.[57] Those kinds of problems could be addressed, at least in theory, by strengthening the legal restrictions on private policing, importing to the private sector the "public law norms" of due process and dignity. The more fundamental problem is that private police are not even nominally committed, as public police are, to the egalitarian project of protecting all citizens from private violence. The defining characteristic of private policing is its "client-driven mandate."[58] Take, for example, the more than one hundred private guards now employed by business improvement districts in downtown Los Angeles. The president of the largest of these groups brushes off calls for stronger public oversight of the guards: "If people are saying more accountability, then I say accountability to whom? It's not the city's money; it's the property owner's money."[59]

Rhetoric like this gives credence to the concern that privatization can make policing less egalitarian in two ways: by reducing the demand for public policing officially committed to protecting everyone, and by reducing the political pressure on public police forces to comply with norms of due process and dignity. The result may be a two-tiered system of policing worrisomely congruent with broader patterns of social hierarchy. Here is how two leading police scholars have described the prospect: "The rich will be increasingly policed preventively by commercial security while the poor will be policed reactively by enforcement-oriented public police," with both the public and private sectors working to "protect the affluent from the poor—the one by barricading and excluding, the other by repressing and imprisoning."[60] That is a troubling prospect not just because it seems harsh, but because it seems radically anti-democratic—something much easier to see with a rounded view of democracy, incorporating a strong element of anti-inegalitarianism.

Bifurcation of the policing function—gentle private cops for the rich, hard-nosed public policing of the poor—is one way the private police could wind up *transforming* the public police, in addition to augmenting or displacing them. But there are other ways, as well. One possibility, for which there is already some evidence, is that the public police may find themselves copying the strategies, rhetoric, and self-conception of the private police—much as Henry Fielding's Bow Street Runners brought the entrepreneurial spirit of thief-taking to the eighteenth-century London magistracy, and J. Edgar Hoover later mimicked the marketing tactics of Alan Pinkerton.[61] Instead of public norms being extended into the private sector, private norms may be imported into the public sphere. Borrowing terms from Philip Selznick, Elizabeth Joh suggests that at bottom the difference between private policing and public policing may be the difference between "management" and "governance"—between organizations that emphasize "efficiency and goal achievement," and organizations that "take[] into account broader values such as integrity, the accommodation of interests, and morality."[62] Selznick wanted governance to supplant management, to some extent, in the internal operation of large-scale private organizations, and he was reasonably optimistic that this could happen. But the opposite is also possible: public agencies can gravitate away from governance toward management.

Some police departments may already be drifting in this direction, pulled along by the mounting tendency for the public and private police to see themselves as partners, sharing similar objectives. In principle the expanding cooperation between public law enforcement and the private security industry, and the growing feeling of affinity between the two sectors, could facilitate a transfer of norms in either direction. In practice, though, there is little evidence so far of private security firms becoming more mindful of values beyond efficiency and the achievement of narrowly defined goals. It is much easier to find signs of police departments becoming more "managerial," both in their practices and in their sense of organizational mission.[63]

As we have seen, even community policing can be understood as the "client-driven mandate" of private security firms crossing over into the public sector, with patrol officers treating their beats the way security guards treat their clients' property. But we have also seen that this definition misses an important, countervailing feature of many "community policing" reforms. In many departments, "community policing" has meant reducing the organizational insularity by opening new channels of communication and cooperation with a variety of outside groups, both governmental and nongovernmental. Officers in these departments have been forced, regularly and systematically, to confront and to accommodate conflicting views of their mission and conflicting notions of how best to balance liberty and security.[64] They have been pushed away, in other words, from a single-minded focus on a narrow set of performance goals; they have been driven from management toward governance. There is no corresponding trend in the private security industry.

There are grounds for skepticism about how strongly the official ethos of a police organization, public or private, shapes the behavior of officers out on the streets. Private security guards hired to patrol a housing project can wind up thinking and acting, in certain respects, much like public law enforcement officers engaged in similar work.[65] But even nominal commitments are important. Walking the talk begins with talking the talk. Moreover, some aspects of organizational style depend quite heavily on decisions made at the top. Among those aspects, ironically, is the treatment of the organization's employees, including the degree to which employees are given a collective voice in the shaping of their vocation.

We will take that matter up in Chapter 8. For now, there is one final point to be made about community policing and private policing, one final point of tension between the two. Funding levels affect not just the amount of policing the state provides, but also the kind of policing. Efforts to open up channels of communication between the police and traditionally marginalized groups—like the "beat meetings" that have apparently achieved some success in Chicago—are expensive. Efforts to involve police officers themselves in departmental reform—like the Oakland violence study of the early 1970s—are expensive. Alternatives to racial profiling can be expensive. So can effective institutions of civilian oversight. The history of police reform is littered with promising innovations abandoned when budgets tightened. The Peer Review Panel that grew out of the Oakland violence study is a good example. High funding levels certainly do not guarantee innovative policing, but low funding levels make it much less likely. The kind of protection the police provide, no less than the amount of protection they provide, is thus partly—although only partly—a matter of the resources they are given. This means that the success of things like community policing, and the other forms of police reform we will explore in the next two chapters, is in part a budgetary matter. And *that* means, in turn, that if private policing undermines political support for generously funding public police, it could threaten not just the quantity of policing but the quality of policing. This is yet another way that police privatization could transform public policing.

CHAPTER 7

Police and Equality

The last chapter focused on one aspect of democratic policing—the relationship between police forces and the communities they serve. It explored the how that relationship might be affected by a broader, more eclectic theory of democracy, one incorporating, in particular, more ambitious ideas about broad political participation and a greater sensitivity to the oppositional tradition of "anti-inegalitarianism." This chapter moves that oppositional tradition to center stage. If democracy consists partly in ongoing resistance to entrenched patterns of illegitimate domination, what does that mean for police practices?

We will explore three sets of implications in turn. The first set has to do with the problems ordinarily brought to mind when equality and policing are jointly discussed. These are the problems associated with disproportionate targeting of minority suspects by the police. Over the past decade these problems have been discussed chiefly in connection with allegations of "racial profiling." The first part of this chapter will examine the issue of racial profiling, and the broader issue of police practices that disproportionately target members of racial and ethnic minorities, through the lens of the eclectic account of democracy we developed in Chapter 5.

The second part of the chapter will explore the flip side of disproportionate targeting—disproportionate neglect. Minority communities have long complained, with justification, that they suffer not just from unduly harsh policing but also, at the same time, from inadequate police protection. The legal scholar Alexandra Natapoff describes "overenforcement" and "underenforcement" as "twin symptoms of a deeper democratic failure of the criminal system: its non-responsiveness to the needs of the poor, racial minorities, and the otherwise politically vulnerable."[1] As Natapoff points out, underenforcement has received much less attention from scholars, judges, and activists than overenforcement. But one important way to deepen the "democratic" in "democratic policing" is by worrying not just about police malfeasance but also police nonfeasance. The second part of this chapter will therefore explore how the agenda of democratic policing might be augmented with a commitment to provide all citizens minimally adequate police protection.

The largest part of this chapter, though, will take up concerns about equality inside police departments, exploring the ramifications of the remarkable but still incomplete transformation of the workforce demographics of American law enforcement agencies. Discussions of equality in policing generally spend even less time on police workforces than they do on the problem of inadequate police protection. But the diversification of policing—the gradual demise of the homogeneously white, male departments that were the norm as recently as the early 1970s—has far greater implications than are generally recognized for the agenda of democratic policing.

We will want to focus in this chapter not just on problems but also on solutions. Broadly speaking, inequitable policing can be attacked in three different ways—the same three ways any kind of improper or undesirable police practice can be remedied. The first way is by substantive mandates imposed from without—typically in the form of a court ruling. This was the strategy, of course, of the Warren Court's "criminal procedure revolution," and it is by no means a thing of the past. By and large the mandates the Supreme Court has promulgated for police have aimed at controlling officer discretion and protecting the dignity of suspects. Concerns about equality—particularly racial equality—have often lurked in the background, but they have stayed in the background. That is partly because equality has been marginalized in prevalent ideas about democracy, and therefore in prevalent ideas about democratic policing. But in principle the same kinds of judicial interventions that gave us *Miranda* warnings could give us protections against forms of inequitable policing. Whether this is the best strategy to pursue is another matter.

The second broad strategy for addressing inequalities in policing is by restructuring the political environment in which police departments operate in order to make them more broadly accountable to the communities they serve. This is the strategy of civilian review boards, for example. Despite all the controversy they have inspired, civilian review boards represent a fairly small intrusion into the autonomy of police departments—even smaller, in some respects, than the informal "partnering" and "consultation" at the heart of the community policing movement, which are not limited, as civilian review boards typically are, to disciplinary matters. But external political control of police departments could be expanded and reconfigured in much more ambitious ways.

The third and final way to address inequalities in policing, or any other problem in policing, is by reconstituting police departments themselves—changing their internal structure and, equally or more important, changing the makeup of police workforces, the kinds of people that police officers are. For the internal composition of police forces is not just a measure of one aspect of egalitarianism in policing; it is also a strategy for advancing other aspects of egalitarianism in policing.

These three strategies overlap. Court orders and the external political environment of police departments, for example, can help change the internal composition of police departments and their internal structure and operating procedures. But it will help to keep in mind, as we proceed, that there are multiple dimensions not just to the problems of inequality in policing, but also to the possible solutions. And because the importance of equality inside police departments has received far less attention than it deserves in recent academic discussions of law enforcement, it will receive the lion's share of attention in this chapter.

Racial Profiling and "Overenforcement"

While not nearly so ill-defined as "community policing," the term "racial profiling" has been applied to a spectrum of different police practices, relying on race to various degrees, in assorted ways, in a range of factual settings.[2] As with community policing, a rounded view of democracy cannot tell us precisely what to think about all of these practices, or even what to think of the paradigmatic case: the systematic use of race (almost always along with other factors) in selecting subjects for investigative attention. Once again, though, it can highlight some important questions and help guard against certain kinds of mistakes.

It can warn us, in particular, not to be too quick to minimize the social costs, and more specifically the democratic costs, of systematically focusing law enforcement scrutiny on members of traditionally disfavored minorities. For reasons I will explain, a rounded view of democratic policing casts doubt on two related notions about racial profiling. The first is that racial profiling is tangential to the central concerns of criminal procedure; this is a view to which the Supreme Court has appeared sympathetic.[3] The second notion is that racial profiling is troubling chiefly to the extent that it is irrational—to the extent, that is to say, that it reflects raw racial animus, a "taste for discrimination,"[4] or fails to take into account the ways that racial profiling can wind up posing practical problems for law enforcement.

What these ways of thinking overlook is the heavy burdens that racial profiling can place on democracy. Those costs are hard to appreciate without a view of democracy that includes a healthy element of anti-inegalitarianism. For an unreconstructed pluralist, racial profiling presents no special problem: racial minorities, like all other groups, are assumed to be capable of defending themselves through the political process. For a believer in participatory democracy—even in its watered-down, mainstream version—things are more complicated. By insulting its targets, undermining their trust in law enforcement, and giving them a sense of second-class citizenship, racial profiling could alienate them from the whole project of collective self-government. On the other hand, perhaps the sting of unfairness will galvanize the victims of racial profiling, making them *more* likely to become politically active. It could go either way.

Once democracy is understood as in large part a matter of anti-inegalitarianism, the democratic costs of racial profiling become more apparent. Racial profiling threatens to re-entrench patterns of social hierarchy—and not just any patterns of hierarchy, but the ones based on race. It may reinforce, that is to say, those systems of illegitimate dominance most notorious, at least in America, for their severity, pervasiveness, and intractability. It could do this in three different ways.

The first way racial profiling may reinforce racial hierarchy is through sheer numbers, imprisoning and otherwise bringing within penal supervision a greatly disproportionate number of minority group members, with a range of familiar, impoverishing consequences for their families and neighborhoods. Bernard Harcourt has shown that the disproportion in rates of arrest and incarceration can greatly exceed any preexisting difference in rates of offending, even if profiling is assumed to be a "rational" policy, pursued only to the point at which minority rates of offending match those among the wider population—a result he calls the "ratchet effect."[5] The second way racial profiling can reinforce racial hierarchy is by training members of minority groups in patterns of public subservience. Stopped by the police again and again, they learn to adopt roles of exaggerated deference and severely diminished self-agency—roles that can easily carry over to other arenas of social life.[6] The third way is by confirming racial stereotypes: suggesting, through higher rates of arrest, prosecution, and incarceration, that the profiled groups really are more prone to crime.[7]

Several things are worth noting about the mechanisms through which racial profiling threatens to reinforce racial hierarchy. First, they are mutually reinforcing. The ratchet effect can exacerbate the disproportionate numbers of African Americans and Latinos in prisons and on probation or parole, and thereby worsen the apparent confirmation of racial stereotypes.[8] The diminished self-agency taught through repeated contacts with the police may wind up reinforcing racial stereotypes, too. In turn, racial stereotypes—particularly the assumption that certain groups are more prone to criminality—can raise the level of subservience that members of those groups feel obliged to perform for the police.[9]

Second, profiling threatens to re-entrench dominance in the ways I have described only to the extent that it targets a traditionally disadvantaged group. Selectively stopping white motorists, for example, will not trigger these mechanisms of hierarchy reinforcement. (It might trigger *other* mechanisms of hierarchy reinforcement, depending on why the white motorists are stopped and what happens after they are stopped. Imagine, for example, that they are stopped in a minority neighborhood to warn them that the area is unsafe.) So it is probably a mistake to lump tactics of that kind together with the targeting of racial minorities under the term "racial profiling." On the other hand, profiling on the basis of a characteristic such as religion or national origin could easily re-entrench dominance in the same way as profiling on the basis of race: applying selective scrutiny to Muslims or to Arab-Americans is, in this respect, very much like applying selective scrutiny to African Americans.[10]

Third, the concerns that racial profiling raise for democracy by threatening to reinforce racial hierarchy do not depend on the fact that profiling involves conscious discrimination by law enforcement officers. Any law enforcement tactic resulting in heavily disproportionate rates of arrest, conviction, and incarceration of members of racial minorities may reinforce racial hierarchy by disrupting minority neighborhoods and reinforcing racial stereotypes. Minority group members are most likely to feel the need to adopt roles of exaggerated deference and subservience if they believe that they attract suspicion because of their race, but that impression can be created by the presence of pervasive stereotypes of minority criminality, with or without a conscious policy of racial profiling. Accordingly, the problems that racial profiling poses for democracy may also be posed by other law enforcement practices that lack the element of conscious targeting but nonetheless have a lopsided impact on minority suspects. A plausible argument can be made, for example, that much of the opprobrium directed at racial profiling should be applied more broadly to the war on drugs.[11]

Fourth and finally, though, there is another side to the equation, just as with order-maintenance policing. Crime hurts minority neighborhoods, too. Higher rates of criminal victimization, in fact, are probably among the worst of the multiple inequalities suffered by members of racial minorities. So if racial profiling, or other tactics that focus law enforcement disproportionately on racial minorities, succeeds in reducing crime in minority neighborhoods, the gains for democracy—both in terms of wider participation and in terms of diminished inequality and the amelioration of hierarchy—may be greater than the costs. This is an empirical question; it is a question that no theory of democracy, no matter how sophisticated, can hope to resolve. Again, what a richer account of democracy does is make clearer the questions that need to be asked, and what turns on the answer.

Understanding the harm of racial profiling (and of disproportionate enforcement more generally) is one thing; finding remedies for it is another. Broadly speaking, there are three possible lines of attack for this or any other threat posed by police practices: judicially enforced rights against the evil to be prevented, external systems of political accountability, and internal reconstitution of police forces. These three approaches sometimes overlap: judges and elected officials, for example, can put pressure on police departments to reconstitute themselves. External pressure of this kind has in fact been responsible for most of the dramatic changes in police forces over the past several decades—a point to which we will return later in this chapter. But distinguishing among these three lines of attack is nonetheless helpful. They suggest different, but complementary, responses to the problems of racial profiling and disproportionate enforcement.

The first response is doctrinal. The elaborate set of rules the Supreme Court began promulgating for police departments in the early 1960s focuses overwhelming on issues of fairness writ small: reining in the discretion of individual law enforcement officers and protecting the dignity of individual suspects. Distributional justice has largely been left out of the picture. A search or seizure, for example, cannot be challenged as "unreasonable" under the Fourth Amendment on the ground that it was motivated by prejudice; the Supreme Court has said that claims of discriminatory policing must be brought under the Equal Protection Clause, not the Fourth Amendment.[12] But that approach has costs. Equal protection doctrine treats claims of inequitable policing the same as any other claim of inequality; it gives no recognition to the special importance of evenhanded law enforcement. As a result, challenges to discriminatory police practices will fail without the *sine qua non* of a successful claim under the Equal Protection Clause as interpreted and applied by the Supreme Court—proof of conscious animus. The Court has reasoned that the Equal Protection Clause generally prohibits only decisions made with "discriminatory purpose," which is to say decisions made " 'because of,' not merely 'in spite of,' . . . adverse effects upon an identifiable group."[13] All this amounts to saying that the challenges will nearly always fail. Actual animus, even when it occurs, is notoriously difficult to prove. And many of the most troubling forms of discriminatory policing today—including many if not most instances of racial profiling—do not, in fact, reflect conscious animus, but rather a neutral, unobjectionable motive coupled with failure to take into sufficient account the harms posed by the practice.[14]

Constitutional doctrine could take other shapes. Fourth Amendment law, in particular, could be modified to take explicit account of the distributional aspects of search and seizure rules. This is something a wide range of legal scholars have long recommended. A rounded understanding of democratic policing lends support to their arguments.

The second broad strategy for combating inequitable "overpolicing" is changing the external political environment within which police departments operate. Some promising possibilities along these lines were mentioned in the last chapter: restructuring civilian oversight boards to make them more broadly representative, and using increased transparency of police decision making to empower community groups. Much of the progress that has been made over the past decade on the issue of racial profiling has resulted from police departments being pressured to address practices that have come to light through public scrutiny of data on police stops, searches, and arrests. Some of that information has, in turn, been collected pursuant to court orders—a good illustration of the way in which the strategy of court orders can overlap with the strategy of external political control.

The third broad strategy for addressing disproportionate targeting is by changing the insides of police departments: their organizational structures and the composition of their workforces. We will take up that topic at the end of this chapter.

Disproportionate Neglect and Minimally Adequate Policing

If democracy means, in part, opposition to entrenched patterns of illegitimate domination, private as well as public, then inadequate policing can be as much a threat to democracy as overly harsh policing. And there is no doubt that many places and many people in the United States suffer from inadequate police protection.[15] What strategies are available to address that problem? The most obvious strategies, again, are judicial intervention, external political control, and internal reconstitution of police departments. We will consider each in turn.

Start with the judiciary. The Fourteenth Amendment, passed in the aftermath of the Civil War, promises all Americans both "due process of law" and the "equal protection of the laws." The background of these provisions strongly suggests that they were meant to guarantee, in part, protection against private violence; much of what concerned the Reconstruction Congress, which passed the Fourteenth Amendment, was the failure of southern states to protect freed blacks from white vigilantes.[16] But that understanding long ago dropped out of constitutional law. Today the Supreme Court refuses to recognize a right to minimally adequate policing, reasoning that the Constitution protects only against injuries directly inflicted by the government. Due process of law, the Court has said, limits government's "power to act," but does not "guarantee . . . minimal levels of safety and security."[17] In dicta, the Court has read the Equal Protection Clause to prohibit a state's selective denial of "protective services to certain disfavored minorities."[18] But since the Equal Protection Clause generally is violated only by decisions made with "discriminatory purpose"—that is, conscious animus—that clause, too, is of little help in challenging inadequate policing.

State tort law mirrors constitutional law in this respect. The vast weight of case law refuses to impose liability on states, municipalities, or police departments for failing to provide adequate police protection. The reasoning that courts offer for this result varies. Some courts describe it as a matter of governmental immunity; others declare simply that the state has no duty to furnish police protection, or that the duty is owed to the public at large, and not to any individual. But the result is almost always the same: tort law, like constitutional law, provides no remedy for inadequate policing.[19]

Lurking behind these results is a sense that judicial involvement is unnecessary here, because elected officials have strong political incentives to provide adequate levels of police protection. Thus, for example, Judge Richard Easterbrook has reasoned that "[t]he body with the power to create a rule also has the right incentives to police it. Cities and states are not hostile to their own laws; they do not need federal courts to prod them to enforce rules voluntarily adopted."[20]

There are grounds for doubt about that. To begin with, American police departments have a long history of providing more protection, or different kinds of protection, in wealthier areas, with well-connected voters, than in poor areas, with residents who are not citizens, do not vote, or simply have less political clout. This problem is exacerbated by the flight of white, wealthier voters to the suburbs, where they have their own police departments, and by the recent, explosive growth in private policing—both ways for white, wealthy voters to provide police protection for themselves but not for poor, minority neighborhoods.[21]

Both doctrinal and structural responses to this problem deserve consideration. Doctrinally, one path would be to reconsider whether the constitutional guarantee of "equal protection" should be understood to include some kind of right to minimally adequate policing. An obvious analogy here would be to the right to minimally adequate education—also rejected on the federal level, but recognized by some state courts. The effectiveness of school finance litigation remains controversial, but the best evidence suggests that at the very least lawsuits have succeeded in drawing public and legislative attention to problems of educational funding, attention that in several states has led to meaningful reform.[22] Once again, the strategy of judicial intervention turns out to blur into the strategy of political control.

Structurally, there may be ways to reform the political environment within which police departments operate, in order to make Judge Easterbrook's confidence in political checks on inadequate policing more justified. Gerald Frug, for example, has argued cogently for moving significant amounts of law enforcement budgeting and policy making from the local to the regional level, in order to force suburban and urban communities to work together on the problems of policing.[23] Proposals for regional governance are often greeted with suspicion, and justifiably so. There is always the risk that "region" simply means, as Jane Jacobs suggested, "an area safely larger than the last one to whose problems we found no solution."[24] But Frug's proposal is not tied, as similar schemes in the past often have been, to notions that larger governmental units will have greater administrative capacity. His argument is different: it is an attempt to use governmental structure to promote good politics. In this respect it is very much in the tradition of the kind of eighteenth-century political economy at work in *The Federalist Papers*—a tradition worth trying to recover in a rounded theory of democratic policing.

Equality Inside Police Departments

When people think about issues of equality in policing, they usually think about how the police treat suspects, victims, complainants, and witnesses of different races, ethnicities, genders, sexual orientations, and socioeconomic statuses. They focus on what we can call *external* equality, not on equality of treatment *inside* police departments—equal treatment of police personnel themselves. But the two dimensions of equality are closely intertwined. The dramatic but incomplete advances over the past several decades in the desegregation of American police departments turns out to be an important and underappreciated asset in the struggle to make *external* equality more of a reality in policing.

American police forces are far more diverse now than they were in 1970, and far more representative of the communities that they serve. Minority officers, female officers, and openly gay and lesbian officers are slowly but dramatically transforming a profession that thirty-five years ago was virtually all white, virtually all male, and uniformly homophobic.

Blacks, for example, made up somewhere around 6 percent of sworn officers in the three hundred or so largest American police departments in 1970; today the figure is around 18 percent.[25] In cities with populations over 250,000, 20 percent of sworn officers are black, and 14 percent are Latino—up from figures of 18 percent and 9 percent, respectively, in 1990.[26] In 2005, for the first time in the history of the New York City Police Department, a majority of the new officers graduating from its academy were members of racial minorities.[27] In some major cities—including Los Angeles, Detroit, and Washington, D.C.—the entire police force is now majority minority.[28] Minority officers remain concentrated in lower ranks,[29] but not across the board. In Los Angeles, for example, where the black share of the city population in 2000 was 11 percent, black officers that year comprised 14 percent of the police force, 15 percent of supervisors, and 22 percent of command-level personnel.[30]

Women were 2 percent of sworn officers in large police agencies in 1972; today they are close to 13 percent. Again, the figure in some departments is significantly higher, although it tops out around 25 percent. Like minority officers, female officers remain concentrated in lower ranks—although, as with minority officers, the extent and uniformity of the concentration is less than one might expect.[31]

The mere fact that there are *any* openly gay officers, let alone gay police executives, is a sea change from the situation thirty years ago. San Francisco had no openly gay officers as late as 1979; Chicago had none as recently as 1991.[32] Even today, gay and lesbian officers can feel strong pressures to keep their orientation hidden or at least unadvertised. This is particularly true for gay male officers.[33] It is therefore difficult to estimate the number of gay and lesbian police officers, or even those who are, to a greater or lesser extent, open about their status. The latter category is clearly growing, though, to the point where, in some departments, "the presence of self-disclosed gay and lesbian officers has become normalized."[34] Between 1992 and 2001, for example, the number of "self-identified gay men and women" working for the San Diego Police Department increased from five to somewhere between thirty-five and fifty. In San Diego as elsewhere, as the number of "out" cops has risen, their presence on the force has become increasingly taken for granted.[35] The participation of uniformed police officers in gay pride parades is now commonplace, if still at times controversial. And in November 2004, the annual meeting of the International Association of Chiefs of Police included, for the first time, a workshop on gay, lesbian, bisexual, and transgendered officers.[36]

Why Internal Equality Matters

American law enforcement has come a long way from the overwhelmingly white, virtually all-male, pervasively homophobic police forces of thirty or forty years ago—although there is still a good way left to go, and the extent of the changes varies greatly from department to department. What have been the effects of this dramatic, if uneven and incomplete, transformation? It is helpful to distinguish three different kinds of possible effects: *competency effects* (distinctive sets of skills and abilities that minority officers, female officers, and gay and lesbian officers may bring to their work); *community effects* (consequences that integrating a police department may have for the relationship between the department and the community it serves); and *organizational effects* (ways in which the presence of minority, female, and gay and lesbian officers may change the internal dynamics of a police department).

Competency effects have long been an important part of the case for diversifying police departments, dating back at least until the 1960s. *The Challenge of Crime in a Free Society*—the landmark report by President Johnson's Commission on Law Enforcement and the Administration of Justice—blamed much of the difficulties that police experienced in the inner city on white officers' "lack of understanding of the problems and behaviors of minority groups," and on the inability of all-white police departments "to deal successfully with people whose ways of thought and action are unfamiliar."[37] Here, as elsewhere, minority officers were suggested to have two different kinds of special competence: greater *understanding* of minority communities, and greater *credibility* in minority communities.

Minority officers have long believed that they do, in fact, have these special competencies.[38] But the quantitative evidence on this score is actually quite conflicting. There are studies finding that black officers shoot just as often as white officers;[39] that black officers arrest just as often as white officers;[40] that black officers are often prejudiced against black citizens;[41] that black officers get less cooperation than white officers from black citizens;[42] and that black officers are just as likely, or even *more* likely, to elicit citizen complaints and disciplinary actions.[43] But there are also studies concluding that black officers get *more* cooperation than white officers from black citizens;[44] that black officers are less prejudiced against blacks[45] and know more about the black community;[46] and that black officers are more likely to arrest white suspects and less likely to arrest black suspects.[47] On both sides of this debate, many of the findings are hard to interpret. If, for example, black officers draw more complaints, is that because they act more aggressively, or because they are assigned to tougher beats, or because prejudice makes their assertions of authority seem more objectionable, or because minority citizens feel more comfortable complaining about officers from whom they do not fear retaliation?

The fairest summary of the evidence is probably that we simply do not know whether black officers, or minority officers more generally, bring a significantly different set of pertinent abilities and understandings to their work. But that is not the way the evidence is usually understood. Instead, the evidence is typically viewed as demonstrating that minority officers do not, in fact, differ appreciably in their on-the-job behavior from white officers. The scholarly consensus is that "no evidence suggests that African American, Hispanic, and white officers behave in significantly different ways."[48] Or, as Edward Conlon puts it in his recently published memoir of his work as a New York City police officer, "[o]ver time and in the main, cops tend to think like other cops."[49]

The evidence has been understood in this way in part because there is an orthodox, long-standing explanation why minority officers should be expected to behave the same as white officers. The explanation is occupational ethos and organizational culture. As an influential scholar of policing explained in the mid-1970s, "[t]he pressures for conformity are so strong that the new officer will either be forced into the police subculture, with the values and orientation of the larger group replacing his own, or his life will be made so unpleasant that he will decide to resign."[50] This view has become pervasive among scholars who study the police, including legal scholars writing about criminal procedure. The governing assumption is that police behavior is determined by "situational and departmental factors," not by race.[51] Nor, for that matter, by gender: the consensus view is that "male and female officers," like white and black officers, "have been found to behave in roughly similar ways."[52]

In fact, the quantitative evidence regarding the differential performance of women officers, like the corresponding evidence about minority officers, is equivocal. Several studies have found that female officers are slightly less proactive than male officers but otherwise behave substantially the same.[53] Other studies have found no differences whatsoever.[54] Still other studies have concluded that female officers are substantially less apt to shoot or to use excessive force,[55] and significantly more helpful to victims of domestic violence.[56] There are also studies, though, suggesting that women officers may be *more* apt to shoot than male officers.[57] Again, many of these findings are difficult to interpret: the greater helpfulness of female officers to domestic violence victims may simply reflect the fact that female officers tend to be better educated than male officers and are more likely to be single.[58]

Whereas minority officers tend to believe that they do in fact have special competencies—specifically, understanding of their communities and credibility in their communities—female officers appear to be divided on that question. The divide is mirrored in the arguments advanced by advocates of increased hiring and promotion of women in police departments, arguments that reflect, in turn the broader divide between "equality feminism" and "difference feminism." A recent report, for example, from the National Center for Women and Policing argues one the one hand that male and female officers are "equally capable" and, one the other hand, that women are *better* officers in a range of respects: less prone to use excessive force, more skillful at "defusing and de-escalating potentially violent confrontation," better at securing the "cooperation and trust," and more effective in responding to incidents of domestic violence.[59]

There has been virtually no research on the relative competencies of gay and straight officers. Anecdotally, though, claims have been made for gay and lesbian officers that echo claims long made for minority officers: that they bring to their work a valuable understanding of their off-the-job community, as well as greater credibility within that community.[60] There are suggestions, too, that gay and lesbian officers, because of "their own experience in marginalized groups," may be especially skilled in "responding to the needs of other oppressed groups."[61] But there are also suggestions that homosexual officers, like minority officers and female officers, are strongly constrained by the "white, male, heterosexual ethos" of policing and by the overriding determination to be perceived as "good cops," both by their fellow officers and by themselves.[62]

So much for competency effects. What about community effects—the consequences of diversifying a police department in terms of its relations with the communities the department serves? Just as black officers, for example, may have more credibility than white officers in a predominantly black neighborhood, a department that recruits, retains, and promotes a significant number of black officers may find the credibility of its entire force enhanced in black neighborhoods. That prospect has, in fact, long served as a significant part of the case for diversifying police workforces. President Johnson's Crime Commission, for example, argued strongly in the late 1960s that improving relations between the police and minority communities required "recruiting more, many more, policemen from minority groups"— because "every section of the community has a right to expect that its aspirations and problems, its hopes and fears, are fully reflected in the police."[63] A similar argument has been made, more recently, for hiring more gay and lesbian officers. Gay and lesbian officers in San Diego, for example, believe that the success of community policing in San Diego is attributable in part to the involvement of openly homosexual officers. As one gay officer explained, "You gain way more respect from the community that you're policing if you have members of the diverse community working as cops."[64]

As with competence effects, though, the objective evidence regarding community effects is mixed. Just as there is some evidence that black officers get more cooperation than white officers from black citizens, and some evidence that they get less,[65] so there is some evidence that minority citizens think minority officers improve the overall quality of policing, but also some evidence that they perceive no difference.[66]

Again, there is a long-standing, broadly accepted explanation for the lack of any clear effect of police diversity on community relations, and, here as well, the explanation blames the police subculture. That subculture has long been thought to sever a minority officer, for example, "from his community and his roots."[67] An early, influential ethnographic study of black police officers concluded that they forfeited, in becoming officers, much of their credibility as blacks. Occupying "a doubly marginal position between the marginal police and his own [racial] marginality," the black officer was "a man exposed to the shame of his race," because his occupational role was perceived as antagonistic to the interests of the ghetto.[68] A pioneering, equally influential study of female officers found that they, too, suffered from a kind of double marginality, forced to choose between "defeminization" and "deprofessionalization": only by relinquishing much of their identity as women could they fully succeed as police officers.[69] Gay and lesbian officers, too, have been said to lead "double lives"; by joining the ranks of law enforcement they estrange themselves from the gay and lesbian community.[70]

The clearest benefits provided by the growing numbers of minority officers, female officers, and gay and lesbian officers pertain not to what I have called competency effects and community effects but, rather, to the consequences that the new demographics have had for the internal dynamics of police departments. The organizational effects can usefully be subdivided into *one-on-one interactions*, *rival trade groups*, and *social fragmentation*.

By *one-on-one interactions* I mean the way that a minority, female, or openly homosexual officer can change the attitudes and behavior of other officers with whom he or she comes into contact—particularly his or her partner. Minority officers tend to believe these effects are significant.[71] So do gay officers[72] and appreciable numbers, if not a majority, of female officers. Quantitative studies of this matter are limited, but they do suggest that the officers are correct. There is evidence, for example, that biracial teams of partners use less force,[73] and men partnered with women handle domestic violence calls as well as women.[74] These results are broadly consistent with the large body of research on integration outside of policing, which suggests on the whole that "the experience of working together across lines of social division . . . though not untroubled by prejudice and hostility, tends to reduce prejudice and hostility."[75]

By *rival trade groups* I mean groups that compete for membership with the long-standing police benevolent associations, which generally serve today not only as social and fraternal organizations but also as collective bargaining agents and lobbying groups. The police benevolent associations now coexist with a range of organizations, many highly vocal, representing the interests of minority officers.[76] In Los Angeles, for example, the Police Protective League competes for members with the Oscar Joel Bryant Foundation, which represents black officers, and the Latin American Law Enforcement Association, known informally as "La Ley." On the national level, there is the National Black Police Association, the National Organization of Black Law Enforcement Officers, the National Organization of Black Law Enforcement Executives, the Hispanic National Law Enforcement Association, and the National Latino Peace Officers Association.

At both the local and national levels, these organizations often take positions at dramatic variance with the position of mainline police organizations—not just on hiring and promotion policies, but on issues such as racial profiling and police brutality,[77] and on questions of police leadership. In Los Angeles, for example, when Chief Bernard Parks was being considered for reappointment in 2002, he was strongly opposed by the Police Protective League, supported by the Oscar Joel Bryant Foundation, and opposed by La Ley.[78] Another, earlier example: in 1991, after Milwaukee's police chief suspended three officers in the fallout from the Jeffrey Dahmer case, the Milwaukee Police Association voted "no confidence" in the chief, but the League of Martin—an organization of black officers—pointedly distanced itself from the vote and defended the suspensions.[79]

One-on-one interactions and rival trade groups are important, but not nearly as important as the third subcategory of organizational effects, *social fragmentation*—the decline of the monolithic police subculture. This is something that older officers—particularly white, male, heterosexual officers—talk about a lot. A white male officer interviewed by sociologist Robin Haarr in the mid-1990s put it this way: "It used to be we were all 'blue,' but that has changed over the past years. Today there is black, white, and female segregation."[80] Haarr agrees. Expressing what seems to be the emerging consensus among police ethnographers, she reports that "unified occupational subculture" of policing is being replaced by workplaces marked by "division" and "segmentation."[81]

This is exactly what many people feared thirty years ago, when courts began imposing race- and gender-conscious hiring plans on police departments. Samuel Williams, a black lawyer serving as president of the Los Angeles Board of Police Commissioners, warned in 1975 that "[t]he entrance of minorities into a department under a judge-fashioned statistical umbrella can only lead to an organization . . . torn by faction and laced with angry mutterings," an organization "deprived of that crucial cooperation among brother officers so critically essential to effective service."[82]

The factions and angry mutterings have come. Police officers today report lines of division, distrust, and resentment not only between white officers and minority officers, but also between male and female officers, between gay and straight officers, and sometimes between black officers and Latino officers, Latino officers and Asian-American officers, and so on. It is not clear how much of this can be laid at the feet of the courts; some of it may have happened no matter what route police departments took to greater workforce diversity. But the decline in solidarity is everywhere apparent. The good news is that it has turned out to be a much more beneficial development than Williams and others anticipated. The decline in solidarity does not seem to have impaired police effectiveness. For operational purposes, it appears still to be true that "blue is blue."[83] In between calls to service, police officers are a less cohesive group than they used to be. But that appears to be a very good thing. It makes the internal cultures of police departments less stifling, and it opens up space for dissent and disagreement. Studies of police departments today read far differently than those of thirty or forty years ago: instead of a single police perspective on any given issue, investigators today typically find a range of conflicting perspectives.[84]

Moreover, the social fragmentation has gone hand in hand with a decline in police insularity, for identity binds as well as divides.[85] Minority officer organizations frequently work closely with minority organizations outside law enforcement; to a lesser extent, female officers sometimes form organizational ties with women working in other historically male professions. The National Center for Women and Policing, for example, is part of Eleanor Smeal's Feminist Majority Project. Organizational alliances like this coexist with and help to foster less formal ties of affinity between minority cops and minority citizens, female cops and women more broadly, and gays and lesbians inside and outside law enforcement.[86] Both the formal, organizational alliances and the less formal ties of affinity create channels for expanding civilian involvement in the shaping and directing of law enforcement.[87] The social fragmentation I have been discussing might more accurately be described, therefore, as social realignment.

The benefits of social realignment would come at a steep cost if, as people like Williams predicted, the decline in police solidarity meant the police did a worse job controlling crime. But that does not seem to have happened. John Lott concluded several years ago that affirmative action in policing had raised crime, particularly in black neighborhoods. He attributed this effect not to a decline in solidarity but the relaxed hiring standards that he claimed had been part and parcel of affirmative action in policing.[88] Lott's results, though, have never been duplicated, and more recent work casts them in serious doubt.[89]

The growing, still far from complete acceptance of openly gay and lesbian officers may contribute in a particularly powerful way to the social realignment of law enforcement—in part by accelerating the fragmentation of the police subculture, in part by creating new channels of communication with groups outside of law enforcement, and in part by challenging the endemic homophobia of law enforcement.[90] There is good reason to think that the suppression of homosexuality has played a central role in cementing police solidarity, in part by rendering professional male–male partnerships sexually unthreatening, and in part by helping to shape a whole, hypermasculinized professional ethos.

When William Westley did his pioneering ethnography of an American police department in the 1950s, for example, he found that the rampant condoning of illegal violence among police officers owed a good deal to the experiences that officers had policing "sex cases"—a category which for him, and for the officers he studied, lumped homosexuals together with rapists, peeping toms, and exhibitionists. Westley thought the police correctly understood the public to approve "extremely rough treatment" in sex cases, but to want that treatment carried out unofficially and without their involvement. The experience of the police in these cases, Westley concluded, "enourage[d] them to use violence as a general resource," and left them embittered and cynical about what the public expected of them. It helped to convince them that their jobs required them to exercise discretion in a way that could not be publicly acknowledged—that police work was essentially and necessarily outside the law.[91]

The presence of openly gay and lesbian officers, particularly once they begin to rise through the ranks, challenges the easy, taken-for-granted homophobia of the law enforcement, and all that it has helped to foster—the nominally desexualized police workplace, the hyper-masculinized ethos of the profession, and the tacit acceptance of extra-legal violence. All of that is on top of the ways in which gay and lesbian officers, like minority officers and female officers, will help to fragment the police subculture and to build identity-based bridges to groups outside of law enforcement. The social realignment of policing—the decline in the solidarity and insularity of the police—has turned out to be the most important effect of the profession's growing diversity.

Taking Stock

Unfortunately, it is far from certain that police forces will continue to diversify at the rate they have over the past three decades. Much of the past progress was produced by court-ordered programs of affirmative action, which are now growing less common. The overwhelming weight of the evidence suggests these programs played a pivotal role in the diversification of American police departments.

Some of the most striking evidence is the progress over time in particular departments. In Pittsburgh, for example, the percentage of women officers went from 1 percent in 1975, when court-ordered hiring quotas were imposed, to 27.2 percent in 1990, the highest figure at the time for any large

city in the nation. When the quota was lifted in 1991, the female share of
new hires plummeted from 50 percent (required under the court order) to
8.5 percent, and by 2001 the percentage of women in the rank of police
officer had dropped to 22 percent and was continuing to decline.[92]

Justin McCrary has compiled a more extensive set of data about the integration of the Chicago Police Department. A lawsuit challenging racial
discrimination in police hiring in Chicago was filed in 1970 by the Afro-
American Patrolmen's League; it was joined by the United States Department of Justice in 1973, and it resulted in 1974 in a court-ordered hiring
quota, made permanent in 1976. The black share of new hires rose from
roughly 10 percent in 1971–1973 to 40 percent in 1975.[93] (The percentage
of black officers on the force as a whole rose much more slowly, even following the hiring change. There is a lesson here: police departments have low
turnover. The annual quit rate is around 4 percent.[94] So it takes a while for
changes in hiring practices to alter the composition of the workforce.)

McCrary also conducted a more systematic comparison of changes in
what he calls the "representation gap"—the difference between the percentage of black officers and the black share of the relevant city population. He
compared changes in this figure in two groups of cities: those that were sued
for discriminating against blacks in hiring, and those that were not. The
bulk of the lawsuits were filed in the 1970s, and they were concentrated
in big cities with large black populations—populations that were growing
faster than the black share of the local police workforce. Many of the hiring
quotas remained in effect into the 1990s, and some are still in place.[95] Mc-
Crary found that the representation gap in the 1970s was much more sizeable in litigated cities than in unlitigated cities, but that in the 1980s and
1990s, when hiring quotas would be expected to begin having an effect on
workforce composition, the gap in litigated cities improved markedly, while
there was relatively little change in the unlitigated cities.[96]

McCrary's study is the most sophisticated and wide-ranging work to date
on the relationship between affirmative action decrees and either racial or
gender integration of police departments. But the broad conclusion he
reaches—that affirmative action has played a large role in the demographic
transformation of American police forces—is the same conclusion reached
by virtually everyone who has studied these questions. Fifteen years ago, for
example, William Lewis ran regressions on black police employment in

forty-six municipal police departments between 1975 and 1985. He found that the most powerful variables associated with increases in the black percentage of the police force were "Black majors, Black police chiefs, and affirmative action consent degrees."[97] Even John Lott is in agreement on this point. Reviewing data on the race and gender composition of 189 American police forces in 1987 and 1993, Lott concluded that the median change in the percentage of black officers was 3.2 percent in cities with consent decrees as opposed to 0.73 percent in other cities, and that the 90th percentile change in the percentage of black officers was 18.2 percent in cities with consent decrees and 6.0 percent in cities without them.[98]

The available statistical work on women officers points in a similar direction. After surveying 446 departments in the mid-1980s, Susan Martin reported that police forces with consent decrees addressing gender in hiring or promotion were 10.1 percent female, compared with 8.3 percent for forces with voluntary affirmative action programs, and 6.1 percent for all other departments.[99] Based on a smaller survey, the National Center for Women in Policing estimated in 2003 that 17.8 percent of the officers in municipal police departments with consent decrees were women, compared to 10.1 percent in surveyed departments without consent decrees, and 14.2 percent of all municipal departments.[100] Tim Sass and Jennifer Troyer, performing a regression analysis of EEOC hiring, concluded that prior anti-discrimination rulings were associated in the 1980s with an increase of 7–10 percent in the female proportion of newly hired officers.[101] Lott reported that, in his sample of 189 large departments, the median increase in the percentage of female officers between 1987 and 1993 was 2.8 percent in departments with consent decrees and 1.1 percent in departments without decrees.[102]

Because the statistics regarding gay and lesbian officers are so paltry, it is much more difficult to assess the role of lawsuits here. Anecdotally, however, lawsuits appear to have played a significant role in spurring departments to become more welcoming to, and tolerant of, openly gay and lesbian cops,[103] just as earlier lawsuits were pivotal in bringing more race and gender diversity to policing.

The heavy role that court-ordered affirmative action has played in integrating police departments provides reason to be concerned that progress may stall, or even be reversed, as consent decrees expire or are rescinded—often well before departments are fully integrated. (The court-ordered hiring quotas in Boston, for example, were rescinded in 2004, despite the fact that the minority representation gap remained around 6–8 percent: racial minorities make up 38–40 percent of the population in Boston, but only 32 percent of the police force.) The worry is that the Pittsburgh experience will be replicated nationwide.

There is some evidence that this is already occurring. Figures on the female percentage of departments with one hundred or more officers suggest that gender integration of American police departments has stalled and even suffered a slight reversal since 2000. The researchers who compiled this set of figures for the National Center for Women and Policing believe that the decline is in fact real, and that it reflects the expiration of consent decrees.[104]

All of this suggests that safeguarding and expanding the gains already achieved in diversifying police departments should be a central component of the police reform agenda, and of what we mean by "democratic policing." The evidence regarding the competence and community effects of police integration is equivocal, but certainly not sufficiently negative to warrant discounting the belief, very broadly held by minority, female, and openly gay officers, that they bring special understandings and special credibility to their work. All the more so when much of the reason for skepticism about these benefits has stemmed from concern about the insular and monolithic police subculture—a subculture that is itself now being transformed, segmented, and rendered more porous by the growing diversity of the police workforce. By weakening the social solidarity of the police, the growing diversity of law enforcement workforces makes it more likely that departments will be able to take advantage of the special competencies of minority officers, female officers, and openly gay and lesbian officers. It also paves the way for bolder experiments with participatory management and workplace democracy in policing—matters to be taken up in the next chapter. And by weakening the *political* solidarity of the police, and the uniformity of viewpoints within police departments, police diversity greatly facilitates other reforms, including civilian oversight, community policing, and systematic efforts to ameliorate racial bias in policing—the *external* dimension of equality in policing.

CHAPTER 8

Police and Participation

The sweeping changes over the past half century in ideas about the police and ideas about democracy have altered the meaning of "democratic policing" in a range of important ways. But one assumption has stayed constant: democratic policing means making the police *answerable* to democracy, not bringing the benefits of democracy to police officers *themselves*. The democracy in democratic policing is external, not internal, to law enforcement. Democracy *within* police organizations has long been thought at best peripheral and at worst antithetical to the more pressing task of reconciling law enforcement with democracy *outside* police organizations. Despite the large changes in the makeup of police forces over the past several decades, and in their operational philosophy, workplace democracy has remained largely absent from discussions of police reform. It formed no part of the ideology of police professionalism, and it plays almost no role in the ideology of community policing. It is off the agenda.

In this chapter I want to examine this absence and to ask whether it is consistent with the rounded theory of democracy sketched in Chapter 5. Obviously, the police cannot be freed from outside oversight. That would be impossible to reconcile not just with a credible account of democracy but with any sane approach to governance. My interest is in the long-term failure of a narrower claim—that rank-and-file police officers should participate collectively in the shaping of their work—to gain significant traction. What accounts for that failure, and does it warrant correction?

I will argue that it does. Participatory democracy in the management of police departments has many of the same attractions that it has elsewhere. Some of those attractions, in fact, are heightened in the context of policing.

In many ways, of course, police officers already *do* participate collectively in the shaping of the work. Partners assigned to the same patrol car discuss how they should spend their time. Teams of officers plan undercover stings and neighborhood sweeps. Policing is heavily unionized, and police unions sometimes take strong positions on matters of departmental policy. Today they may be joined at the table by identity-based caucuses of police officers— groups, for example, of black, or Latino, or gay and lesbian officers. And, even without pressure from below, wise sergeants, lieutenants, and captains— like wise supervisors in any occupation—find ways to enlist the rank and file in processes of cooperative problem-solving.

But in law enforcement all of this occurs at the margins. It cuts against the grain. The dominant mind-set of police departments, police reformers, appellate judges, and criminal justice scholars—the dominant mind-set, in short, of nearly everyone who thinks about policing and its problems—is, and has long been, that policing is a place for top-down management. Good police officers are police officers who follow rules. Police unions, and police organizing more generally, are obstacles, not opportunities.[1] Democracy means the rule of law, and the rule of law means that policing is no place for exercises in workforce empowerment. If law enforcement has turned out, ironically, to be one of the last strongholds of trade unionism, it is also (and not accidentally) a lingering bastion of the Taylorist faith in scientific management. Police work is notoriously rule-bound, so much so that "all cops exist in a state of mild infraction."[2] The particular focus of police rulebooks is often the subject of criticism: too much attention to the proper kind of shoe laces, not enough attention to the grounds for an investigative stop. But outside the ranks of police officers themselves, there is little sentiment for giving line officers more of a say in how policing should be carried out. Even the fiercest foes of authoritarian workplaces tend to make an exception for law enforcement. Indeed, the very same people who usually argue strongly for industrial democracy often tend to favor, again in the name of democracy, subjecting the work of police officers to rigid, comprehensive, and minutely detailed rules, imposed from the outside or at least from the top.

That program—prescribing from above the "one best method" of policing, in the name of democracy and the rule of law—animates our law of constitutional criminal procedure, is taken for granted in most efforts at police reform, and provides a point of continuity in the managerial philosophy of policing, bridging the shift from police professionalism to community policing. "Team policing" and "problem-oriented policing," two important predecessors of community policing, each incorporated elements of participatory management.[3] But those elements became much more muted as time went on and as team policing and problem-oriented policing were absorbed into mainstream thinking about law enforcement. As a result, policing has clung more stubbornly to authoritarian management practices than other, traditionally hierarchical sectors of the American economy—including, ironically, the military.[4]

A comment on terminology: "workplace democracy" and "participatory management" often are distinguished from each other. "Workplace democracy" refers to unionism and other bottom-up efforts at employee empowerment; "participatory management" means efforts at cooperative problem-solving implemented and controlled by management, often over strong objections from unions. Workplace democracy involves an actual *delegation* of power to workers, whereas participatory management typically involves only *consultation*. In keeping with the eclectic account of democracy we have been applying, though, I will use the terms "workplace democracy" and "participatory management" for the most part interchangeably, to refer to efforts to allow employees, whether police officers or otherwise, to participate in the shaping of their work.

Something is lost when workplace democracy is defined so broadly: the reminder that things could be more radically restructured, that employees could be given collective legal powers instead of simply consulted. It is similar to what was lost when "neighborhood policing," the largely unsuccessful movement in the late 1960s and early 1970s to hand over control of police departments to local residents, was replaced by "community policing," the now ubiquitous set of arrangements through which police departments consult with groups outside law enforcement—with the police deciding when to consult, with whom, and about which subjects.[5] Defining democracy to encompass both delegation and consultation risks cheapening the term and obscuring the plainly important distinction between schemes that redistribute legal authority and those that seem to be just about talking. It risks obscuring, too, the ways in which systems of consultation—sometimes intentionally—can threaten to undercut more far-reaching efforts at workplace democracy, by mollifying employees and undercutting their solidarity.

I run these risks here not because I think that underlying arrangements of power are unimportant or immutable—far from it—but because I think that certain formalized systems of consultation can be democratizing in their own right. That is to say, they can advance some (although obviously not all) of what we mean by "democracy." They can allow people to participate collectively in the decisions that shape their lives; they can open up the channels of decision making to new perspectives and new concerns; they can advance John Dewey's project of "securing diffused and seminal intelligence."[6] This is the sense in which it makes sense to call "community policing" democratizing, even when—as almost always—it does little to limit the operational autonomy of the police. And in this sense even schemes of participatory management adopted unilaterally by employers and controlled by employers can, at least in some circumstances, appropriately be called "democratizing."

I also will be taking some liberties in this chapter with Taylorism. Strictly speaking, Taylorism called for simplifying manual tasks by breaking them down and dividing them among employees, and then for controlling employees' every movement in order to eliminate inefficiency. Obviously, policing consists of more than manual labor, and no one has ever tried to break down and to routinize police work the way that Frederick Taylor broke down and routinized factory work.[7] More broadly, though, Taylorism has come to stand for a certain approach to managing work, an approach that shuns reliance on employees' intelligence and emphasizes the control of work through rigid rules promulgated from the top.[8] I will argue that we tend instinctively to take this approach to police work, and that this may be a mistake, for many of the reasons that Taylorism in the narrow sense has been discredited.

I will be contrasting Taylorism with workplace democracy, and this, too, is a simplification. A workplace can be completely undemocratic without having even a touch of Taylorism. (Think of a company run by the kind of mercurial, utterly vacuous despot familiar on television sitcoms.) And some systems of participatory management are entirely compatible with the kind of detailed work rules Taylor favored—a point to which we return. As long as these caveats are kept in mind, though, the crude dichotomy between workplace democracy, loosely defined, and Taylorism, loosely defined, will prove useful in identifying and challenging certain unstated preconceptions underlying almost all discussions of democratic policing.

Taylorism, Anti-Taylorism, and the Police

Top-down workplace regimentation of the kind famously advocated by Frederick Taylor still has fans, many of whom may never have heard of "scientific management."[9] In the low-wage sector of the American economy, Taylorism continues to flourish, bolstered in many workplaces by new technologies of surveillance and monitoring.[10] But among management theorists and other students of employment, Taylor's ideas have long been out of fashion, and for good reasons. Fixed systems of rules that seek to control employees' every action are widely thought today to be bad for management, bad for employees, and bad for society. They are bad for management because they inevitably fail to address the full complexity of the tasks given to employees; because they make employees unmotivated and disloyal; and because they forfeit the knowledge and insights of the workforce—its "diffused and seminal intelligence."[11] They are bad for workers because they are stultifying and immiserating. And they are bad for society because they train workers in habits of alienation and passivity, rather than the habits of engagement, cooperation, and deliberation that help a democratic society flourish.

This multifaceted critique of Taylorism is conventional wisdom today among labor activists and management theorists alike. It has at least three sources: one in social theory, one in democratic theory, and one in management theory. The first source is the "alienation" indictment of industrial and postindustrial employment: the idea, as old as Taylorism itself, that the loss of "meaningful work" has helped to bring about the crippling sense of disconnection and disempowerment that pervades modern collective life.[12]

The second source is the notion that democracy consists not just in elections and representation, but also, and more critically, in a broadly engaged citizenry. This way of thinking about democracy gained especially wide currency in the 1960s, when "participatory democracy" became the catchphrase of the New Left, but its roots are much older. It is the tradition of Rousseau, Tocqueville, and Dewey.[13] There is also a long tradition, revived in the late 1960s and early 1970s, of viewing workplaces as the ideal loci for experiments in participatory democracy: intimate enough for face-to-face conversations, and important enough to make participation manifestly worthwhile.[14] The third source of disenchantment with Taylorism is the widespread enthusiasm among management theorists, beginning in the 1980s and 1990s, for workforces marked by teamwork and cooperation.[15]

The agendas of meaningful work, industrial democracy, and cooperative management do not always coincide. Trade unions, the most familiar form of industrial democracy, can be impediments to management-controlled structures for employee participation in workplace decision making—in part because unions often suspect, sometimes with justification, that these structures are aimed chiefly at pacifying workers and undermining their solidarity.[16] Some tactics of cooperative management—"quality circles," for example—have proven compatible with workplaces arguably as regimented as anything dreamed of by Frederick Taylor, even if the rules change more often, and even if employees participate in their revision.[17] I will return to these points of tension later in this chapter. For now, though, the important thing is that Taylor's agenda of improving workplace performance by minutely regulating job practices from the top down is now widely believed to be bad for management, bad for workers, and bad for society.

Each prong of the modern anti-Taylorist consensus has readily apparent implications for policing. Indeed the standard indictment of Taylorism takes on some special strength in the context of law enforcement. I will discuss that standard indictment, and its application to policing, by first considering the costs to management, then the costs to workers, and then the costs to society. The tripartite division here is artificial: the interests of police managers overlap considerably both with the interests of rank-and-file police officers and with the interests of society. As long as we keep the artificiality in mind, though, separating out the costs to management, to officers, and to the public at large will be analytically useful.

Start with the view, now quite common, that authoritarian workplaces are bad for management. The standard arguments for this view are (a) that predetermined rules cannot possibly address the full complexity of any but the very simplest tasks, (b) that efforts to specify in advance the "one best method" to perform a particular job forfeit the diffused, hands-on knowledge that workers gain by actually doing the job, and (c) that rigid regulation of workers undercuts their loyalty and motivation. All three of these arguments apply at least in part to police officers, and the first and second apply with particular strength.

Ignoring Complexity. In the second half of the twentieth century we made a great discovery about policing: it is a very complicated job. This discovery was made in two stages. First, in the 1950s and 1960s, legal scholars and sociologists documented the extraordinary degree of discretion that police officers exercised in their work. To most of these scholars, the discretion exercised by police officers was alarming. It seemed lawless, arbitrary, and hence undemocratic.[18] The solution was to tame police discretion with rules—maybe rules promulgated by courts (the project taken up with enthusiasm by the Warren Court, and continued half-heartedly by the Burger Court), maybe rules promulgated by legislators or by the police themselves (the solutions urged by some academics), or maybe rules promulgated by civilian oversight boards (the program embraced by many community activists).[19] The second stage began in the 1970s, when skepticism began to mount that any set of rules could ever address, in anything like a comprehensive fashion, the endlessly changing circumstances encountered daily by the police.[20] Today this skepticism is conventional wisdom.

Nowadays almost everyone who thinks seriously about the police recognizes that the job of a patrol officer is complex and demanding, in large part because it is so varied and unpredictable.[21] It might be different if policing was mostly about applying the law—investigating crimes, arresting suspects based on probable cause, and so on. But we have known for decades that most activities of the police do not involve invoking the law.[22] If the police have a core function, it is not law enforcement narrowly defined but rather, in Egon Bittner's influential formulation, employing coercive force or the threat of coercive force "in accordance with the dictates of an intuitive grasp of situational exigencies."[23] This is not the sort of thing that lends itself to rigid regulation.

Plenty of thoughtful people still believe we need stricter rules for the police, if not across the board then at least with regard to particular parts of policing. But almost no one imagines that rules alone can give us better policing. The job of police officers is too varied and too complicated for that. It is surely more varied and more complicated than most factory work—jobs for which the managerial case against Taylorism has been made forcefully and cogently in recent years. If it is futile to try to prescribe in advance all the kinds of problems that an assembly line worker may confront and the solutions to each of those problems, it is even more futile to try to do the same thing for police officers.

Forfeiting Knowledge. Some tasks are complicated but are not the kinds of things about which one can acquire and pass along knowledge. Mastery just comes with practice. Standup comedy may be like that: telling a joke is not simple, but it may not be the kind of thing that can be taught, either. No one would try to run a comedy club by laying down strict rules of comedy technique for the performers to follow. But that is because rules of that kind seem impossible, not because a good comedy club manager gradually refines his theory of comedy by listening to what the comics report back about their experiences.

Policing used to be thought to be like standup comedy in this regard. Maybe it was complicated, but it did not lend itself to the development of craft knowledge. The parts of policing that did not have to do with following rules had to do with instinct—with the gut rather than the head. Lots of people, including many cops, probably still think this way about policing. Certainly the fictional police officers celebrated on television and in movies rely heavily on hunches and intuition.

And police departments, by and large, often seem to operate on some variant of this assumption. New officers spend time in an academy, and most sizeable departments also provide opportunities for in-service training— advanced courses, for example, on developments in forensic science or in the law of search and seizure. But little effort is spent collecting and disseminating the lessons learned by officers on the job—neither the local lessons, about who can or cannot be relied upon in a particular neighborhood, the best routes to follow on patrol, and so forth; nor the global lessons, about how to gain trust on the street, how to calm an agitated suspect, how to protect an informant, and so on.

It remains a "central fact of police work," as Egon Bittner pointed out years ago, that "every individual officer has important information that he does not share with anyone"—"substantive factual information about crime, people, social areas, conditions, etc., which are of use in getting the work of policing done." Writing in 1970, Bitter described a hierarchy of "systematic information denial," ameliorated by a "colossally complicated network of secret sharing": "Teams of partners do not talk about each other in the presence of nonteam members, line personnel do not talk about their peers in the presence of ranking officers and, of course, no members of the department talk about anything remotely connected with police work with any outsiders."[24] Police departments are less insular places today than they were in 1970, for reasons discussed in Chapter 7. But the pattern of "systematic information denial" remains, in large part because departments do little in any organized way to capitalize on the "diffused and seminal intelligence" of the rank and file.[25]

It is not that police officers have nothing interesting and reflective to say about these issues. It is a commonplace of scholarship about the police that individual officers are often far more thoughtful, reflective, and insightful than researchers expect them to be.[26] In places where rank-and-file officers have been asked to participate in policy making, the results have generally been impressive. In the early 1970s, for example, a team of researchers led by the criminologist Hans Toch asked a specially recruited group of Oakland police officers to find ways to reduce violence between officers and citizens. With the outside scholars serving largely as consultants, the officers set their own agenda, carried out their own research, and devised their own proposals. One of those proposals, a "Peer Review Panel" for counseling and assisting officers with a history of violent encounters, in fact proved effective. Toch and his collaborators came away impressed with the ability of rank-and-file officers to serve as "agents of change," not only in the day-to-day operation of the Peer Review Panel, but also in coming up with the idea for the panel, and in carrying out the research on which it was based.[27]

But initiatives are rare. This is a loss, in the same way that it is a loss to the management of a manufacturing facility when insights from the shop floor are systematically ignored. There may be reasons for top-down management of policing that do not apply to manufacturing. We will get to that question later. For now, though, the important point is that in policing, just as in manufacturing and probably more so, failing to enlist line police officers in the ongoing reshaping of their job imposes a cost on management, because it forfeits the diffused understanding and cognitive powers of the workforce—"the vast amount of knowledge, insight, experience, and just plain street savvy that officers acquire," as well as their "constructive thinking, creativity, and resourcefulness."[28]

Undercutting Loyalty and Motivation. A major part of the case that management theorists advanced in the 1980s and 1990s for industrial "cooperativism" was that treating employees just as tools or cogs undercuts their loyalty and motivation. Enlisting the minds and imaginations of employees was good for management not just because rules could not possibly cover all the various situations that arose on the shop floor, and not just because employees often acquired valuable knowledge and insights, but also because treating employees as team members would make them work harder and stay in their jobs longer.[29]

This particular argument against Taylorism applies only in part to policing. Police officers tend to love their jobs and to keep them for a long time. The attrition rate for police departments has always been low—around 4 percent—even during periods when the police feel particularly embattled.[30] It is easy to lose sight of this fact, because police officers are grumblers; the occupation is marked by a kind of culture of complaint.[31] But one of the remarkable things about policing is how officers can hate the daily circumstances of their work and yet still love "the Job."[32] American police departments have many problems, but keeping officers loyal is not one of them.

Nor, in general, is getting officers to work hard. Many if not most cops are attracted to police work in part because of the excitement it promises and in part because of the opportunities it provides for service. They are attracted, in short, by the work, not just by the paycheck and the power.[33] Among their peers, cops gain respect by "good collars," by acts of physical courage, by being "completely gung-ho"[34]—not by cleverly avoiding work.[35] If anything, police tend to be *overly* enthusiastic about their work. Excessive zeal among the workforce is not a problem in most industries, but of course it has long been a major problem in policing. That is why so many of the rules imposed on police officers are aimed not at getting them to work hard but at reining in improper law enforcement tactics, and why officers, especially young officers, tend to complain more bitterly about not being "allowed to do our jobs" than about the hours they have to work or the quotas they are expected to meet.[36]

Still, cynicism and shirking by police officers are hardly unknown. And it is striking how often officers themselves attribute the most notorious manifestations of these problems—the "drive-and-wave" approach to patrolling, for example—to one aspect or another of the top-down management of police departments: either to rules that prevent them from doing their jobs, or to disciplinary codes that do not take sufficient account of the line officer's perspective.[37] Again, there may be good reasons—perhaps bound up with the rule of law—for denying rank-and-file officers a more significant voice in the formulation and application of the rules under which they work. We will address that possibility later. The point for now is simply that in policing, as elsewhere, there is reason to think that rigid top-down management imposes a cost on management by undercutting motivation—even if police departments have largely managed to escape the problems of long-term loyalty that plague other employers.[38]

Law enforcement Taylorism may impose another, related cost on management: it may make it harder to recruit high-caliber officers in the first place. The education credentials of police officers have improved dramatically over the past four decades. The vast majority of police officers in the early 1960s had never attended college; now most officers have at least two years of college education, and a sizeable minority have graduate degrees.[39] Findings are inconclusive on the difference that higher education makes in police officers, but the bulk of the research suggests that, all things being equal, college-educated officers are more responsible, more imaginative, more understanding, more adaptable, better at building trust and confidence, and better at resolving conflicts.[40] For these reasons most police departments would like to hire more college-educated officers. One impediment to doing so, probably, is the lingering perception that policing is not a job that rewards initiative and creativity.[41]

Some departments explicitly defend that view. New London, Connecticut, went to court several years ago to defend, successfully, its policy of refusing to hire applicants who scored too high on a test of "cognitive ability."[42] The publisher of the test recommends its use to screen out employees who will become bored by "unchallenging work"[43] with "rigid procedures"[44]—jobs "where creativity could be a detriment."[45] New London's deputy police chief told a reporter that the department had adopted the test because "[p]olice work is kind of mundane."[46] The president of the test publishing company agreed: "You can't decide not to read someone their Miranda rights because you felt it would be more efficient, or you thought they knew them already."[47] All of this would make perfect sense to Frederick Taylor, who warned that "[t]he man who is mentally alert and intelligent is for this very reason entirely unsuited" for monotonous work. An employee hired to handle pig iron, for example, should "be so stupid and so phlegmatic that he more nearly resembles in his mental make-up the ox than any other type."[48]

Few departments echo New London's in making this view of policing a matter of official policy. The vast majority of law enforcement executives today would endorse the position of police unionists that "[t]he better the caliber of the police officer, the fewer problems you have in the community."[49] But by failing to encourage innovation and collective decision making among line officers, even progressive police departments may not only forfeit some of the advantage of their officers' intelligence, but also send signals to potential recruits that law enforcement is not a field that welcomes thinkers. Those signals may make it hard to recruit the kind of applicants that most departments want.

Alienation. We have spent some time examining the attractions that participatory management in policing may hold for police departments and, by extension, for the communities they serve. But the earliest objections to "scientific management" centered not on its costs to employers but on the toll it took on employees. Those objections, still voiced today, are that rigidly rule-bound workplaces are stultifying, demeaning, and alienating. By "deskilling" workers and turning artisans into machines, Taylorism fosters a sense of powerlessness and disconnection. It fosters, that is to say, what many people see as modernity's defining social ills.[50]

Although police officers rarely become so disenchanted as to quit, there are plenty of reports of police officers who grow to feel alienated and discouraged.[51] And a collective kind of alienation has been well documented in policing—better documented, probably, than alienation in any other occupation. A central theme of police ethnography since the 1950s has been the distinctive sense of estrangement that police officers feel from society. That estrangement—often accompanied by feelings of frustration, bitterness, and cynicism—has been blamed for a host of police pathologies: the "code of silence," the paranoia and insularity, the proclivity to violence, the intolerance and "authoritarianism."[52] This is not precisely the kind of alienation Taylorism is commonly blamed with fostering; it is "us against them" rather than "myself alone." And the estrangement of the police has itself typically been blamed not on the way their work is structured and managed but on their grinding daily encounters with crime and disorder.[53]

Still, there may be connections between the collective estrangement experienced by the police and the sense of anxiety and personal isolation that many officers feel. Even if they are separate phenomena, they may well feed on and worsen each other. The widespread impression that police officers are especially prone to domestic violence and suicide has been hard to confirm statistically,[54] but there is no doubt that many officers suffer seriously from job-related stress, that their families often suffer along with them, and that a frustrated, alienated police officer is more likely to be a violent and abusive police officer. The stultification and immiseration of any group of employees should be a matter of social concern, but there are special reasons to be worried about unhappy police officers.

Are there reasons to think, though, that unhappy police officers can be blamed in part on the rigid, top-down management of policing? Police officers regularly complain, and often bitterly, that their views are never consulted, that they are subject to arbitrary and irrational directives from above and without, and that the rules under which they operate are absurdly unrealistic—rules that could never have been promulgated by anyone familiar with the daily realities of law enforcement. Cops often seem to take a kind of subversive glee in the inanity of what they endure, and their shared sense of the thanklessness of their work can contribute in an odd way to *esprit de corps*. But police officers also tell researchers that they find the administrative and organizational aggravations of their work more stressful than the physical danger and psychological trauma.[55] It stands to reason that the ongoing experience of insult and voicelessness can take a toll, and that police officers—like any other group of employees—would feel more positive about their work if they participated in its management.

And, in fact, when police departments have experimented with participatory management, this has been the result. The Madison, Wisconsin, Police Department, which began experimenting with participatory decision making in the 1980s, found that it increased job satisfaction, made officers more open to reform, and improved the level of police service in the eyes of the public.[56] More recently, the police department in Broken Arrow, Oklahoma, has turned much of its policy making over to a twelve-member committee of management officials, union leaders, and rank-and-file officers, a move that appears to have contributed to greater productivity (as measured by arrest and clearance rates), a sharp drop in citizen complaints, and higher levels of job satisfaction.[57]

Teaching democracy. The costs that law enforcement Taylorism imposes on management and officers it also imposes on the public, because the public has an interest in the effective management of police forces and in the happiness and psychological well-being of individual police officers. But there is another potential cost to the public of rigid, top-down management of policing. It forfeits the opportunity to train police officers in the values and habits of democratic citizenship: values of openness, tolerance, and compromise; habits of engagement, cooperation, and deliberation.

There is long tradition of viewing the workplace as the ideal training ground for democratic citizenship. There are hints of the idea in the later work of John Stuart Mill and a sustained development of the notion in the early twentieth-century writings of G. D. H. Cole.[58] The idea went into something of a dormancy with the rise of democratic pluralism in the 1940s and 1950s. The pluralists, as we have seen, thought mass participation in democratic governance was not unnecessary but was positively pernicious. But in the 1960s and 1970s, when the idea of "participatory democracy" regained favor, there was renewed appreciation for the possibility that rigid, autocratic workplaces can stunt the political development of employees, not only depriving them of full, satisfying lives but also weakening democracy in the broader society.[59]

That thesis has remained controversial. But even if democracy does not depend on fostering the political growth of *all* employees, there are special reasons to want *police officers* to internalize democratic values and habits. There are two points here. First, the police are often placed in positions where they can actively support or actively threaten democratic activities: they can protect political protesters, for example, or they can attack them; they can help create a climate of respect for individual privacy and autonomy, or they can make privacy insecure and nonconformity difficult; they can enforce norms of tolerance, or they can reinforce bias and prejudice;

they can teach citizens that authority may safely be challenged, or they can teach the opposite.[60] Second, there are reasons to think that effective policing *in general*—at least the forms of effective policing most congenial to a free and open society—depends on some of the same values and skills often thought important for democratic citizenship more broadly.

This is the great lesson of William Ker Muir's classic study of Oakland police officers in the early 1970s. Muir's book remains unusual. Nearly every other police sociologist, before and after Muir, has sought to explain why the police, in general, are the way they are. Muir asked a different question, if anything more pressing: what makes some police officers more effective and more trustworthy than others? His answer was that good police officers had democratic virtues: a comfort with moral ambiguity, an ability to see shades of gray, a broad capacity for tolerance and empathy, and, perhaps most important, "an enjoyment of talk"—that is to say, an affinity for conversation, argument, deliberation, advocacy, and compromise.[61]

Police officers developed these virtues, in part, by working in a department that itself embraced them. Among the heroes of Muir's book, remember, was Chief Charles Gain, the legendary reformer who ran Oakland's police force from 1967 to 1973. Gain ruled with a heavy hand and was never popular with the rank and file; in 1972 the Oakland Police Officers' Association voted no confidence in his administration.[62] Muir admired him nonetheless for infusing the department "with a sense of purpose from which his men derived dignity and moral meaning."[63] Much of that was accomplished, Muir thought, through a training style and a workplace climate that invited "participation, discussion, argument, and questioning."[64] What Muir liked about the Oakland Police Department, in short, was the way it seemed to operate as a school for democratic citizenry—or, more precisely, democratic leadership. Muir saw police officers as "streetcorner politicians," and they were most likely to grow in that that role if they worked in departments that within themselves fostered "widespread political participation."[65] His touchstone here was Tocqueville.[66]

As we have seen, Muir was not alone in thinking workplace democracy was particularly important for police officers. The pioneering police ethnographer William Westley suggested in 1970 that the remedy for the alienated and repressive mentality of the police was, in large part, "participatory democracy." "Police organizations," he argued, "must be democratized by involving as many policemen as possible in decision-making on all aspects of the department's job."[67] Westley was echoing George Berkley, who had argued a year earlier in *The Democratic Policeman* that strong, democratic police unions and broad participation by officers in departmental decision making were critical for training the police in the "rules and values" of democracy.[68] Berkley reasoned that a police force "cannot hope to function in a manner with a democratic society if its internal operations deviate from that society's norms and values." Only by "participating in the give-and-take of . . . deliberations" were police officers "likely to develop the respect for accommodation and conciliation along with the attitudes of patience and tolerance which are indispensable to the democratic process."[69] And the criminologist John Angell took an even stronger line in 1971, suggesting that the "basic hope for correcting the dysfunctional trends of American police organizations" was to bring law enforcement in line with the participatory, "humanistic-democratic values of the United States," especially as reflected in "the trend toward employee involvement in decision-making processes."[70]

By the end of the 1970s, though, arguments like Westley's, Berkley's, and Angell's had dropped out of sight. Except among police officers themselves, and often even there, enthusiasm largely vanished for bringing even the mildest forms of workplace democracy to American law enforcement.[71] With isolated exceptions, it has yet to reappear.

The Missing Strand in Democratic Policing

What happened? Why did the arguments for giving police officers a voice in the shaping of their work—arguments that attracted such thoughtful and well-informed supporters in the early 1970s—disappear by the decade's end? To be sure, a certain amount of disenchantment emerged by the 1980s about workplace democracy in general.[72] But shared decision making in the workplace soon found new fans among management theorists. And the case for participatory democracy had seemed in the early 1970s to apply with special urgency to law enforcement, because of the strong social interest in fostering democratic values and habits in the police. Why, then, did sentiment for workplace democracy in policing vanish so completely, and why has it never rematerialized? And why, for that matter, did the sentiment take until the 1960s to emerge in the first place? Why has internal democracy nearly always been the missing strand in discussions of democratic policing?

Much of the explanation was bad timing. As we have seen, at the very point in the twentieth century when interest in workplace democracy reached its zenith—the late 1960s and early 1970s—American police departments seemed peculiarly inhospitable places for experiments in participatory management. Police forces at that time were almost uniformly white, male, and politically reactionary.[73] Grassroots activism among police officers was in fact on the rise, but it took discouraging forms: contempt for civilian authority, fierce opposition to outside oversight of any kind, organized brutality against student protesters, vigilante attacks on black militants, and active participation in far-Right organizations.[74] As a result, the very scholars and community activists who might otherwise have been most sympathetic to calls for participatory management of law enforcement agencies instead concluded that democracy required tight, top-down control of the police.

The spirit of Frederick Taylor hovered over the police professionalism movement of the middle decades of the twentieth century. The characteristic reforms of this era were "*bureaucratic*—strong lines of administrative control and oversight, extensive rules and regulations, pre- and in-service training provided by police departments, elimination of discretion, and simplification of work tasks."[75] One might add to this list the heavy reliance on "integrity testing" and workplace spies for internal discipline.[76] None of this had much to do with viewing line police officers as "professionals" in the normal sense of that term; indeed it was incompatible even "with the recognition of the police as *craftspersons*."[77] Police professionalism sought to give individual officers less of a say in the shaping of their work, not more.

This aspect of police professionalism never encountered significant resistance, in part because police officers were poorly respected by the public; they seemed to need more direction, not more of a say in how they did their jobs. Throughout the first half of the twentieth century, police officers were widely viewed as slow-witted at best and venal at worst.[78] Improving this image was one of the express goals of police professionalism. But popular perceptions reinforced the ideology of progressive law enforcement administrators in steering police reform away from any experiments with participatory management.

And, of course, the middle decades of the twentieth century were also the heyday of democratic pluralism, which downplayed the importance of widespread political participation and stressed the threats to democracy posed by the "authoritarian personality." Democratic pluralism reinforced the tendency of mid-twentieth-century police reformers to think that police officers should follow rules, not make them. Workplace democracy, like participatory democracy more generally, was off the pluralist agenda. And police officers, drawn from the working class and hardened by the nature of their work, seemed especially prone to the authoritarian personality feared by the pluralists[79]—and especially important to bring under elite control, given their license and assignment to use coercive force.

The unraveling of police professionalism and democratic pluralism in the late 1960s might have cleared space for proposals to bring a degree of workplace democracy to policing. And it did, briefly: witness the writings of George Berkley, William Westley, William Muir, and John Angell in the late 1960s and early 1970s. But the moment quickly passed, for reasons having much to do with the extraordinary politics of the time, and with the incendiary role the police played in those politics.

By the end of the 1970s, when policing was among the most heavily organized of all public occupations, police unions had joined "the mainstream of American trade unionism," devoting the bulk of their attention to working conditions, job security, and the "bread-and-butter . . . issues that have been near and dear to the hearts of U.S. trade unionists for decades."[80] But by then the damage had been done. The frightening forms taken by police activism in the late 1960s and early 1970s had dulled the appetite of virtually all scholars and police reformers for bringing workplace democracy to law enforcement.

There were isolated exceptions. Herman Goldstein, in particular, continued to argue for a version of "problem-oriented policing" that, among other things, "engage[d] rank-and-file officers more fully in the operation of the police agency"[81] and gave them "more of a say in policies affecting [their] own role[s]."[82] With Goldstein's encouragement, the Madison, Wisconsin, Police Department began experimenting with participatory management in the 1980s, and the results appeared promising.[83] But by then the police reform agenda had become monopolized by community policing, which except at the margins has had little to say about the role of ordinary officers in shaping departmental policy.

In 1990, following years of "community policing" reforms, Goldstein complained that the "dominant form of policing" continued "to view police officers as automatons."[84] It still does today. Even the mildest versions of workplace democracy for police officers have stayed largely off the table. Encouraging patrol officers to be thoughtful and creative about their work is often said to be part of community policing, and even more so of problem-solving policing.[85] In practice, though, this has rarely amounted to more than placing additional discretion in the hands of individual officers. There are a few efforts to give officers a collective, deliberative voice in how policing is carried out, or to enlist police unions or identity-based police organizations as partners in police reform. The "community" in "community policing" rarely includes police officers themselves.

Reassessing Police Departments as Sites for Workplace Democracy

The idea of bringing participatory management and rank-and-file intellectual engagement to policing was bandied about in the late 1960s and early 1970s, and tried out cautiously and successfully in some places, but it never caught on. There were two basic reasons. The first was an accident of history: at the time when workplace democracy was most in vogue, police officers were monolithically white, male, and reactionary, and they were organizing themselves in ways that seemed to threaten democracy rather than support it. The second was a matter of principle: the "rule of law" seemed to require police officers to be followers, not innovators. Democracy inside police departments, even in small doses, seemed—and may still—incompatible with external democratic control of the police.

The accident of history is now . . . well, history. As we saw in the last chapter, police departments today are far more diverse than they were in the late 1960s and early 1970s. Police forces are no longer monolithically white, male, homophobic, and reactionary. Desegregation of American police departments still has far to go, and there are reasons to fear that progress may be stalling. But much of the transformation has already occurred. And among the most important consequences of the new demographics of American law enforcement is a dramatic decline in the solidarity and insularity of the police—hard to quantify, but widely remarked upon by police officers and the scholars who study them. The notion of police departments as insular, homogeneous bastions of unchallenged patriarchy, racism, and authoritarianism is seriously out of date. Police departments today are more socially complex, more open to debate and disagreement, and more reflective of the divisions in the communities they serve. Along with the vastly increased numbers of college-educated police officers, the demographic and cultural transformation of American law enforcement suggests that police departments are much safer places today for experiments in rank-and-file participation in organizational decision making.

But what about the rule of law? Jerome Skolnick's influential account of democratic policing, as we have seen, stressed the rule of law as the key to reconciling the "fundamentally authoritarian character" of the police "with the democratic society they were policing."[86] And he suggested that the rule of law required police to follow the directions laid down for them by the courts, elected officials, and the public at large; it was therefore inconsistent, in the context of policing, with "the extent of initiative" ordinarily "contemplated by nontotalitarian norms of work."[87] Skolnick never quite said that collective innovation by police officers should be discouraged, but his account left little room for it. Individual "strategies of independence" were inconsistent with "the principle of legality." So was police activism. Programs of participatory management controlled from above—say, some kind of law enforcement equivalent of "quality circles"—were not ruled out, but neither did Skolnick show any enthusiasm for them. The police reform agenda suggested by his work was controlling the police from above and from outside. And that is largely the police reform agenda we have had since the 1960s. Police professionalism and community policing, despite their differences, have both been versions of this agenda.

Here is the difficulty in assessing whether workplace democracy in law enforcement really *is* inconsistent with the rule of law: no one knows precisely what the "rule of law" means. Like most scholars who invoke the concept, Skolnick was unapologetically vague about its details, but seemed influenced by Lon Fuller's account.[88] Fuller identified eight elements in the rule of law: (1) rules of general application that are (2) publicized, (3) applied prospectively, (4) understandable, (5) noncontradictory, (6) capable of being followed, (7) stable, and (8) faithfully applied.[89] How many of these elements are truly separate is controversial.[90] More importantly, there is dispute about what the elements themselves mean, and about how they should be weighted and combined. Depending on the answers to *those* questions, the "rule of law" can wind up meaning—as Richard Fallon demonstrated several years ago—anything from originalism to formalism to fair process to substantive justice.[91]

As a result, it is not entirely clear what we mean when we talk about reconciling police with the rule of law. Four possibilities suggest themselves. First, the "rule of law" in policing could simply mean that the police do not themselves violate the law. Fuller himself seemed to think that "lawless conduct by the police" was the chief threat they posed to the rule of law.[92] Second, reconciling the police with the rule of law could mean ensuring that the police do not frustrate the application of the law to the people they police—by, for example, failing to arrest offenders. This view emphasizes the role of the police in securing the last of the eight elements Fuller identified in the rule of law, namely, "congruence between the rules as announced and their actual administration."[93] Third, the "rule of law" in policing could mean ensuring that all exercises of power by the police are governed by law, rather than simply being arbitrary exercises of discretion. This view seems consistent with Hayek's famous definition of the rule of law: "stripped of all technicalities this means that government in all its actions is bound by rules fixed and announced beforehand—rules which make it possible to foresee with fair certainty how the authority will use its coercive powers in given circumstances, and to plan one's individual affairs on the basis of this knowledge."[94] Fourth and finally, the "rule of law" in policing could mean that the police are subject to majoritarian control or judicial oversight—or some combination of those two checks. It may dilute the value of the term "rule of law" to employ it as a synonym for democracy or for the protection of civil rights,[95] but there is no doubt that the term is sometimes used in this way.

Fortunately, we do not need to decide for present purposes which of these formulations—or what admixture of two or more of them—best captures our intuitions regarding what it means to reconcile the police with the rule of law. The fact is that none of these four versions of the rule of law in policing, alone or in combination, are inconsistent or even in strong tension with a resolve to greatly increase the voice of rank-and-file officers in the management of their departments.

This is perhaps most obvious with respect to the first formulation of the rule of law in policing, the formulation stressing the obligation of police officers not to break the law. *One* way for police officers to help shape the nature of their work is for them simply to ignore legal directives addressed to them. But this certainly is not the only way, nor is it a particularly powerful way. When we talk about workplace democracy in *any* field, what we typically have in mind is not employees ignoring the rules imposed on them, but (a) employees collectively participating in the shaping of those rules, and (b) the rules being shaped in such a manner that room is left for employees to be creative about how best to further the objectives of the organization. Both these possibilities seem worth exploring in the context of law enforcement. Rank-and-file officers could be involved in the formulation of the rules under which the police operate, and the rules could be designed to leave room for innovation by individual officers and teams of officers. Neither of these would involve *any* violation of the law by the police; they are alternative ideas about how the law governing the police should be hammered out in the first place, and about what that law should look like.

The situation is slightly more complicated with respect to our second version of the rule of law in policing: the notion that police discretion should not be allowed to frustrate the neutral and consistent application of pre-announced legal rules. This version of the rule of law is violated when the police decide on their own, for example, not to enforce a particular prohibition of which they disapprove (think of police during Prohibition refusing to pursue bootleggers), or to ignore violations of the law in a particular area (think of "the time-honored practice of ghetto confinement of deviance"),[96] or to refrain from arresting particular suspects, despite the existence of probable cause (think of the tacit condoning of lynching during Jim Crow). This version of the rule of law could also be violated, if less egregiously, by some of the innovations one might expect if police officers were given a larger say in the nature of their work: decisions by groups of officers, for example, to concentrate their efforts on certain areas or certain kinds of offenses, ignoring other areas or other offenses, or decisions by individual officers to look the other way in particular situations.

But this second formulation of the rule of law in policing is hopelessly unrealistic. Enforcement discretion in policing is unavoidable. Police departments *today* make decisions all the time about where to concentrate their resources; police officers *today* make decisions all the time about whether to look the other way. And very few of the legal rules imposed on officers *today* do anything to rein in enforcement discretion. Mandatory arrest rules for domestic violence suspects are an obvious exception. But these rules have been noteworthy and controversial in part because they are so unusual.[97] If the rule of law means that the police must arrest everyone who there is reason to believe has committed a crime, then the rule of law is pie in the sky, and we might as well stop talking about it. Police discretion, and a massive amount of it, is simply unavoidable.

This is a large part of the attraction of the third formulation of the rule of law in policing: the idea that all exercises of power by the police, including decisions not to invoke their power, should be governed by rules announced in advance. This version of the rule of law seems inconsistent, or at least in tension, with *some* of what I have been calling workplace democracy in policing. It seems in tension with the view that the rules under which the police operate should be structured to allow ample room for *ad hoc* decisions by individual officers—or, for the matter, by groups of officers—about how the mission of the police can best be advanced in particular situations.

But it is fully compatible with other forms of workplace democracy in policing—in particular, with those forms that involve rank-and-file police officers in the formulation of the rules under which they operate. Indeed, those forms of workplace democracy might *bolster* the third version of the rule of law in policing, in two different ways. First, police officers—like other employees—are more likely to comply with rules they think are legitimate, and they are more likely to think that rules are legitimate when they have a say in what the rules are. This role of legitimacy in securing compliance with workplace rules, and the role of procedural regularity in creating legitimacy, has long been a central part of the general argument for workplace democracy.[98] It finds strong support in the recent research psychologist Tom Tyler has conducted on the reasons people obey the law. Law abidance, Tyler concludes, is tied to the perceived legitimacy of the legal system, and perceived legitimacy depends in significant part on opportunities for participation. Control over the results is not as important: "what people want is to feel that their input has been solicited and considered by decision makers."[99] Tyler's research has focused on the compliance of ordinary citizens with the criminal law, but perceived legitimacy seems, if anything, to be even more important in securing the compliance of police officers with the rules under which they are asked to operate. In choosing their jobs, after all, cops have bought into the legal system; they should be especially susceptible to the notion that everyone owes a duty of compliance to rules adopted and applied through fair procedures.

Second, wholly apart from the ways in which rank-and-file participation can make a police department's internal rules seem more legitimate, rules that cops themselves help to fashion may be more likely to be obeyed simply because they will be more sensible. William Simon, among others, has claimed precisely this kind of benefit for systems of workplace governance involving "rolling rules regimes"—sets of formal directives that are revised continuously based on the experience of the workers applying them. Simon argues that systems of this kind (typified by the Toyota Production System, much discussed by management theorists) combine "the normative explicitness associated with formal rules with the continuous adjustment to particularity associated with informal norms," charting a middle course between "the command-and-control model of Fordist bureaucracy" and the "traditional artisanal vision in which work is regulated by tacit norms that can be grasped only by prolonged socialization into guild and local workplace cultures."[100]

"Rolling rules regimes" may be particularly attractive forms of workplace democracy in policing for other reasons, as well. They may be the forms that have the best potential for developing the democratic skills and habits of officers, and for giving officers a greater appreciation of democratic values. I will have a bit more to say about rolling rules later in this chapter. Still, a significant amount of ad hoc improvisation is unavoidable in policing, in part for reasons we have already discussed. So something further should be said, before we move on, about the tension between the third version of the rule of law in policing and the notion that the rules under which police operate should leave them room for creativity.

The fact that police discretion comes into conflict with a coherent and plausible conception of the rule of law does not mean that police discretion should be minimized. There are other things we care about, in addition to the rule of law—especially this particular conception of the rule of law.[101] And compliance with this particular conception of the rule of law in policing will always be a matter of degree. Just as there is no way to eliminate enforcement discretion in policing, there is no way to bring all of that enforcement discretion under the control of rules. Rules simply cannot be drafted that will dictate, without ambiguity, the appropriate exercise of enforcement discretion in every imaginable situation. Nor can rules be drafted to specify, in advance, the proper application of all the other kinds of discretion exercised by the police when applying their coercive powers. Therefore it may make sense to expand even those kinds of workplace democracy that come into conflict with the third version of the rule of law in policing, the notion that all exercises of police authority should be governed by rules.

What about the fourth version of the rule of law in policing—the version that takes the "rule of law" to mean majoritarian control, or judicial oversight, or some combination of the two? The first thing to be said is that any kind of workplace democracy in policing could and should be subject to outside checks, both political and judicial. Giving police officers more of a say does not mean giving them a final say. None of the benefits of workplace democracy would be threatened by allowing for an electoral veto, a judicial veto, or both—so long as the veto power is not exercised excessively.

The caveat is significant, of course. At some point there *is* a trade-off between giving police officers a greater voice and giving the public, or the courts, more control over policing. But trade-offs between different elements of "democratic policing" are unavoidable, even without bringing workplace democracy for police officers into the mix. There is a familiar trade-off, for example, between majoritarian control of policing and judicial control of policing. So the existence of a trade-off between workplace democracy for police officers and outside control of the police is not, by itself, sufficient reason to reject the notion that rank-and-file officers should play a greater role in shaping the nature of their work.

All the more so given how far we are from actually confronting that trade-off. Few of the rules under which police currently operate were imposed by elected officials or adopted through other majoritarian processes. Judicial control of the police is more extensive. But even this is easy to overestimate. By far the largest source of constraints on the police is departmental management.

This is the great legacy of police professionalism: law enforcement agencies run their own shops, largely free from outside interference. Community policing has made departments less insular and more likely to consult with outsiders, but it has almost never meant a decrease in the operational autonomy of law enforcement. With minor exceptions, community policing programs are adopted unilaterally by the police—and that means by police management.[102] Civilian oversight is now an accepted feature of law enforcement in most major American cities, but for the most part the oversight operates at the margins: reviewing selected disciplinary decisions, for example.[103] We could give police officers substantially more voice in shaping their work without diminishing outside control. What would have to yield is the ability of *management* to operate unilaterally. In this respect, at least, policing is not very different from other lines of work.

Imagining Workplace Democracy in Policing

Let me sketch briefly four implications of a commitment to expanding workplace democracy in policing. First, such a commitment will require us to confront the tensions between different approaches to involving line officers in police management and policy making—the tensions, in particular, between the model of police unionism, the model of participatory management, and the model of what I will call "multivalent organizing." Second, any serious effort to bring more participatory democracy to policing should include greater attention to the quality of supervision in law enforcement agencies. Third, judges, policymakers, and the public at large may want to pay more heed to the views of organized groups of police officers—particularly when those groups appear democratic and broadly representative. Fourth and finally, the value of workplace democracy in policing provides an additional reason, beyond the more familiar ones, for worrying about the growing privatization of law enforcement.

Models of Rank-and-File Participation. Up until now I have purposefully put to one side the distinction often drawn between "industrial democracy" and "participatory management": between trade unionism on the one hand and, on the other hand, management-controlled exercises in consulting with workers. ("Participatory management" in this narrower sense is to workplace democracy roughly as community policing is to "neighborhood policing," the umbrella term for various proposals advanced in the 1970s to place police departments under a strong version of neighborhood control.)[104] I now want to turn my attention to that distinction, as well as to the possibility that the best model for workplace democracy in policing may differ both from traditional trade unionism and from traditional forms of "participatory management," narrowly defined.[105]

There are at least three different models for giving rank-and-file officers more say in how policing is carried out. The first is by strengthening police unions and giving them a greater role in the setting of policy. The second is through management-controlled initiatives at participatory policy making—initiatives that might look roughly like "quality circles" in manufacturing, the "rolling rules regimes" typified by the Toyota Production System, or the bottom-up experiment in police reform that Hans Toch and his collaborators carried out in Oakland in the 1970s. The third is by building on the pattern of multivalent organizing that seems to have developed over the past few decades in policing—the patchwork quilt of police unions and identity-based police organizations. Some but not all of the police unions are now affiliated with broad-based labor organizations like the Teamsters or the AFL-CIO. Some but not all of the identity-based police organizations are associated, formally or informally, with identity-based groups outside of policing.

These models can tend in a variety of ways to crowd each other out. Management-led efforts at participatory decision making can wind up marginalizing and undercutting bottom-up exercises in participatory democracy, sometimes by design. Unions, partly for that reason, often oppose top-down exercises in participatory management. Unions can be threatened, as well, by the proliferation of groups that compete with them for the allegiance of the rank and file. Nor is this simply a matter of institutional competition: groups representing minority officers, or female officers, or gay and lesbian officers, offer a different kind of solidarity than traditional police unions, a solidarity that sweeps less broadly within policing but also builds bridges with groups outside of policing.[106]

At the same time, the incompatibility of the three models should not be overstated. They need not work at cross-purposes. Some employees join and support both unions and identity-based caucuses, drawing from them different but complementary forms of solidarity.[107] And unions can participate in the design and operation of processes of participatory management. The police union in Madison, Wisconsin, for example, played a significant consultative role in shaping that department's unusual and apparently successful experiments in participatory management.[108] There are reasons to believe, moreover, that both multivalent organizing and management-led exercises in participatory decision making could help to change the shape of police unionism, making it a stronger and more productive instrument of workplace democracy.

I will not attempt in this chapter to identify the ideal admixture of the three models of rank-and-file participation I have described. I do want to note, though, several distinct attractions of the multivalent organizing model, because it is the least familiar of the three, and I want to say a word or two about the possibility of combining that model with "rolling rules regimes" in policing. Along the way I will note some ways in which both of these models of bottom-up police reform might reinforce rather than weaken the third model, police unionism.

The special attractions of the multivalent organizing model are these. First, it is already emerging of its own accord. Efforts to capitalize on it will be swimming with the current.[109] Second, multivalent organizing offers the familiar advantages of competition. Precisely because they are often rivals for the allegiance of the rank and file, organizations of police officers today help to keep each other honest.[110] Third and finally, multivalent organizing in police forces does double duty, not only fostering solidarity among police officers, but also breaking down the traditional insularity of policing by building bridges to outside groups. A hint of the good that might do, outside as well as inside police departments, may be found in the critical role that organizations of black police officers in South Africa have played not only in reforming law enforcement but also in the broader struggle for racial equality[111]—or, closer to home, the role that organizations of minority police officers, working with groups outside law enforcement, have played in debates over racial profiling. It is true that multivalent organizing does not foster occupation-wide solidarity of officers to the same degree as traditional police unionism. But this may well be a price worth paying, particularly given how prone law enforcement has been to excessive insularity.

In theory, police unions could be bridges to groups outside of policing, too. In the early 1970s, when police unions were emerging from a decades-long period of dormancy, some people hoped that unionism would build solidarity between police officers and other working-class employees.[112] For the most part it has not happened: the ideology of collective bargaining and class solidarity has proved too weak to alter the traditional insularity and law-and-order ideology of the police.[113] All the more striking, then, that identity politics, for all its faults, seems to have managed that trick.

Even more striking, competition from identity-based groups may be prompting some mainstream police unions to build their own bridges to civilian groups, both inside and outside the labor movement. Local police unions arose in late 1960s and early 1970s from local "benevolent associations" and "protective leagues." They tended to keep their old names, avoid the term "union," and steer clear of affiliation with other labor organizations. In recent years, though, a growing number of police unions have affiliated either with the Teamsters or with the AFL-CIO's International Union of Police Associations, and some have formed more surprising alliances. A case in point is the Los Angeles Police Protective League, a notoriously inward-looking organization that five years ago found itself struggling against Bernard Parks, an African-American chief of police strongly supported by the Oscar Joel Bryant Foundation, which represents black officers in Los Angeles. To challenge the lessons Chief Parks drew from the Rampart Division corruption scandal, the PPL commissioned a report by Erwin Chemerinsky, a law professor long active in the ACLU.[114] Two years later, the PPL's efforts to oust Parks triggered a decertification drive by dissent officers supported by the Teamsters; in response the PPL joined the IUPA.[115]

There are reasons, then, to think that efforts to democratize the internal operations of police departments have been helped rather than hindered by the emergence of identity-based groups of police officers, rivaling and at times directly challenging traditional police unions and benevolent associations. I now want to examine the reasons for thinking that the multivalent organizing model should make room, as well, for efforts at participatory management organized and coordinated by the command structure. More specifically, I want to examine, briefly, the attractions for policing of the "rolling rules regimes"—systems of workplace rules revised continually and collaboratively by employees and their supervisors.

The Toyota Production System—a particularly well-studied example of such a regime—has the following elements, in William Simon's suggestive account. First, it "emphasizes the goals of learning and innovation." Second, it "combines the normative explicitness associated with formal rules with the continuous adjustment to particularity associated with informal norms," because "rules get re-considered and re-written when they come in tension with unanticipated contingency." Third, it "treats normative decision-making in hard cases as presumptively collective and interdisciplinary." Fourth, it "fosters a style of reasoning that is intentionally destabilizing of settled practices." Fifth and finally, it "attempts to bracket or sublimate issues of individual and retrospective fairness."[116]

To a striking degree, many of these elements were present in the successful approach the Oakland Police Department briefly took in the 1970s to the problem of violent police–citizen encounters. The Peer Review Panel—and even more so the bottom-up process through which it was developed—emphasized learning; treated the task at hand as collaborative and interdisciplinary; sought progressive improvement rather than stabilized solutions; and focused less on blame than on prevention.[117] The only TPS element missing in the Oakland violence reduction project is the distinctive compromise we discussed earlier, in our discussion of the rule of law, between hard-and-fast rules and flexible, ad hoc decision making—the rejection of both "the command-and-control model of Fordist bureaucracy" and the "traditional artisanal vision" of "tacit norms" that resist articulation.[118]

Since debates about police reform often focus precisely on the relative merits of "command-and-control" regulation versus policing as craftwork, the middle course that Simon associates with TPS deserves our attention. Here is how Simon describes it:

> Toyota formality is not designed to restrict discretion. . . . Rather, the purpose of formal norms is to facilitate learning. . . . "Say what you do, and do what you say," is a basic premise of Toyota-style engineering. . . . The duty to articulate forces the actors to reflect on what they are proposing to do and to communicate it as precisely as possible to their peers. . . . An articulated norm is more readily criticized and debated both because it is more easily grasped and because criticism is less likely to risk personal offense when the norm is divorced from particular people.[119]

The system thus "discourages ad hoc adjustments," but "formalization is . . . strongly associated with revisability."[120]

Simon associates the "rolling rules regimes" of TPS with the regulatory approaches that other scholars have praised as "experimentalist" government.[121] He sees the TPS approach to rules, for example, in provisions of the safety standards developed by the Institute of Nuclear Power Plant Operation.

Those standards instruct that whenever an employee "cannot or believes he should not" comply with an existing rule, the employee should inform the appropriate supervisor and hold off further activity governed by the rule until a decision is made about whether the rule should be modified. In emergency situations, employees are instructed to take whatever actions they think necessary, but also to *document* what they do, so that it can be incorporated, "if appropriate . . . into a revision of the affected procedure."[122]

In the context of policing, this kind of collaborative, heuristic rulemaking could simultaneously give officers a collective voice in the shaping of their work, preserve their ability to respond flexibly to unforeseen circumstances, and—in ways we have previously explored—promote the rule of law by minimizing arbitrary exercises of discretion. It could also encourage patrol officers to think critically, explicitly, and systematically about how they go about their work, and help them over time to improve a whole range of their practices through collective learning—generalizing and institutionalizing what took place in Oakland in the 1970s with regard to violent encounters between police and citizens.

Plainly, there are limits. Ad hoc improvisation, as we have discussed, is inherent in policing—although maybe not to the degree we have sometimes thought. More importantly, "rolling rules" developed collaboratively within a police department, like any set of internal, departmental directives, would need to operate within the confines of rules imposed on the department from the outside—constitutional limitations on police actions, statutory regulation of law enforcement, and local ordinances affecting the police. This, though, is a standard feature of the kind of experimentalist regime Simon uses TPS to illustrate.[123]

The role of labor unions in a "rolling rules" regime of participatory management is a large and heavily debated subject. I do not want to enter this debate here, except to reiterate and expand on a point made earlier: unionism and participatory management do not necessarily work at crosspurposes. In policing as in other fields, union support has sometimes helped participatory management succeed. There is also room to hope that participatory management can, over time, change unions for the better. In policing as elsewhere, unions may stick to bread-and-butter issues of salary, seniority, and security because management practices, along with the compromises struck by labor relations law, have conditioned employees to think that larger questions of organizational policy are none of their business.[124] When employees begin to think otherwise, unions may as well.

The Role of Supervision. Efforts to expand workplace democracy in policing will depend heavily on skillful and enlightened leadership with the police hierarchy, both among command staff and among mid-level supervisors. This is true most obviously of management-driven exercises in participatory decision making. But it is also true, perhaps paradoxically, of efforts to foster "bottom-up" forms of workplace democracy, including both stronger and more productive police unions and what I have been calling multivalent organizing of the rank and file. Grassroots efforts at workplace democracy in policing are most likely to flourish, and to be channeled in productive directions, when they are welcomed. It is naïve to think that repression, either in a workplace or in society at large, helps nurture movements for change.[125] Departments that make clear their desire and ability to work with organizations of rank-and-file officers in reexamining policies and improving operations are more likely to elicit that kind of productive engagement. But sending signals of this sort, and making good on them, requires skillful managers and supervisors.[126]

Facilitating workplace democracy is not the only reason to want better managers and supervisors in policing. Even aside from this benefit, more skillful supervision—particularly at the sergeant level—has long been thought, by many informed observers, to be one of the best ways to improve the quality of policing. Good supervision can do much of what the criminal procedure revolution tried, with only limited success, to accomplish with rules: make the day-to-day work of policing less arbitrary, more accountable, and more enlightened.[127] One alternative to Taylorism *other* than workplace democracy is, in fact, greater reliance on responsible and flexible supervision. There is a case to be made for this kind of thing throughout government, including in policing.[128] For reasons I have tried to make clear in this chapter, I think it should be combined in policing with an expanded role for workplace democracy.

Fortunately, these two alternatives to law enforcement are not in strong competition; instead, they can complement each other. Not only can skillful supervision facilitate workplace democracy, but workplace democracy can help responsible supervisors: by tapping them into the street-level expertise of the rank and file, by strengthening the attachment of the rank and file to the department's objectives, and by developing in officers the kinds of habits and temperaments that should ease relations with the communities served by the department.

Paying Heed. It is not clear there is much courts can or should do to expand workplace democracy in policing, even assuming that goal is worth pursuing. This is mainly a task for police officers themselves and for enlightened law enforcement management. Courts could take one small step, though. They could start to pay heed to the views of organized groups of police officers in the same way they pay heed to the views of law enforcement management. It is common for courts, including the United States Supreme Court, to give heavy weight to the official views of state and federal law enforcement agencies when ruling on questions of police procedure.[129] It is far less common for courts to give weight to the views of organizations of rank-and-file police officers. Doing so is one straightforward way for courts to give line officers a greater voice in the nature of their work.

In determining how much weight to give the views of a particular organization of police officers, courts may want to take into account not only the number of and kinds of officers involved in the organization, but also how democratically it is run, and to what degree positions adopted by the organization are the products of deliberation and debate.[130] Drawing distinctions along these lines will not only help courts identify those organizations whose views are likely to be better informed and more representative of the views of police officers more broadly; it may also help to push organizations of police officers—unions as well as identity-based organizations—toward greater openness and more careful deliberation. If there are reasons to democratize the insides of police departments, there are also reasons to try to democratize the insides of the organizations claiming to represent the views of rank-and file-police officers.

Police Privatization. Over the last thirty-five years, as police departments have transformed the demographics of their workforces and changed their operational philosophy from police professionalism to community policing, they have also lost their monopoly. Growth in public law enforcement has slackened, and the private security industry has exploded. Private guards today greatly outnumber sworn law enforcement officers throughout the United States, and the gap continues to widen.

Chapters 6 and 7 examined some of the concerns that police privatization raises for democratic policing—concerns about undermining the public accountability of policing and about linking physical security to wealth. These issues deserve far more attention than they have received. But even less thought has been given to the threats that police privatization may pose to the halting, unfinished project of democratizing the internal operations of police departments. In a recent, illuminating study of a large Canadian security firm, George Rigakos found a workplace marked by extraordinary efforts at monitoring, controlling, and disciplining employees, and by levels of alienation and cynicism remarkable even in comparison with what we have come to expect from public law enforcement officers.[131] There is no reason to think other security firms would look strikingly different in these regards.[132]

Things could change, of course. The private security industry is currently the target of a major organizing campaign,[133] and workplace democracy could be imposed by statute on private security firms—just as on any other private firm. At bottom, though, what a private security firm offers its customers is, as Rigakos puts it, "a management system for hire."[134] This will likely make public norms regarding the *internal* operation of police forces the hardest to export to the private sector. Their internal operations— overwhelmingly nonunion, unburdened by civil service rules and "police officer bills of rights," relentlessly focused on efficiency and narrowly drawn performance goals—are precisely what the private firms have to offer.[135] It is what distinguishes one firm from another, and what still, despite the spread of public sector managerialism,[136] most strongly distinguishes private policing as a whole from public law enforcement. If the current trend toward police privatization has any single point, after all— other than retreating from a collective commitment to equalitarian protection against illegal force—the point is to escape, to circumvent, or to limit the domain of the organizational styles associated with public law enforcement, and to move the internal operations of policing toward a more thoroughgoing form of managerialism.

Conclusion

We have spent so much time in this book tracing and connecting two stories of intellectual transformations—the rise and fall of democratic pluralism, and the shift from police professionalism to community policing—that it is easy lose sight of what has stayed constant. For virtually all of the past half century, the central task of police reform in the United States has been understood to be reconciling law enforcement with the principles of a democratic society—in a phrase, "democratic policing." Today democratic policing is the stated goal not just of U.S. police reform, but of police reform throughout the world.[1] The phrase and its equivalents are thrown around so often, and with so little reflection, that it is easy to assume it means nothing. It is easy to assume that democratic policing, like democracy itself, has become simply a term of "vague endorsement" for whatever practices we find praiseworthy.[2]

If this book has done nothing else, I hope it has shown that assumption wrong. Defining democratic policing is difficult not because the concept is empty but because it is so rich. Saying we are in favor of democratic policing raises more questions than it answers. But the questions it raises are crucial: what are our core political ideals, and how can policing best advance those ideals?

Democratic policing has altered its meaning over the past four decades as our ideas about democracy and our ideas about policing have changed. The changes have been complex and intertwined; ideas about the police have reflected ideas about democracy, and vice versa. Democratic pluralism cohered so well with police professionalism that they produced what I called, in Chapter 2, "pluralist policing." Community policing fits snugly with participatory democracy and deliberative democracy—particularly so with the watered-down amalgam of those theories that is now the closest thing we have to an orthodox, commonsense account of the American political ideal. And the continuities in our thinking about the police are linked with continuities in our thinking about democracy. The continued de-emphasis of equality in the constitutional regulation of the police, for example, fits with the de-emphasis of "anti-inegalitarianism" in democratic theory. The relative neglect of structural issues in police reform, in favor of a focus on occupational culture, is of a piece with a broader tendency to see democracy as more a matter of culture than of institutions. And the ongoing tendency to view the police as a breed apart, unsuited both by role and by temperament for participation in democratic decision making, reflects in part the lingering emphasis on personality in democratic theory, and in part the continuing focus on the democratic value of compromise—the continuing assumption that democracy mixes poorly with force, confrontation, and dissensus.

We can deepen the "democratic" in democratic policing by questioning some of these ongoing assumptions, and by selectively recovering some of the orthodoxies we have discarded. The insights of democratic pluralism, for example, can help us guard against the naïve reification of "community" found in some strands of community policing. The pluralists can remind us, too, of the democratic attractions of modern urban life—often obscured in discussions of policing today by a sentimental, suburban nostalgia. Eighteenth-century political economy, with its focus on channeling and capitalizing on ambition and self-interest, can help us balance our concern for the cultural aspects of democratic policing with attention to the internal structure of police departments and external systems of accountability. Participatory democracy, as it was articulated and defended in the 1960s and 1970s, can enrich community policing by making community involvement in policing more meaningful and, as importantly, by including rank-and-file police officers themselves in the "community," valuing their experience and tapping into their collective intelligence. And sensitivity to the oppositional side of democracy—the tradition of anti-inegalitarianism—can help to keep us focused on the ways in which policing can buttress, or alternatively can destabilize, entrenched patterns of illegitimate domination.

This book has not provided a final, definitive account of democratic policing or a fixed agenda for reforming law enforcement. No such account is possible, and no such agenda can make much sense. The meaning of democratic policing will remain in flux—because our ideas about democracy and our ideas about the police will remain in flux; and because, as we have seen, democracy is in part a context-specific matter of oppositional politics and improvisational self-governance, of resistance to the forms of illegitimate hierarchy we find around us at a given place and time, and of collaborative responses to the challenges of the moment.

That is one reason this book has focused on the United States, largely ignoring debates about democratic policing in the rest of the world. Another reason, noted in the introduction, is more practical; the American experience is the one I know best, and it has been quite enough to fill a book. Giving up a comparative perspective is giving up something valuable. But I hope that something has been gained in exchange: a thick and nuanced exploration of the ways that debates about democracy and policing have played out in the particular context of the United States in the second half of the twentieth century and the beginning of the twenty-first century.

That context includes, of course, the terrorist attacks of September 11, 2001. The "war on terror" has stayed in the background throughout this book. I promised in the introduction that taking a longer view of democratic policing—tracing the roots of current controversies in debates and development over the past half century—would help us respond intelligently to the law enforcement challenges of our day, including but not limited to global terrorism. I hope I have made good on that promise. It is hard to assess the significance, for example, of rollbacks on the warrant requirement and other systems of judicial oversight without understanding the role those rules play in advancing particular conceptions of democratic policing. In the same manner, it is difficult to judge the wisdom of investigative tactics focused on people of particular races, ethnicities, and religious affiliations without appreciating the democratic costs of this kind of profiling—including the ways in which it can reinforce patterns of inequality, and the implications it may have for community policing. No one thinks police departments do well to alienate large segments of the communities they serve, but the nature and extent of those costs depend heavily on what kind of relationship the police want to have with those communities. The answer to *that* may have much to do with what kind of threat we think terrorism poses, and what responses we think will prove most effective.[3] But it will turn, too, on our notions about the relationship between policing and democracy.

Those notions may have even broader implications for the "war on terror." Many ideals commonly associated with democracy—human dignity, procedural regularity, the "rule of law"—are wrapped up with ideas about the police, and more precisely with the distinctive, mid-twentieth-century dystopia of the "police state." As we saw in Chapter 4, the trope of the police state lost much of its power when democratic pluralism began to unravel. It is worth remembering, though, how some of our most valorized ideals have been defined in reaction against particular forms of overbearing state authority, executed by and symbolically identified with police forces notorious for their brutality and lawlessness. It was a staple of political rhetoric during the Cold War that the United States must take care, in its struggle against communism, not to "become what we are fighting against." The fear, of course, was not that fighting communism abroad would push the United States away from free enterprise at home. The fear—distinctly pluralist—was that the United States might begin to mimic the police tactics of communist dictatorships, and in so doing forfeit much of what it was trying to defend. That is fear worth keeping in mind in assessing not only workaday law enforcement practices in the shadow of terrorism, but also the extraordinary policies and practices the United States has put into place for investigating, interrogating, and incapacitating "enemy combatants" and other individuals suspected of collaborating with terrorist groups.

But the most important lessons of this book are closer to home. They concern the rich and productive debates over the past half century about the proper shape of prosaic, everyday policing in the United States, the way in which those debates have been linked to changing ideas about the nature of American democracy, and the possibilities for enriching those debates in the future. Sharpening our thinking about democracy will sharpen our thinking about democratic policing. And reexamining our hopes and fears about the police can help clarify our ideas about democracy.

REFERENCE MATTER

Notes

1. *See* GEORGE E. BERKLEY, THE DEMOCRATIC POLICEMAN 1 (1969); HERMAN GOLDSTEIN, POLICING A FREE SOCIETY (1977); JEROME H. SKOLNICK, JUSTICE WITHOUT TRIAL: LAW ENFORCEMENT IN DEMOCRATIC SOCIETY (1966) [hereinafter SKOLNICK, JUSTICE WITHOUT TRIAL]; JAMES Q. WILSON, VARIETIES OF POLICE BEHAVIOR: THE MANAGEMENT OF LAW AND ORDER IN EIGHT COMMUNITIES (1968). The President's Commission on Law Enforcement and Administration of Justice was appointed in 1965, the National Advisory Commission on Civil Disorders in 1967, and the National Commission on the Causes and Prevention of Violence in 1968. *See* GOLDSTEIN, *supra* at 5. Skolnick's report to the National Commission on the Causes and Prevention of Violence was itself published in 1969, continuing his exploration of the predicaments the police posed for American democracy. *See* JEROME H. SKOLNICK, THE POLITICS OF PROTEST 241–92 (Ballantine Books 1969).

2. Amy Waldman, *U.S. Struggles to Transform a Tainted Iraqi Police Force*, N.Y. TIMES, June 30, 2003, at A; *see also, e.g.*, Carlotta Gall, *In Warlord Land, Democracy Tries Baby Steps*, N.Y. TIMES, June 11, 2003, at A4; Peter S. Green, *Kosovo Pins Its Hopes on Rule of Law*, N.Y. TIMES, May 19, 2003, at A8; Todd S. Purdum, *It's Democracy, Like It or Not*, N.Y. TIMES, Mar. 9, 2003, at D1, D3.

3. *See* SKOLNICK, JUSTICE WITHOUT TRIAL, *supra* note 1, at 1–22; Jerome Hall, *Police and Law in a Democratic Society*, 28 IND. L.J. 133, 143–45, 170 (1953); Herbert Packer, *Two Models of the Criminal Process*, 113 U. PA. L. REV. 1 (1964); Jonathan Simon, *Speaking Truth and Power*, 36 LAW & SOC. REV. 37, 39 (2002). In a widely influential formulation, Packer contrasted the "due process model" of criminal procedure with the "crime control model" and, without explicitly invoking democracy, found the former model rooted in a "complex of values" that included equality and anti-authoritarianism. Packer, *supra*, at 16–18.

4. *See, e.g., Harris v. United States,* 331 U.S. 145, 160 (1947) (Frankfurter, J., dissenting) (calling constitutional limits on search and seizure by the police "an indispensable need for a democratic society").

5. Patrick J. McDonnell, *Searches of Homes Just Plain Rude, Iraqis Say,* L.A. TIMES, July 1, 2003, at A5.

6. *See, e.g.,* Dan M. Kahan, *Reciprocity, Collective Action, and Community Policing,* 90 CAL. L. REV. 1513, 1535–37 (2002); Tracey L. Meares, *Praying for Community Policing,* 90 CAL. L. REV. 1593, 1598 (2002).

7. *See, e.g.,* GOLDSTEIN, *supra* note 1, at 141–42; Gerald Frug, *City Services,* 73 N.Y.U. L. REV. 23, 81 (1998); Jerome Skolnick, *Neighborhood Police,* THE NATION, Mar. 22, 1971, at 372; Arthur L. Waskow, *Community Control of the Police,* TRANS-ACTION, Dec. 1969, at 4.

8. *See, e.g.,* BERKLEY, *supra* note 1, at 30–35; WILLIAM A. WESTLEY, VIOLENCE AND THE POLICE: A SOCIOLOGICAL STUDY OF LAW, CUSTOM, AND MORALITY xvii (1970).

9. *See* Waldman, *supra* note 2, at A1.

10. *See* WILSON, *supra* note 1, at 200–26. Wilson himself was skeptical that the "service style" of policing could be employed effectively in large, heterogeneous communities. *See id.* at 249–57, 290. Other scholars, writing around the same time, expressed similar doubts. *See* Maureen Cain, *Trends in the Sociology of Police Work,* 7 INT. J. SOC. L. 143, 151 (1979).

11. Community policing often seems "less a program than a set of aspirations wrapped in a slogan," David H. Bayley, *Community Policing: A Report from the Devil's Advocate, in* COMMUNITY POLICING: RHETORIC OR REALITY 225, 225 (Jack R. Green & Stephen D. Mastrofski eds., 1988)—albeit a set of aspirations that has become "the new orthodoxy for cops"; John E. Eck & Dennis Rosenbaum, *The New Police Order: Effectiveness, Equity, and Efficiency in Community Policing, in* THE CHALLENGE OF COMMUNITY POLICING: TESTING THE PROMISES 3, 3 (Dennis P. Rosenbaum ed., 1994). Still, "[f]or all the diverse definitions of community policing, it may boil down to this: police treating a neighborhood the way a security guard treats a client property." Lawrence W. Sherman, *The Police, in* CRIME 327, 338–39 (James Q. Wilson & Joan Petersilia eds., 1995). On the roots of community policing in Wilson's "service style," see DOROTHY GUYOT, POLICING AS THOUGH PEOPLE MATTER 5–7 (1991).

12. Waldman, *supra* note 2, at A11.

13. BERKLEY, *supra* note 1, at 196 (quoting Woodrow Wilson). For similar sentiments, see Hall, *supra* note 3, at 156; Lawrence W. Sherman, *Consent of the Governed: Police, Democracy, and Diversity, in* POLICING, SECURITY AND DEMOCRACY: THEORY AND PRACTICE 17, 18 (Menachem Amir & Stanley Einstein eds., 2001).

14. *See* David A. Sklansky, *Quasi-Affirmative Rights in Constitutional Criminal Procedure,* 88 VA. L. REV. 1229, 1286–92 (2002).

15. WILLIAM JAMES, PRAGMATISM 61–74, 77 (Bruce Kuklick ed., Hackett Publ'g 1981) (1907); HORACE M. KALLEN, CULTURE AND DEMOCRACY IN THE UNITED STATES: STUDIES IN THE GROUP PSYCHOLOGY OF THE AMERICAN PEOPLE 11, 41–43,

115–25 (1924); Alain Locke, *Pluralism and Intellectual Democracy, in* 1942 Conf. on Sci., Phil. & Relig. 196, *reprinted in* The Philosophy of Alain Locke: Harlem Renaissance and Beyond 53 (Leonard Harris ed., 1989); John Rawls, Political Liberalism 36–37 (paperback ed. 1996).

16. *See* C. Wright Mills, The Power Elite 244–45 (1956). On this theme see also the justly acclaimed treatment of democratic pluralism in Michael Paul Rogin, The Intellectuals and McCarthy: The Radical Specter 268 (1967).

17. Despite the dangers of ambiguity, I will often, as here, use "pluralism" as a synonym for democratic pluralism.

18. Ian Shapiro, Democratic Justice 30 (1999); *see also* Ian Shapiro, The State of Democratic Theory 3–4, 50–52 (2003).

19. Ed Zern, Hunting and Fishing from A to Zern 311 (1985).

20. Jack Lively, Democracy 1 (1975).

21. Robert A. Dahl, Democracy and Its Critics 2 (1989).

22. Lively, *supra* note 20, at 1. Dan Kahan, for example, seems to take this position when he suggests that sensible arguments about institutional structures must "be grounded in normative considerations outside the concept of democracy." Dan M. Kahan, *Democracy Schmemocracy*, 20 Cardozo L. Rev. 795, 800 (1999). But he may only be claiming that we should be clear about our particular conception of democracy. *See id.* at 796–97. This would be consistent with Kahan's own work in criminal procedure, which, as we will see in Chapter 4, draws heavily on a specific set of ideas about democracy.

23. For an extended argument along precisely these lines, see Edward L. Rubin, *Getting Past Democracy*, 149 U. Pa. L. Rev. 725 (2001).

24. This is the gist, for example, of Fareed Zakaria's recent argument about "illiberal democracy." He contends that both the United States and the world in general suffer from an excess of democracy—which he takes to require only free and fair elections—and a deficit of what he calls "constitutional liberalism": a "bundle of freedoms" including "the rule of law, a separation of powers, and the protection of basic liberties of speech, assembly, religion, and property." Fareed Zakaria, The Future of Freedom: Illiberal Democracy at Home and Abroad 17 (2003). His primary prescription is to delegate more governmental decisions to institutions insulated from politics, like the Supreme Court and the Federal Reserve Board. *See id.* at 248–54. "What we need in politics today," he argues, "is not more democracy but less." *Id.* at 248.

25. *See, e.g.*, Philip Pettit, *Is Criminal Justice Politically Feasible?* 5 Buff. Crim. L. Rev. 427 (2002). Zakaria's ideas are closely paralleled by Pettit's proposal for establishing "penal policies board[s]" that would "operate[] at arm's length from parliament and government," much "[l]ike a central bank."

26. W. B. Gallie, *Essentially Contested Concepts, in* The Importance of Language 121, 135 (Max Black ed., 1962) (reprinted from 56 Proc. Aristotelian Soc'y 167 (1955–56)); *cf.* Lively, *supra* note 20, at 1–2 (concluding that "the very fact that the

term is so persistently and so ardently canvassed in the ordinary language of politics creates a need for it to be given as great a coherence and clarity as possible," and that there is "no compulsion on us to allow bad usages to drive out the good").

27. *See* Franklin E. Zimring, *The Necessity and Value of Transnational Comparative Study: Some Preaching from a Recent Convert*, 5 CRIMINOLOGY & PUB. POL'Y 615 (2006).

28. *See, e.g.*, Samuel R. Gross & Debra Livingston, *Racial Profiling Under Attack*, 102 COLUM. L. REV. 1413 (2002).

29. For thoughtful arguments along these lines, see William J. Stuntz, *Local Policing After the Terror*, 111 YALE L.J. 2137 (2002).

30. *See* Daniel C. Richman, *The Right Fight: Local Police and National Security*, BOSTON REV., Dec. 2004/Jan. 2005, at 6.

NOTES TO CHAPTER 1

1. ROBERT A. DAHL, 1 TOWARD DEMOCRACY: A JOURNEY: REFLECTIONS: 1940–1997, at 6 (1997); *see also id.* at 33.

2. *See* MARK LAWRENCE KORNBLUH, WHY AMERICA STOPPED VOTING: THE DECLINE OF PARTICIPATORY DEMOCRACY AND THE EMERGENCE OF MODERN AMERICAN POLITICS (2000).

3. JEFFREY SKLANSKY, THE SOUL'S ECONOMY: MARKET SOCIETY AND SELFHOOD IN AMERICAN THOUGHT, 1820–1920, at 5, 11 (2002). On this theme, see also JAMES LIVINGSTON, PRAGMATISM AND THE POLITICAL ECONOMY OF CULTURAL REVOLUTION, 1850–1940 (1994).

4. Theodore J. Lowi, *Foreword* to KENNETH PREWITT & ALAN STONE, THE RULING ELITES: ELITE THEORY, POWER, AND AMERICAN DEMOCRACY vii, vii (1973). Mancur Olson noted in 1965 that parts of the pluralist account were sufficiently uncontroversial that they were "passed on to the young in the textbooks almost without qualification." MANCUR OLSON, THE LOGIC OF COLLECTIVE ACTION: PUBLIC GOODS AND THE THEORY OF GROUPS 124 n.54 (1965) (citing JAMES MACGREGOR BURNS & JAMES WALTER PELTASON, GOVERNMENT BY THE PEOPLE 310–11 (4th ed. 1960)).

5. William E. Connolly, *The Challenge to Pluralist Theory*, *in* THE BIAS OF PLURALISM 3 (William E. Connolly ed., 1969). For similar, contemporary assessments, see CAROLE PATEMAN, PARTICIPATION AND DEMOCRATIC THEORY 14 (1970); PREWITT & STONE, *supra* note 4, at 114; Darryl Baskin, *American Pluralism: Theory, Practice, and Ideology*, 32 J. POLITICS 71, 80 (1970).

6. Connolly, *supra* note 5, at 21–22. On this theme, see also EDWARD A. PURCELL, JR., THE CRISIS OF DEMOCRATIC THEORY: SCIENTIFIC NATURALISM AND THE PROBLEM OF VALUE (1972), and Richard Primus, Note, *A Brooding Omnipresence: Totalitarianism in Postwar Constitutional Thought*, 106 YALE L.J. 423 (1996).

7. *See* BRIAN CHAPMAN, POLICE STATE 11–32 (1970).

8. *Id.* at 50.

9. SLAUGHTER-HOUSE CASES, 83 U.S. 36, 49–50 (1873); *see generally* Markus Kirk Dubber, *"The Power to Govern Men and Things": Patriarchal Origins of the Police Power in American Law*, 52 BUFF. L. REV. 1277 (2004).

10. CHAPMAN, *supra* note 7, at 114; *see also* Robert Gellately, *Situating the 'SS-State' in a Social-Historical Context: Recent Histories of the SS, the Police, and the Courts in the Third Reich*, 64 J. MODERN HIST. 338, 338 (1992).

11. CHAPMAN, *supra* note 7, at 114 ("[T]he professional skepticism of policemen becomes elevated to a theory of the state. . . . [A]ll is suspect, everyone a potential traitor."); HANNAH ARENDT, THE ORIGINS OF TOTALITARIANISM 430 (1968 ed.) ("The category of the suspect . . . embraces under totalitarian conditions the total population."); *id.* at 433–34 ("The totalitarian secret police . . . has given up the traditional old police dream which the lie detector is supposed to realize. . . . The modern dream of the totalitarian police, with its modern technologies, is incomparably more terrible."); *see also* GHITA IONESCU, THE POLITICS OF THE EUROPEAN COMMUNIST STATES 105 (1967).

12. ARENDT, *supra* note 11, at 431.

13. *Id.* at 433.

14. CHAPMAN, *supra* note 7, at 81.

15. *See* MICHAEL PAUL ROGIN, THE INTELLECTUALS AND McCARTHY: THE RADICAL SPECTER 1–31, 216–82 (1967); PATEMAN, *supra* note 5, at 1–21; and PURCELL, *supra* note 5, at 235–72. Not all pluralists saw McCarthyism as a mass phenomenon. *See, e.g.*, Nelson W. Polsby, *Toward an Explanation of McCarthyism*, *in* NELSON W. POLSBY, ROBERT A. DENTIER & PAUL A. SMITH, POLITICS AND SOCIAL LIFE, at 809 (1963); Nelson W. Polsby, *Down Memory Lane with Joe McCarthy*, COMMENTARY, Feb. 1963, at 55. But in the conventional pluralist understanding, McCarthy was "the heir of LaFollette." EDWARD A. SHILS, THE TORMENT OF SECRECY: THE BACKGROUND AND CONSEQUENCES OF AMERICAN SECURITY POLICIES 99 (1956) (Elephant Paperbacks ed. 1996).

16. CHAPMAN, *supra* note 7, at 135.

17. ALEXIS DE TOCQUEVILLE, DEMOCRACY IN AMERICA 232 (Harvey C. Mansfield & Delba Winthrop trans. & eds., 2000) (1835).

18. *Id.* at 233.

19. MAX WEBER, *Bureaucracy*, *in* FROM MAX WEBER: ESSAYS IN SOCIOLOGY 196 (H. H. Gerth & C. Wright Mills trans. & eds., 1946).

20. ROBERT MICHELS, POLITICAL PARTIES: A SOCIOLOGICAL STUDY OF THE OLI-GARCHICAL TENDENCIES OF MODERN DEMOCRACIES 342–56 (Eden & Cedar Paul trans., Free Press 1962) (1911).

21. On that decline, see KORNBLUH, *supra* note 2.

22. DAVID B. TRUMAN, THE GOVERNMENTAL PROCESS: PUBLIC INTERESTS AND PUB-LIC OPINION 356 (2d ed. 1971) (1951).

23. *Id.* (quoting Joseph Wood Krutch, *Whom Do We Picket Tonight?*, HARPER'S,

Mar. 1950, at 66, 67. Krutch said he found himself "looking backward with a certain sense of nostalgia into all those ages of Western civilization when no one supposed that being a good citizen was more than a part-time job." Krutch, *supra*, at 68.

24. ROBERT A. DAHL, WHO GOVERNS? DEMOCRACY AND POWER IN AN AMERICAN CITY 279 (1961).

25. *Id.* at 305; *see also, e.g., id.* at 225 (*"Homo civicus* is not, by nature, a political animal.*"*).

26. ANGUS CAMPBELL, PHILLIP E. CONVERSE, WARREN E. MILLER & DONALD E. STOKES, THE AMERICAN VOTER 543 (1960). Dahl and Truman both served on the Social Science Research Council's Committee on Political Behavior, which helped plan the 1952 study and thereafter remained associated with the work at Michigan. *See id.* at vi. The Committee on Political Behavior also included V. O. Key, Jr., whose *Politics, Parties, & Pressure Groups*, first published in 1942, did much to popularize democratic pluralism.

27. *Id.*

28. *Id.* at 544. Similar results were reached in an earlier, influential study of how voters in Elmira, New York, made up their minds in the 1948 presidential election. Like *The American Voter*, the Elmira study found average citizens uninformed, uninvolved, and uninterested in politics. But the system still worked impressively well. "Where the rational citizen seems to abdicate, nevertheless angels seem to tread." BERNARD R. BERELSON, PAUL F. LAZARFELD & WILLIAM N. McPHEE, VOTING: A STUDY OF OPINION FORMATION IN A PRESIDENTIAL CAMPAIGN 306–11 (1954).

29. PETER BACHRACH, THE THEORY OF DEMOCRATIC ELITISM: A CRITIQUE 7–9 (1967); ROGIN, *supra* note 15, at 25; Jack L. Walker, *A Critique of the Elitist Theory of Democracy*, 60 AM. POL. SCI. REV. 285, 286–89 (1966).

30. *See* ROGIN, *supra* note 15, at 45.

31. *See id.* at 46; SKLANSKY, *supra* note 3, at 16–27.

32. *See, e.g.,* CHRISTOPHER LASCH, THE AGONY OF THE AMERICAN LEFT 171 (1969); PURCELL, *supra* note 15, at 197–217.

33. David B. Truman, *The American System in Crisis*, 74 POL. SCI. Q. 481, 486 (1959); *see also, e.g.,* ROBERT A. DAHL, A PREFACE TO DEMOCRATIC THEORY 50 (1956) ("Philosopher kings are hard to come by."). For a good discussion of Lippman's writings on democracy, see PURCELL, *supra* note 15, at 104–07. The key works are WALTER LIPPMAN, PUBLIC OPINION (1922), and WALTER LIPPMAN, THE PHANTOM PUBLIC (1925).

34. *See* ROGIN, *supra* note 15, at 18.

35. SKLANSKY, *supra* note 3, at 228. The authors of the Elmira study, for example, sought ultimately to understand "the social psychology of the voting decision." *See* BERELSON ET AL., *supra* note 28, at 277.

36. THE FEDERALIST No. 51, at 262 (James Madison) (Bantam Books 1982).

37. DAHL, *supra* note 33, at 4, 18.

38. *See* TRUMAN, *supra note* 22, at 3–13 (quoting THE FEDERALIST No. 10).

39. DAHL, *supra* note 33, at 82; *see also, e.g.*, SEYMOUR MARTIN LIPSET, POLITICAL MAN: THE SOCIAL BASES OF POLITICS 9 (1960); TRUMAN, *supra note* 22, at xli, 529–31; Truman, *supra* note 33, at 493.

40. DAHL, *supra* note 33, at 143 (emphasis added).

41. *See, e.g.*, WILLIAM LEACH, LAND OF DESIRE: MERCHANTS, POWER, AND THE RISE OF A NEW AMERICAN CULTURE 231–44, 288–91, 372–78 (1993); SKLANSKY, *supra* note 3, at 178–91.

42. *See, e.g.*, GARY CROSS, AN ALL-CONSUMING CENTURY: WHY COMMERCIALISM WON IN MODERN AMERICA 17–65 (2000).

43. Assuming, of course, that consumers could be counted on to prefer good detergent, which Veblen famously doubted. *See* THORSTEIN VEBLEN, THE THEORY OF THE LEISURE CLASS (1899). But even Veblen gave consumers a degree of collective agency, albeit an agency they were apt to use foolishly. *See* SKLANSKY, *supra* note 3, at 185.

44. JOSEPH A. SCHUMPETER, CAPITALISM, SOCIALISM AND DEMOCRACY 269 (HarperPerennial 1976) (1942).

45. *Id.* at 273.

46. *Id.* at 263. Schumpeter was not, of course, the first to draw this comparison. The pioneering publicist Edward Bernays, for example, had called politics "the first big business in America," and had suggested that politicians could learn a great deal from businessmen about "methods of mass distribution of ideas and products." ED-WARD BERNAYS, PROPAGANDA 95 (1928). On Bernays, see LEACH, *supra* note 41, at 319–22; LARRY TYE, THE FATHER OF SPIN: EDWARD L. BERNAYS AND THE BIRTH OF PUBLIC RELATIONS (1998).

47. SCHUMPETER, *supra* note 44, at 271.

48. *Id.* at 282.

49. *Id.* at 261.

50. *Id.*

51. *See, e.g.*, BACHRACH, *supra* note 29, at 17–25; JACK LIVELY, DEMOCRACY 35–41, 76 (1975); PATEMAN, *supra* note 5, at 3, 5. The authors of the Elmira study dissented from "the usual analogy" between voting and "the more or less carefully calculated decisions of consumers or businessmen or courts"; they thought political "preferences" were more like "cultural tastes" in "music, literature, recreational activities, dress, ethics, speech, social behavior." *See* BERELSON ET AL., *supra* note 28, at 311. But classifying voting with clothing choices rather than with calculated economic decisions was very much in keeping with a mass-market view of elections. (Elsewhere the authors compared political views with food selections in a cafeteria. *See id.* at 318.) Moreover, investigations of "voting behavior" like the Elmira study and *The American Voter* themselves reflected, in their very methodology and choice of subject matter, a consumerist view of politics. They brought to political science "the theory and techniques of market research." Robert B. Westbrook, *Politics as Consumption: Managing the Modern American Election, in* THE CULTURE OF CONSUMPTION: CRITICAL

ESSAYS IN AMERICAN HISTORY, 1880–1980, at 143, 163 (Richard Wightman Fox & T. J. Jackson Lears eds., 1983).

52. CAMPBELL ET AL., *supra* note 26, at 541; *see also, e.g.*, DAHL, *supra* note 33, at 131–32 & n.12; ROBERT A. DAHL & CHARLES E. LINDBLOM, POLITICS, ECONOMICS AND WELFARE 283 n.15 (1953).

53. SCHUMPETER, *supra* note 44, at 242.

54. *Id.* at 242–43.

55. *See id.* at 243, 271–72, 290.

56. BACHRACH, *supra* note 29, at 95.

57. SCHUMPETER, *supra* note 44, at 270.

58. *Id.* at 262.

59. *Id.*

60. *Id.* at 263. The pluralists' divergence from Schumpeter on this point was consistent with the emerging position of social scientists in the 1950s that public attitudes resisted easy manipulation—a position that itself was based in part on the Elmira study of voting behavior. On this so-called law of minimal effects, see BERELSON ET AL., *supra* note 28, at 248; V. O. KEY, JR., POLITICS, PARTIES, & PRESSURE GROUPS 483–85 (5th ed. 1964) (1942); JOSEPH T. KLAPPER, THE EFFECTS OF MASS COMMUNICATION 4–9, 43–47 (1960); Westbrook, *supra* note 51, at 164.

61. SCHUMPETER, *supra* note 44, at 290–96.

62. *Id.* at 290.

63. *Id.* at 293–94.

64. *Id.* at 291–92. This is, of course, precisely the suggestion made today by people like Fareed Zakaria and Philip Pettit. (See notes 24 and 25 to the Introduction.) Interestingly, Schumpeter's example of an issue that should be placed beyond politics was similar to Pettit's: the detailed content of a criminal code. Crime, he pointed out, "is a complex phenomenon," the "popular slogans about it are almost invariably wrong," and it is prone to be approached in "fits of vindictiveness" or "fits of sentimentality." Schumpeter used the Bank of England, the Interstate Commerce Commission, and "certain of our . . . state universities" to illustrate the point that "[d]emocracy does not require that every function of the state be subject to its political method." SCHUMPETER, *supra* note 44, at 292–93.

65. SCHUMPETER, *supra* note 44, at 294.

66. *Id.* at 301.

67. *Id.* at 294.

68. *Id.*

69. *Id.* at 295.

70. *See, e.g., id.* at 275–81 & nn.16–19, 21–22.

71. *See id.* at 293.

72. *Id.* at 294.

73. *See, e.g., id.* at 300–02.

74. *Id.* at 263, 298. Schumpeter accepted political parties, which he saw as

opportunistic alliances for the purpose of achieving political power. The political process needed them, in the same way that the mass market needed department stores. *See id.* at 283. But he had no use for groups actually united by a common interest: "groups with an axe to grind." *Id.* at 263.

75. *See* Baskin, *supra* note 5, at 73–79.

76. ARTHUR F. BENTLEY, THE PROCESS OF GOVERNMENT: A STUDY OF SOCIAL PRESSURES 222 (Transaction Publishers 1995) (1908). On Bentley's influence, see OLSON, *supra* note 4, at 117–31; PURCELL, *supra* note 15, at 254.

77. *See* R. JEFFREY LUSTIG, CORPORATE LIBERALISM: THE ORIGINS OF MODERN AMERICAN POLITICAL THEORY, 1890–1920, at 109–49 (1982); SKLANSKY, *supra* note 3, at 131.

78. KORNBLUH, *supra* note 2, at 117.

79. BENTLEY, *supra* note 76, at 208–09.

80. *See id.* at 220–21.

81. *See id.* at 211, 258–59.

82. *See id.* at 226–27.

83. *Id.* at vii.

84. *Id.* at 448.

85. *Id.* at 452.

86. *Id.* at 307; *see also id.* at 447–59.

87. *Id.* at 305–06.

88. *Id.* at 453.

89. *See* DAHL & LINDBLOM, *supra* note 52, at 330 n.7; Thelma Z. Lavine, *Introduction* to BENTLEY, *supra* note 76, at xiv.

90. *See* JOSÉ ORTEGA Y GASSET, THE REVOLT OF THE MASSES (1930).

91. The insight is Michael Rogin's. Rogin persuasively characterized pluralism as in part "a theory of history in which industrialization is the major actor." ROGIN, *supra* note 15, at 10. "For the modern pluralists, industrial society destroys old groups and loyalties, but it also creates new ones"—"more utilitarian than traditional," but stabilizing nonetheless. *Id.* at 12. Indeed, it was precisely "the success of industrialization" that allowed "group politics to dominate a society." *Id.* at 10.

92. JANE JACOBS, THE DEATH AND LIFE OF GREAT AMERICAN CITIES 19 (1961) (Vintage Books ed. 1992). For all her contempt for traditional urban planning, Jacobs shared with many of her targets a bedrock faith in the "freedom of the city"; it was in part because of this shared commitment that her attack on traditional planning principles resonated so widely. *Id.* at 50; *see also id.* at 116, 150, 340, 379, 444. On Jacobs's influence, *see, e.g.*, Douglas Martin, *Jane Jacobs, 89, Who Saw Future in Cities, is Dead*, N.Y. TIMES, Apr. 26, 2006, at A1.

93. PURCELL, *supra* note 15, at 211; David A. Hollinger, *Ethnic Diversity, Cosmopolitanism and the Emergence of the American Liberal Intelligentsia*, 27 AM. Q. 133 (1975). Hollinger describes the "cosmopolitan ideal" of mid-century intellectuals as "a desire to transcend the limitations of any and all particularisms in order to achieve

a more complete human experience and a more complete understanding of that experience." Hollinger, *supra*, at 135, 150. He makes the intriguing suggestion that the rise of this ideal may have been linked to the rise of elitism. Cosmopolitanism, he argues, "is difficult to maintain as a prescription for society at large unless one is willing—as most American intellectuals have not been—to attribute to the general populations a prodigious capacity for growth. The cosmopolitan ideal commanded the widest allegiance from American intellectuals when it was implicitly understood to be their peculiar possession, when members of the intelligentsia did not feel obliged—as many of them did after the mid-1960s—to adopt values that could be justified in the wider context of general social theory." *Id.* at 150–51.

94. TRUMAN, *supra* note 22, at 507–519.

95. DAHL, *supra* note 33, at 150. Similar claims may also be found in, e.g., KEY, *supra* note 60, at 6–8.

96. EARL LATHAM, THE GROUP BASIS OF POLITICS: A STUDY IN BASING-POINT LEGISLATION 226–27 (1952).

97. *Id.* at 13, 28.

98. TRUMAN, *supra* note 22, at 17–21.

99. *See* DAHL, *supra* note 33, at 18.

100. LATHAM, *supra* note 96, at 10; *see also, e.g.,* KEY, *supra* note 60, at 17.

101. *See, e.g., id.* at 38–49; DAHL, *supra* note 33, at 136–37, 145; KEY, *supra* note 60, at 690–712.

102. LATHAM, *supra* note 96, at 49.

103. DAHL, *supra* note 33, at 145.

104. TRUMAN, *supra note* 22, at 7 (quoting 1 ALEXIS DE TOCQUEVILLE, DEMOCRACY IN AMERICA 191 (Phillips Bradley ed., Knopf 1945) (1835)); *see also, e.g.,* ROBERT A. DAHL, DEMOCRACY AND ITS CRITICS 295 (1989).

105. LATHAM, *supra* note 96, at 10; *see also, e.g.,* TRUMAN, *supra* note 22, at 31–35, 51–52. Truman, *supra* note 33, at 488. Latham thought this ceaseless activity was "fully in accord with the American culture pattern which rates high in the characteristics of optimism, risk, experimentalism, change, aggressiveness, acquisitiveness, and a colossal faith in man's ability to subdue and bend nature to his desire." LATHAM, *supra* note 96, at 35. Presumably it was rhetoric like Latham's that C. Wright Mills had in mind when he dismissed the pluralists as "romantic," caught up in "a kind of bewildering, Whitmanesque enthusiasm for variety." C. WRIGHT MILLS, THE POWER ELITE 244 (1956).

106. Thus, for example, Robert Dahl concluded in his study of New Haven politics that "[p]robably the most striking characteristic of influence in New Haven is the extent to which it is *specialized*; that is, individuals who are influential in one sector of public activity tend not to be influential in another sector; and, what is probably more significant, the social strata from which individuals in one sector tend to come are different from the social strata from which individuals in other sectors are drawn." DAHL, *supra* note 24, at 169. Like "a number of old American cities," New

Haven had evolved "from a system in which resources of influence were highly concentrated to a system in which they are highly dispersed," from "a system of *cumulative inequalities* in political resources to a system of noncumulative or *dispersed inequalities* in political resources." *Id.* at 227–28.

107. Baskin, *supra* note 5, at 73–79. On the importance of overlapping memberships, see especially BERELSON ET AL., *supra* note 28, at 318–20; TRUMAN, *supra note* 22, at 168, 514, 520.

108. *E.g.*, DAHL, *supra* note 33, at 84.

109. *Id.* at 145; *see also id.* at 150 (suggesting that "perhaps in no other national political system in the world is bargaining so basic a component of the political process"); LATHAM, *supra* note 96, at 224 (stressing centrality of "the principle of toleration and compromise, without which the democratic process would not function at all").

110. DAHL, *supra* note 33, at 133.

111. *Id.* at 146.

112. Connolly, *supra* note 5, at 13; *see also, e.g.*, BACHRACH, *supra* note 29, at 62–63. Thus George Berkley, drawing on pluralist scholarship in 1969 for insight into democratic policing, took it as uncontroversial that democracy "first of all requires consensus." GEORGE E. BERKLEY, THE DEMOCRATIC POLICEMAN 2 (1969).

113. DAHL, *supra* note 33, at 132; *see also id.* at 77–80; BERELSON ET AL., *supra* note 28, at 313, 319; KEY, *supra* note 60, at 227; LATHAM, *supra* note 96, at 225.

114. TRUMAN, *supra note* 22, at xli, 159, 512, 524; *cf., e.g.*, SHILS, *supra* note 15, at 160, 231.

115. DAHL, *supra* note 33, at 47, 76–77; *see also* KEY, *supra* note 60, at 12–13; TRUMAN, *supra* note 22, at 512–13, 524.

116. Truman, *supra* note 33, at 490; *see also, e.g.*, BERKLEY, *supra* note 112, at 4 (noting that "[a]lthough in former days the contract theory was often viewed as expressing the essence of democracy, more contemporary thinkers focus on . . . the affirmation of individual worth. Adlai Stevenson, for example, felt that the essence of democracy is the dignity of man").

117. *E.g.*, SHILS, *supra* note 15, at 160; TRUMAN, *supra* note 22, at xxxvii, 512–13.

118. DAHL, *supra* note 24, at 90–94.

119. TRUMAN, *supra* note 22, at xxxviii.

120. *See* DAHL, *supra* note 24, at 91.

121. BACHRACH, *supra* note 29, at 47–64.

122. TRUMAN, *supra* note 22, at 535; *see also* Truman, *supra* note 33, at 495–97. In the words of sociologist Edward Shils, pluralist politics required "a sense of affinity among the elites and a common attachment to the institutions and apparatus through which political life is carried on." SHILS, *supra* note 15, at 158. The authors of the Elmira study similarly stressed the importance of "opinion-leading relationships," through which "the total information and knowledge possessed in the group's present and past generations can be made available for the group's choice." BERELSON ET AL.,

supra note 28, at 321; *see also id.* at 322–23. Opinion leaders were thus the "angels" that seemed to intercede when "the rational citizen seems to abdicate." *Id.* at 311.

123. ROGIN, *supra* note 15, at 25. The same point is made, e.g., in PREWITT & STONE, *supra* note 4, at 201, and Walker, *supra* note 29, at 287.

124. T. W. ADORNO, ELSE FRANKEL-BRUNSWIK, DANIEL J. LEVINSON & R. NEVITT SANFORD, THE AUTHORITARIAN PERSONALITY (1950); *see also, e.g.*, DAHL, *supra* note 33, at 18; LIPSET, *supra* note 39, at 105; Morris Janowitz & Dwaine Marvick, *Authoritarianism and Political Behavior*, 17 PUB. OP. Q. 185 (1953); Robert E. Lane, *Political Personality and Electoral Choice*, 49 AM. POLITICAL SCI. REV. 173 (1955). For assessments of the role of personality in pluralism, see PURCELL, *supra* note 15, at 253–54; ROGIN, *supra* note 15, at 18.

125. ADORNO ET AL., *supra* note 124, at ix.

126. *Id.* at 228; *see also, e.g.*, Lane, *supra* note 124, at 176. On reactions to *The Authoritarian Personality*, and on the study's roots in earlier work by Adorno and other members of the Frankfurt School, see MARTIN JAY, THE DIALECTICAL IMAGINATION: A HISTORY OF THE FRANKFURT SCHOOL AND THE INSTITUTE OF SOCIAL RESEARCH, 1923–1950, at 219–52 (1996 ed.) (1973).

127. *See, e.g.*, DAHL, *supra* note 33, at 18, 81–82; LIPSET, *supra* note 39, at 97–130; Janowitz & Marvick, *supra* note 124, at 191, 195, 199.

128. DAHL, *supra* note 33, at 89.

129. BERELSON ET AL., *supra* note 28, at 319. See also the extended juxtaposition of pluralism with extremism in SHILS, *supra* note 15, at 223–38.

130. LASCH, *supra* note 32, at 172. For the classic declaration of "the end of deep political conflict in the West, the end of utopian attempts to reconstruct society," *id.* at 171, see Daniel Bell's collection of essays, THE END OF IDEOLOGY: ON THE EXHAUSTION OF POLITICAL IDEAS IN THE FIFTIES (1961).

131. BERELSON ET AL., *supra* note 28, at 314, 323.

132. *Id.* at 321, 323; *see also, e.g.*, Walker, *supra* note 29, at 287.

133. SHILS, *supra* note 15, at 21.

134. *See* JOHN DEWEY, THE PUBLIC AND ITS PROBLEMS 205 (1946 ed.) (1927); *supra* note 122 and accompanying text. On Dewey's influence, see PURCELL, *supra* note 15, at 197–217.

135. *See, e.g.*, BERELSON ET AL., *supra* note 28, at 306; DAHL, *supra* note 33, at 18; TRUMAN, *supra* note 22, at 14–44.

136. David Truman, for example, opened his essay on McCarthyism—the same essay in which he dismissed Lippman as a Platonist—by warning that America's failure in China, together with the Sputnik crisis, had "produced a variety of responses, a good many of which were inappropriate in the sense that they were not adequately based on reality," although they may have been "comforting" and "psychologically useful." Truman, *supra* note 33, at 481. Later he suggested that "psychoanalytic examination" of Lippman himself "might be revealing," although Truman did not propose to carry it out. *Id.* at 487.

137. This tendency of pluralism, present from the outset, grew more pronounced after October 1957. Pluralism was always a response to the felt realities of the times, and few realities were felt as sharply as Sputnik. *See* PAUL DICKSON, SPUTNIK: THE SHOCK OF THE CENTURY 108–33, 223–34 (2001); ROBERT A. DIVINE, THE SPUTNIK CHALLENGE 3–96 (1993); WALTER A. MCDOUGALL, THE HEAVENS AND THE EARTH: A POLITICAL HISTORY OF THE SPACE AGE 137–65, 227–30 (1985); Walter A. McDougall, *Technocracy and Statecraft in the Space Age—Toward the History of a Saltation*, 87 AM. HIST. REV. 1010, 1023–24 (1982).

138. *See, e.g.*, LIVELY, *supra* note 51, at 82; PATEMAN, *supra* note 5, at 1–2.

139. Here is Dahl, for example: "Probably this strange hybrid, the normal American political system, is not for export to others." DAHL, *supra* note 33, at 151.

140. *See id.*; LATHAM, *supra* note 96, at 35.

141. Alan Taylor, *The Exceptionalist*, NEW REPUBLIC, June 9, 2003, at 33, 33; *cf.* MILLS, *supra* note 105, at 25 (criticizing "[t]hose who have abandoned criticism for the new American celebration"); *id.* at 358 n.* (calling American history the "common denominator of the conservative mood in America today").

142. PURCELL, *supra* note 15, at 271; *see also, e.g.*, Hollinger, *supra* note 93, at 147.

NOTES TO CHAPTER 2

1. *See* Olmstead v. United States, 277 U.S. 438 (1928).

2. *See* Carroll v. United States, 267 U.S. 132 (1925).

3. *See* Sorrells v. United States, 287 U.S. 435 (1932).

4. *See, e.g.*, Daniel C. Richman, *The Changing Boundaries Between Federal and Local Law Enforcement*, 2 CRIM. JUST. 81 (2000).

5. *See., e.g.*, CRAIG BRADLEY, THE FAILURE OF THE CRIMINAL JUSTICE REVOLUTION 18 (1993).

6. *See, e.g.*, Robert M. Cover, *The Origins of Judicial Activism in the Protection of Minorities*, 91 YALE L.J. 1287, 1305–06 (1982); Michael J. Klarman, *The Racial Origins of Modern Criminal Procedure*, 99 MICH. L. REV. 48 (2000); Louis Lusky, *Minority Rights and the Public Interest*, 52 YALE L.J. 1, 26–30 (1942); Carol S. Steiker, *Second Thoughts About First Principles*, 107 HARV. L. REV. 820, 841–44 (1994).

7. Moore v. Dempsey, 261 U.S. 86 (1923).

8. Powell v. Alabama, 287 U.S. 45 (1932).

9. Norris v. Alabama, 294 U.S. 587 (1935).

10. Brown v. Mississippi, 297 U.S. 278 (1936).

11. ROBERT A. DAHL, A PREFACE TO DEMOCRATIC THEORY 142–43 (1956).

12. *See, e.g., id.* at 121, 138; ROBERT A. DAHL, WHO GOVERNS?: DEMOCRACY AND POWER IN AN AMERICAN CITY 293–96 (1961); DAVID B. TRUMAN, THE GOVERNMENTAL PROCESS: PUBLIC INTERESTS AND PUBLIC OPINION 103–04, 511, 518 (2d ed. 1971) (1951).

13. *See* Watts v. Indiana, 338 U.S. 49 (1949); Haley v. Ohio, 332 U.S. 596 (1948); Malinski v. New York, 324 U.S. 401 (1945); Ashcraft v. Tennessee, 322 U.S. 143 (1944).

14. *See, e.g.*, HERMAN GOLDSTEIN, POLICING A FREE SOCIETY 2–3 (1977); DOROTHY GUYOT, POLICING AS THOUGH PEOPLE MATTER 5–7 (1991). The canonical works are AUGUST VOLLMER, THE POLICE AND MODERN SOCIETY (1936) and O. W. WILSON, PO-LICE ADMINISTRATION (1950). Vollmer was the chief of police in Berkeley, California, until 1932 and then taught police administration at U.C. Berkeley. Wilson, Vollmer's protégé, was the Dean of the School of Criminology at U.C. Berkeley and later directed the police departments in Fullerton, Wichita, and Chicago. On Wilson's influence, see Lawrence W. Sherman, *The Sociology and the Social Reform of the American Police: 1950–1973*, 2 J. POLI. SCI. & ADMIN. 255, 256 (1974).

15. *See, e.g.*, GOLDSTEIN, *supra* note 14, at 2–3, 133–34, 144.

16. *See id.*

17. *See, e.g.*, BRADLEY, *supra* note 5, at 9–10.

18. Vollmer was an important exception, in this respect and in others. *See supra* note 14.

19. ROBERT M. FOGELSON, BIG-CITY POLICE 167–92 (1977).

20. *See, e.g.*, WILSON, *supra* note 14, at 8; William H. Parker, *The Police Challenge in Our Great Cities*, 291 ANNALS AM. ACAD. POL. & SOC. SCI. 5, 6 (1954).

21. FOGELSON, *supra* note 19, at 161; Parker, *supra* note 20, at 7–8.

22. *See, e.g.*, BANTON, *supra* note 49, at 1 (quoting police administrators); WILSON, *supra* note 14, at 421 (advising that "[t]he solution of most police problems involves influencing mass attitudes, which can only be molded, directed, and controlled by the force of public opinion"). Vollmer, too, had stressed the importance of public opinion. *See* VOLLMER, *supra* note 14, at 6–7.

23. *See, e.g.*, GOLDSTEIN, *supra* note 14, at 2.

24. Parker, *supra* note 20, at 6–7.

25. *See* FOGELSON, *supra* note 19, at 141–66. Fogelson argues the first wave re-formers had a military model for the police rather than the professional model adopted by the second wave. *See id.* at 40–66, 154. The distinction between the two models may be overdrawn, *see* Egon Bittner, *The Rise and Fall of the Thin Blue Line*, 6 REV. AM. HIST. 421, 424–27 (1978), and Fogelson makes clear, in any event, that some of the early reformers, including Vollmer, favored a professional model, *see* FO-GELSON, *supra* note 19, at 154.

26. Bittner, *supra* note 25, at 426; *see also* GUYOT, *supra* note 14, at 5–10.

27. 384 U.S. at 483–86.

28. Tennessee v. Garner, 471 U.S. 1, 18–19 (1985).

29. *See* Illinois v. Lafayette, 462 U.S. 640 (1983); South Dakota v. Opperman, 428 U.S. 364 (1976).

30. *Lafayette*, 462 U.S. at 648.

31. GEORGE E. BERKLEY, THE DEMOCRATIC POLICEMAN 21–22 (1969).

32. John Edgar Hoover, *The Basis for Sound Law Enforcement*, 291 ANNALS AM. ACAD. POL. & SOC. SCI. 39, 41–42 (1954).

33. Wolf v. Colorado, 338 U.S. 25, 32–33 (1949). It was partly on this basis that *Wolf* refused to apply the exclusionary rule to state criminal proceedings. The Supreme Court reversed that decision in Mapp v. Ohio, 367 U.S. 643 (1961), but not because it had come to doubt the wisdom of decentralized policing.

34. *See, e.g.,* JAMES Q. WILSON, VARIETIES OF POLICE BEHAVIOR: THE MANAGEMENT OF LAW AND ORDER IN EIGHT COMMUNITIES 289 (1968).

35. *See, e.g.,* GOLDSTEIN, *supra* note 14, at 131.

36. James Q. Wilson, *The Police and Their Problems: A Theory*, 12 PUB. POL'Y 189, 191 (1963).

37. The second category included, e.g., RAYMOND B. FOSDICK, AMERICAN POLICE SYSTEMS (1920). The third category included most notably the work of August Vollmer, *see supra* note 14, as well as, e.g., ARTHUR WOODS, POLICEMAN AND PUBLIC (1919). For an important but limited exception to the generalization in the text, see the discussion of police graft in WILLIAM FOOTE WHYTE, STREET CORNER SOCIETY: THE SOCIAL STRUCTURE OF AN ITALIAN SLUM 123–46 (1943).

38. *See* Jerome Hall, *Police and Law in a Democratic Society*, 28 IND. L.J. 133 (1953); William Westley, *Violence and the Police*, 59 AM. J. SOC. 34 (1953).

39. *See* WILLIAM A. WESTLEY, VIOLENCE AND THE POLICE: A SOCIOLOGICAL STUDY OF LAW, CUSTOM, AND MORALITY (1970). In addition to the part of the dissertation published in 1953, a second portion appeared as William A. Westley, *Secrecy and the Police*, 34 SOC. FORCES 254 (1956).

40. Hall, *supra* note 38, at 145–46.

41. Westley, *supra* note 38, at 41; *see also* WESTLEY, *supra* note 39, at 10.

42. Hall, *supra* note 38, at 146.

43. *See, e.g.,* Maureen Cain, *Trends in the Sociology of Police Work*, 7 INT. J. SOC. L. 144–48 (1979).

44. WESTLEY, *supra* note 39, at 9; *see also* Westley, *supra* note 38, at 34; Westley, *supra* note 39, at 256–57.

45. Westley, *supra* note 39, at 256.

46. Westley, *supra* note 38, at 35.

47. Westley, *supra* note 39, at 256.

48. WESTLEY, *supra* note 39, at 10.

49. Maureen Cain, *Some Go Forward, Some Go Back: Police Work in Comparative Perspective*, 22 COMP. SOC. 319, 320 (1993); *see also, e.g.,* Stuart A. Scheingold, *Cultural Cleavage and Criminal Justice*, 40 J. POL. 865, 881–82 (1978); John Van Maanen, *Working the Street: A Developmental View of Police Behavior, in* THE POTENTIAL FOR CRIMINAL JUSTICE REFORM 83, 84–85 (Herbert Jacob ed., 1974). For a skeptical review, see Robert W. Balch, *The Police Personality: Fact or Fiction?*, 63 J. CRIM. L. CRIMINOLOGY & POLICE SCI. 106 (1972). For an early, dissenting perspective, see MICHAEL BANTON, THE POLICEMAN IN THE COMMUNITY 215–68 (1964).

50. *See* JEROME H. SKOLNICK, JUSTICE WITHOUT TRIAL: LAW ENFORCEMENT IN DEMOCRATIC SOCIETY 45 n.4, 49–59, 231 (1966); Wilson, *supra* note 36, at 191–94.

51. WILSON, *supra* note 34, at 33–34, 47.

52. SKOLNICK, *supra* note 50, at 61.

53. *See* SKOLNICK, *supra* note 50, at 259–62.

54. *See, e.g.*, BRIAN CHAPMAN, POLICE STATE 96 (1970); ARTHUR NIEDERHOFFER, BEHIND THE SHIELD: THE POLICE IN URBAN SOCIETY 103–51 (1967); *cf.* Balch, *supra* note 49, at 107 (noting that "the typical policeman, as he is portrayed in the literature, is almost a classic example of the authoritarian personality").

55. *See id.* at 192.

56. SKOLNICK, *supra* note 50, at 61. "Therefore it is preferable to call the police officer's a conventional personality." *Id.*

57. *See, e.g.*, CHRISTOPHER LASCH, THE AGONY OF THE AMERICAN LEFT 207 (1969); Thomas R. Brooks, *New York's Finest*, COMMENTARY, Aug. 1965, at 29, 31; James Ridgeway, *The Cops & the Kids*, NEW REPUBLIC, Sept. 7, 1968, at 11; Arthur L. Waskow, *Community Control of the Police*, TRANS-ACTION, Dec. 1969, at 4.

58. 333 U.S. 10, 14 (1948).

59. *Id.*

60. *See, e.g.*, Coolidge v. New Hampshire, 403 U.S. 443, 449 (1971); Chapman v. United States, 365 U.S. 610, 614 (1961).

61. Herbert L. Packer, *The Courts, The Police, and the Rest of Us*, 57 J. CRIM. L. CRIMINOLOGY & POLICE SCI. 238, 241 (1966).

62. Herbert Jacob, *Introduction, in* THE POTENTIAL FOR REFORM OF CRIMINAL JUSTICE 9, 10 (Herbert Jacob ed., 1974).

63. *See* Frank v. Maryland, 359 U.S. 360 (1959).

64. *See* Camara v. Municipal Court, 387 U.S. 523 (1967); See v. City of Seattle, 387 U.S. 541 (1967).

65. *See* United States v. Biswell, 406 U.S. 311 (1972); Colonade Catering Corp. v. United States, 397 U.S. 72 (1970).

66. *E.g.*, O'Connor v. Ortega, 480 U.S. 709, 720 (1987); New Jersey v. T.L.O., 469 U.S. 325, 351 (1985) (Blackmun, J., concurring).

67. *See, e.g.*, 4 WAYNE R. LaFAVE, SEARCH AND SEIZURE §10.1(b), at 373–80 (3d ed. 1996).

68. *See* Skinner v. Railway Labor Executives' Ass'n, 489 U.S. 602, 650 (1989) (Marshall, J., dissenting).

69. *Camara*, 387 U.S. at 530.

70. *See, e.g.*, Michigan Dep't of State Police v. Sitz, 496 U.S. 444 (1990); New York v. Burger, 482 U.S. 691, 717 (1987).

71. Illinois v. Lidster, 540 U.S. 419, 424–25 (2004).

72. Samson v. California, 126 S. Ct. 2193, 2200 (2006).

73. Hall, *supra* note 38, at 153, 156, 171.

74. *See supra* TRUMAN, *supra* note 12, at xli, 159, 512, 524.

75. WESTLEY, *supra* note 39, at 10.

76. *See, e.g.*, Herbert Packer, *Two Models of the Criminal Process*, 113 U. PA. L. REV. 24–38 (1964); Charles A. Reich, *Police Questioning of Law Abiding Citizens*, 75 YALE L.J. 1161, 1164–70 (1966).

77. Samuel Walker, *Origins of the Contemporary Criminal Justice Paradigm: The American Bar Foundation Survey, 1953–1969*, 9 JUST. Q. 47, 51, 56–58, 63 (1992).

78. *See id.* at 68–69; WAYNE R. LaFAVE, ARREST: THE DECISION TO TAKE THE SUSPECT INTO CUSTODY (1965); Herman Goldstein, *Police Discretion: The Ideal Versus the Real*, 23 PUB. ADMIN. REV. 148 (1963); Joseph Goldstein, *Police Discretion Not to Invoke the Criminal Process: Low-Visibility Decisions in the Administration of Justice*, 69 YALE L.J. 543 (1960); Sanford H. Kadish, *Legal Norm and Discretion in the Police and Sentencing Processes*, 75 HARV. L. REV. 904, 906–15 (1962); Wayne R. LaFave, *The Police and Nonenforcement of the Law* (pts. 1 & 2), 1962 WISC. L. REV. 105, 180; Frank Remington, *The Law Relating to "On the Street" Detention, Questioning and Frisking of Suspected Persons and Police Arrest Privileges in General*, 51 J. CRIM. L., CRIMINOLOGY, & POLICE SCI. 386 (1960).

79. Hall, *supra* note 38, at 154.

80. Jonathan Simon, *Speaking Truth and Power*, 36 LAW & SOC. REV. 39 (2002).

81. *See* SKOLNICK, *supra* note 50, at 199–202, 227–29. On the tendency of scholars in the 1960s to favor judicial control of the police, see, e.g., Egon Bittner, *The Police on Skid-Row: A Study of Peace Keeping*, 5 AM. SOC. REV. 699, 699–700 (1967). In his widely admired lectures at the University of Minnesota in 1974, Anthony Amsterdam urged the use of police administrators as intermediaries; expanding on an earlier suggestion by the administrative law scholar Kenneth Culp Davis, Amsterdam argued that police discretion should be reined in by police rulemaking. But he stressed that police rulemaking could be "created and maintained in working order only by the stimulation and the oversight of courts enforcing constitutional law." Anthony G. Amsterdam, *Perspectives on the Fourth Amendment*, 58 MINN. L. REV. 349, 380 (1974); *see also* KENNETH CULP DAVIS, DISCRETIONARY JUSTICE 65, 95 (1969).

82. Mapp v. Ohio, 367 U.S. 643 (1961).

83. Terry v. Ohio, 392 U.S. 1 (1968).

84. United States v. Wade, 388 U.S. 218 (1967); Miranda v. Arizona, 384 U.S. 436 (1966).

85. *Miranda*, 384 U.S. at 444–45.

86. Katz v. United States, 389 U.S. 347 (1967).

87. Chimel v. California, 395 U.S. 752 (1969).

88. Camara v. Municipal Court, 387 U.S. 523 (1967); See v. City of Seattle, 387 U.S. 541 (1967).

89. *See* United States v. Rabinowitz, 339 U.S. 56 (1950).

90. The most explicit rejection of *Rabinowitz* came in *Chimel*, 395 U.S. at 759–68.

91. *E.g.*, *Katz*, 392 U.S. at 20.

92. *See Rabinowitz*, 339 U.S. at 70 (Frankfurter, J., dissenting); Harris v. United

States, 331 U.S. 145, 161–62 (1947) (Frankfurter, J., dissenting); Davis v. United States, 328 U.S. 582, 595 (1946) (Frankfurter, J., dissenting); Amsterdam, *supra* note 81, at 396–97.

93. *See, e.g.,* Payton v. New York, 455 U.S. 573 (1980); United States v. Chadwick, 433 U.S. 1 (1977); United States v. United States District Court, 407 U.S. 297 (1972).

94. SKOLNICK, *supra* note 50, at 229.

95. Robert A. Dahl, *Decision-Making in a Democracy: The Supreme Court as a National Policy-Maker*, 6 J. PUB. L. 279, 291 (1957).

96. *See* Thomas W. Merrill, *Capture Theory and the Courts: 1967–1983*, 72 CHI.-KENT L. REV. 1039, 1056–59 (1997).

97. ALEXANDER M. BICKEL, THE LEAST DANGEROUS BRANCH: THE SUPREME COURT AT THE BAR OF POLITICS 16 (1962).

98. Dahl, *supra* note 95, at 294.

99. Hall, *supra* note 38, at 160.

100. William E. Connolly, *The Challenge to Pluralist Theory, in* THE BIAS OF PLURALISM 3, 22–23 (William E. Connolly ed., 1969).

101. *See* Malinski v. New York, 324 U.S. 401 (1945); Ashcraft v. Tennessee, 322 U.S. 143 (1944); Chambers v. Florida, 309 U.S. 227, 236 (1940); *cf.* Goldman v. United States, 316 U.S. 114, 142 (1941) (Murphy, J., dissenting) (stressing importance of protecting civil liberties, including Fourth Amendment rights, "[a]t a time when the nation is called upon to give freely of life and treasure to defend and preserve the institutions of democracy and freedom").

102. Hall, *supra* note 38, at 140.

103. *See* Irvine v. California, 347 U.S. 128, 149 (1954) (Douglas, J., dissenting); *Rabinowitz*, 339 U.S. at 82 (Frankfurter, J., dissenting); *Harris*, 331 U.S. at 171 (Frankfurter, J., dissenting). On the general subject of anti-totalitarian rhetoric in postwar criminal procedure, see Margaret Raymond, *Rejecting Totalitarianism: Translating the Guarantees of Constitutional Criminal Procedure*, 76 N.C. L. REV. 1193 (1998).

104. 333 U.S. 10, 17 (1948); *cf.* Wolf v. Colorado, 338 U.S. 25 (1949). Writing for the Court in *Wolf*, Justice Frankfurter called protection from "arbitrary" police intrusions "basic to a free society." *Id.* at 27. It did not take "the commentary of recent history," he noted, for the "knock at the door . . . as a prelude to a search, without authority of law but solely on the authority of the police . . . to be condemned as inconsistent with the conception of human rights enshrined in the history and the basic constitutional documents of English-speaking peoples." *Id.* at 28.

105. *See, e.g.,* Osborn v. United States, 385 U.S. 323, 343, 349, 352 (1966) (Douglas, J., dissenting); Lopez v. United States, 373 U.S. 427, 466, 470 (1962) (Brennan, J., dissenting).

106. *See, e.g.,* Escobedo v. Illinois, 378 U.S. 478 (1964); Spano v. New York, 360 U.S. 315 (1959).

107. 384 U.S. 436, 457 (1966).

108. Boyd v. United States, 116 U.S. 616, 630 (1886). On the fading of *Boyd*, a decision praised as late as the 1940s and 1950s as the leading interpretation of the Fourth Amendment, see, e.g., Note, *The Life and Times of* Boyd v. United States *(1886–1976)*, 76 MICH. L. REV. 184 (1977).

109. Katz v. United States, 389 U.S. 347, 362 (1967) (Harlan, J., concurring); *accord, e.g.*, Terry v. Ohio, 392 U.S. 1, 9 (1968).

110. *See, e.g.*, Raymond, *supra* note 101, at 1210–20.

111. David B. Truman, *The American System in Crisis*, 74 POL. SCI. Q. 481, 490 (1959); *see also, e.g.*, BERKLEY, *supra* note 31, at 4 (noting that "[a]lthough in former days the contract theory was often viewed as expressing the essence of democracy, more contemporary thinkers focus on . . . the affirmation of individual worth. Adlai Stevenson, for example, felt that the essence of democracy is the dignity of man.").

112. Dahl, *supra* note 95, at 295.

113. I describe this shift in greater detail in David A. Sklansky, *Back to the Future: Kyllo, Katz, and Common Law*, 72 MISS. L.J. 143, 149–60 (2002).

114. Katz v. United States, 389 U.S. 347, 352 (1967).

115. *See id.* at 362 (Harlan, J., concurring); *Terry*, 392 U.S. at 9.

116. *See Terry*, 392 U.S. at 19.

117. Amsterdam, *supra* note 81, at 395; *see also, e.g.*, Peter Arenella, *Fourth Amendment*, *in* ENCYCLOPEDIA OF THE AMERICAN CONSTITUTION 223 (Leonard Levy et al. eds., Supp. I 1992).

118. *Cf.* Reynolds v. Sims, 377 U.S. 533, 567 (1964) (noting that the United States, "once primarily rural in character," had become "predominantly urban"). In requiring that state legislative districts be of roughly equal population, the Court understood itself to be preventing the unfair advantaging of rural areas at the expense of cities and suburbs. The Court purported, of course, to care only about evenhandedness: Chief Justice Warren's majority opinion warned that "[m]alapportionment can, and historically has, run in various directions." *Id.* at 562 n.43. Still, the opinion had a faint but unmistakable air of urban condescension: "Legislators represent people, not trees or acres. . . . [P]eople, not land or trees or pastures, vote." *Id.* at 562, 580.

119. Papachristou v. City of Jacksonville, 405 U.S. 156, 164 (1972); *see also* Reich, *supra* note 76, at 1172 (warning that although "safety requires measures" so do "independence, boldness, creativity, high spirits"). The Court's opinion in *Papachristou*, written by Justice Douglas, cited Reich's article and plainly shared its spirit.

120. *See, e.g.*, William J. Stuntz, *The Uneasy Relationship Between Criminal Procedure and Criminal Justice*, 107 YALE L.J. 1, 24–25 (1997).

121. U.S. DEP'T OF JUSTICE, BUREAU OF JUSTICE STATISTICS, HOMICIDE TRENDS IN THE UNITED STATES (revised 2002).

122. *See, e.g.*, Parker, *supra* note 20; O. W. Wilson, *Police Authority in a Free Society*, 56 J. CRIM. L. CRIMINOLOGY & POLICE SCI. 175 (1963). On the relative lack of alarm

about crime in this period, despite rising crime rates, see DAVID GARLAND, THE CUL-
TURE OF CONTROL: CRIME AND SOCIAL ORDER IN CONTEMPORARY SOCIETY 66,
146–47, 152–54 (2001). Garland suggests that, starting in the 1970s, the threat of
crime began to be experienced as a "normal social fact," an "everyday risk" compa-
rable with traffic accidents. *Id.* at 106, 109. This seems to me to get things back-
wards. What happened in the 1970s was that crime *ceased* to be accepted as a normal,
everyday risk. But Garland's larger point about this social transformation seems
plainly right: crime became, beginning in the 1970s, "much more salient as a social
and cultural fact." *Id.* at 148.

123. *See, e.g.*, PRESIDENT'S COMM'N ON LAW ENF'T & THE ADMIN. OF JUSTICE, THE
CHALLENGE OF CRIME IN A FREE SOCIETY 12 (1967) (setting forth "the foundations of
a crime control program"). On the transformation of crime from a "challenge" to a
"crisis," to be eliminated rather than managed, see also Markus Dirk Dubber, *Criminal Justice Process and War on Crime, in* THE BLACKWELL COMPANION TO CRIMINOL-
OGY 49 (Colin Sumner ed., 2004).

124. David Luban, *The Adversary System Excuse, in* THE GOOD LAWYER: LAWYERS'
ROLES AND LAWYERS' ETHICS 83, 92 (David Luban ed., 1983); *see also, e.g.*, Murray
L. Schwartz, *The Zeal of the Civil Advocate,* 1983 AM. BAR FOUND. RES. J. 543, 553
(suggesting that "the basic purpose" of criminal procedure is "to avoid one type of
error"). By 1983, when both these pieces were published, homicide rates were significantly higher than in the 1950s or today—suggesting, again, that crime rates go
only so far in explaining levels of concern about crime and disorder.

125. *See* Cain, *supra* note 43, at 148–49. The seminal work was HOWARD S.
BECKER, OUTSIDERS: STUDIES IN THE SOCIOLOGY OF DEVIANCE (1963).

126. The change also reflected, in part, changes in urban life itself, and particularly
changes in patterns of urban crime. Unlike national homicide rates, big-city homicide
rates really did begin to skyrocket in the late 1960s. *See* Eric Monkkonen, *Homicide Over
the Centuries, in* THE CRIME CONUNDRUM: ESSAYS ON CRIMINAL JUSTICE 163, 166–67
(Lawrence M. Friedman & George Fisher eds., 1997). On other contributions to the
decline of the "cosmopolitan ideal," see David A. Hollinger, *Ethnic Diversity, Cosmopolitanism and the Emergence of the American Liberal Intelligentsia,* 27 AM. Q. 149–51 (1975).

127. *See, e.g.*, Akhil Reed Amar, *Fourth Amendment First Principles,* 107 HARV. L.
REV. 757 (1994).

128. *See, e.g.*, Louis Michael Seidman, Brown *and* Miranda, 80 CAL. L. REV. 673,
718–47 (1992).

129. *See, e.g.*, Tracey Maclin, Terry v. Ohio's *Fourth Amendment Legacy: Black Men
and Police Discretion,* 72 ST. JOHN'S L. REV. 1271 (1998).

130. *See* GOVERNOR'S COMM'N ON THE LOS ANGELES RIOTS, VIOLENCE IN THE
CITY—AN END OR A BEGINNING? (1965); NATIONAL ADVISORY COMM'N ON CIVIL DIS-
ORDERS, REPORT (1968); NATIONAL COMM'N ON THE CAUSES AND PREVENTION OF VIO-
LENCE, TO ESTABLISH JUSTICE, TO ENSURE DOMESTIC TRANQUILITY (1969);
PRESIDENT'S COMM'N ON CAMPUS UNREST, THE SCRANTON REPORT (1970).

131. *See* THE POLITICS OF RIOT COMMISSIONS, 1917–1970, at 3–54, 259–527 (Anthony M. Platt ed., 1971).

132. WILSON, *supra* note 34, at 289; *see also, e.g., id.* at 250 (characterizing voters as "political consumer[s]").

133. *E.g., id.* at 233.

134. Wilson, *supra* note 36, at 200–12 (quoting RICHARD HOFSTADTER, THE AGE OF REFORM (1960)).

135. *Id.* at 215. A fair amount might be said about Wilson's use of the term "jungle" to refer to the inner city. Among its tamer connotations, the term signaled Wilson's concern for orderliness, and his rejection of the pluralist enthusiasm for the hurly-burly of modern urban life. These themes grew more pronounced in his later writings, most famously in James Q. Wilson & George L. Kelling, *Broken Windows*, ATLANTIC MONTHLY, Mar. 1982, at 29. On that essay's "aesthetic of orderliness, cleanliness and sobriety," see BERNARD E. HARCOURT, ILLUSION OF ORDER: THE FALSE PROMISE OF BROKEN WINDOWS POLICING 23–27 (2001). On the broad influence of the essay, see Chapter 4.

136. WILSON, *supra* note 34, at 140–226.

137. *See id.* at 227–99.

138. *Id.* at 299.

139. *Id.* at 288.

140. *Id.* at 289; *see also* JAMES Q. WILSON, THINKING ABOUT CRIME 132–34 (1975).

141. WILSON, *supra* note 34, at 285 n.5.

142. WILSON, *supra* note 140, at xix.

143. On the critical role that proposals for citizen review boards played as focal points for police organizing in the late 1960s, see, e.g., STEPHEN C. HALPERN, POLICE-ASSOCIATION AND DEPARTMENT LEADERS: THE POLITICS OF CO-OPTATION 11–88 (1974); SKOLNICK, *supra* note 50, at 278–81; SAMUEL WALKER, POLICE ACCOUNTABILITY: THE ROLE OF CITIZEN OVERSIGHT 27–29 (2002).

144. *See* SKOLNICK, *supra* note 50, at 286–88; JEROME H. SKOLNICK, JUSTICE WITHOUT TRIAL: LAW ENFORCEMENT IN DEMOCRATIC SOCIETY 249–50, 258–62 (2d ed. 1975). An important development in this regard was the 1971 vote of no confidence in Chief Charles Gain of the Oakland Police Department by the local Police Officers' Association. Gain was a committed reformer who won the respect not only of Skolnick but also other scholars who used the Oakland department for sociological research on the police. *See* WILLIAM KER MUIR, JR., POLICE: STREETCORNER POLITICIANS (1977); HANS TOCH, J. DOUGLAS GRANT & RAYMOND T. GALVIN, AGENTS OF CHANGE: A STUDY IN POLICE REFORM (1975); Byron Michael Jackson, Leadership and Change in Public Organization: The Dilemmas of an Urban Police Chief (1979) (unpublished Ph.D. dissertation, University of California, Berkeley) (on file with author). Berkley, too, was favorably impressed with Gain's reforms. *See* BERKLEY, *supra* note 31, at 97, 103, 168, 198. More about Gain later in chapter 4, *infra*.

145. *See* WALKER, *supra* note 143.

146. On that theme, see, e.g., Dan M. Kahan & Tracey L. Meares, *The Coming Crisis of Criminal Procedure*, 86 GEO. L.J. 1153, 1156–59 (1998); and Louis Michael Seidman, *Akhil Amar and the (Premature?) Demise of Criminal Procedure Liberalism*, 107 YALE L.J. 2281, 2315–17 (1998).

147. Seidman, *supra* note 128, at 673; *see also* Tracey L. Meares, *What's Wrong with Gideon*, 70 U. CHI. L. REV. 215, 230 (2003). Consider, for example, the Court's deliberate downplaying of race in *Miranda*. *See* Seidman, *supra*, at 751 n.254.

148. *See, e.g.*, Gerald E. Frug, *The Ideology of Bureaucracy in American Law*, 97 HARV. L. REV. 1276 (1984).

149. *See, e.g.*, Connolly, *supra* note 100, at 13; MICHAEL PAUL ROGIN, THE INTELLECTUALS AND MCCARTHY: THE RADICAL SPECTER 269 (1967).

NOTES TO CHAPTER 3

1. On Jack Webb and *Dragnet*, see MICHAEL J. HAYDE, MY NAME'S FRIDAY: THE UNAUTHORIZED BUT TRUE STORY OF *DRAGNET* AND THE FILMS OF JACK WEBB (2001); DAVID MARC, DEMOGRAPHIC VISTAS: TELEVISION IN AMERICAN CULTURE 73–79 (rev. ed. 1984); Steven D. Stark, *Perry Mason Meets Sonny Crockett: The History of Lawyers and the Police as Television Heroes*, 42 U. MIAMI L. REV. 229, 244–45 (1987); Paul A. Jorgensen, *The Permanence of Dragnet*, 12 FILM Q. 35 (1958). On Friday as the "prototypical police professional," see also STEVE HERBERT, CITIZENS, COPS, AND POWER: RECOGNIZING THE LIMITS OF COMMUNITY 21 (2006).

2. *Jack, Be Nimble!*, TIME, Mar. 15, 1954, at 47.

3. *See* HAYDE, *supra* note 1, at 42, 60, 122, 172. When Webb died in 1982, the department flew its flags at half-mast and retired Joe Friday's badge number. *See id.* at 236.

4. *Id.* at 182.

5. *See id.* at 181–203; MARC, *supra* note 1, at 78–79.

6. MARC, *supra* note 1, at 74.

7. *See, e.g.*, HAYDE, *supra* note 1, at 174.

8. *See id.* at 118; MARC, *supra* note 1, at 75.

9. Arnold S. Kaufman, *Human Nature and Participatory Democracy*, *in* NOMOS III: RESPONSIBILITY 266 (Carl J. Friedrich ed., 1960).

10. *Id.* at 272, 289.

11. *See, e.g.*, HANNAH ARENDT, THE HUMAN CONDITION (1958).

12. JAMES MILLER, DEMOCRACY IS IN THE STREETS: FROM PORT HURON TO THE SIEGE OF CHICAGO 44, 111, 119 (paperback ed. 1994).

13. Port Huron Statement, *reprinted in id.* at 329, 333.

14. KIRKPATRICK SALE, SDS 69 (1973).

15. MILLER, *supra* note 12, at 142, 153. Kaufman remained convinced that it was "both possible and desirable vastly to extend the frontiers of participatory institutions

in many areas of social and political life," but by the late 1960s he warned that "uncritical exuberance" about participatory democracy had obscured "the nature and limits of a democracy of participation. For if participation provides an answer to many problems, it does not answer every problem; nor does it serve in any old form." Arnold S. Kaufman, *Participatory Democracy: Ten Years Later, in* THE BIAS OF PLURALISM 201, 203–04, 206 (William E. Connolly ed., 1969).

16. *See, e.g.*, MILLER, *supra* note 12, at 5, 55–61.

17. Port Huron Statement, *supra* note 13, at 333.

18. MILLER, *supra* note 12, at 310.

19. Port Huron Statement, *supra* note 13, at 333.

20. *See* Port Huron Statement, *supra* note 13, at 330–31. This theme in the Port Huron Statement drew heavily on the work of C. Wright Mills. *See* MILLER *supra* note 12, at 78–91; C. WRIGHT MILLS, THE POWER ELITE 298–324 (1956). It was influentially expanded from a neo-Marxist perspective in HERBERT MARCUSE, ONE-DIMENSIONAL MAN: STUDIES IN THE IDEOLOGY OF ADVANCED INDUSTRIAL SOCIETY (1964).

21. *See, e.g.*, GARY CROSS, AN ALL-CONSUMING CENTURY: WHY COMMERCIALISM WON IN MODERN AMERICA 146–55 (2000). The best-selling works of Vance Packard were particularly influential in this regard. *See* VANCE PACKARD, HIDDEN PERSUADERS (1957); VANCE PACKARD, THE WASTE MAKERS (1960); VANCE PACKARD, THE STATUS SEEKERS (1961); DANIEL HOROWITZ, VANCE PACKARD AND AMERICAN SOCIAL CRITICISM 148–52 (1994).

22. KENNETH PREWITT & ALAN STONE, THE RULING ELITES: ELITE THEORY, POWER, AND AMERICAN DEMOCRACY 195 (1973); *see also* DAVID HALBERSTAM, THE BEST AND THE BRIGHTEST (1973).

23. *See, e.g.*, CHRISTOPHER LASCH, THE AGONY OF THE AMERICAN LEFT 189 (1969) ("The system no longer responds to the expressed wishes of the voters. If they elect Lyndon Johnson as a dove, he turns into a hawk; if they try to end the war by voting for Robert Kennedy, the arbitrary, unpredictable, and meaningless act of an assassin thwarts this choice as well.").

24. E. E. SCHATTSCHNEIDER, THE SEMI-SOVEREIGN PEOPLE: A REALIST'S VIEW OF DEMOCRACY IN AMERICA 35 (1960).

25. MANCUR OLSON, THE LOGIC OF COLLECTIVE ACTION: PUBLIC GOODS AND THE THEORY OF GROUPS 127–28 (1965).

26. Port Huron Statement, *supra* note 13, at 329, 330. Here, too, the influence of C. Wright Mills was apparent.

27. SCHATTSCHNEIDER, *supra* note 24, at 68.

28. JEFFREY SKLANSKY, THE SOUL'S ECONOMY: MARKET SOCIETY AND SELFHOOD IN AMERICAN THOUGHT, 1820–1920, at 228 (2002).

29. Richard Flacks, *The Liberated Generation: An Exploration of the Roots of Student Protest*, 23 J. SOC. ISSUES 52, 56–57 (1967). On Flacks and SDS, see MILLER, *supra* note 12, at 157–83.

30. *See, e.g.*, CAROLE PATEMAN, PARTICIPATION AND DEMOCRATIC THEORY 24–25 (1970); William E. Connolly, *The Challenge to Pluralist Theory, in* THE BIAS OF PLURALISM 3, 10 (William E. Connolly ed., 1969).

31. *See, e.g.*, ABRAHAM H. MASLOW, MOTIVATION AND HUMAN PERSONALITY (1954); CARL R. ROGERS, ON BECOMING A PERSON (1961). On the influence of humanistic psychology on New Left ideology, see LASCH, *supra* note 23, at 181–82; Harry R. Targ, *Social Science and a New Social Order*, 8 J. PEACE RES. 207, 218 n.6 (1971).

32. MILLER, *supra* note 12, at 101 (quoting Tom Hayden).

33. *Id.* at 146.

34. *Id.* at 147.

35. *Id.*

36. For the former, see, e.g., JANE J. MANSBRIDGE, BEYOND ADVERSARY DEMOCRACY (1980); PATEMAN, *supra* note 30; MICHAEL J. SANDEL, DEMOCRACY'S DISCONTENT: AMERICA IN SEARCH OF PUBLIC PHILOSOPHY (1996). For the latter, see, e.g., Gerald E. Frug, *The Ideology of Bureaucracy in American Law*, 97 HARV. L. REV. 1276, 1295–96 (1984); Phillip Green, *'Democracy' as a Contested Idea, in* DEMOCRACY 2, 14–18 (Phillip Green ed., 1999); Hannah Fenischel Pitkin & Sarah M. Shumer, *On Participation*, 2 DEMOCRACY 43 (1982). Some work continued to straddle the divide, most notably BENJAMIN BARBER, STRONG DEMOCRACY: PARTICIPATORY POLITICS FOR A NEW AGE (1984).

37. *See, e.g.*, SANDEL, *supra* note 36; Cass R. Sunstein, *Beyond the Republican Revival*, 97 YALE L.J. 1539 (1988).

38. AMY GUTMANN & DENNIS THOMPSON, DEMOCRACY AND DISAGREEMENT 14 (1996); *see also, e.g.*, Joshua Cohen, *Procedure and Substance in Deliberative Democracy, in* DELIBERATIVE DEMOCRACY: ESSAYS ON REASON AND POLITICS 407 (James Bohman & William Rehg eds., 1997); Robert C. Post, *Racist Speech, Democracy, and the First Amendment*, 32 WM. & MARY L. REV. 267, 279–85 (1991). For a helpful overview, see Samuel Freeman, *Deliberative Democracy: A Sympathetic Account*, 29 PHIL. & PUB. AFF. 371 (2000). For a skeptical treatment, see Christopher H. Schroeder, *Deliberative Democracy's Attempt to Turn Politics into Law*, 65 LAW & CONTEMP. PROBS. 95 (2002).

39. Frug, *supra* note 36, at 1296.

40. ROBERT A. DAHL, AFTER THE REVOLUTION?, at 81 (1970).

41. RICHARD M. NIXON, *Toward an Expanded Democracy* (June 27, 1968), *in* NIXON SPEAKS OUT: MAJOR SPEECHES AND STATEMENTS BY RICHARD M. NIXON IN THE PRESIDENTIAL CAMPAIGN OF 1968, at 9, 15 (1968).

42. State of the Union (Jan. 22, 1971), *in* 7 WEEKLY COMP. PRES. DOCS. 89, 96 (Jan. 25, 1971). The development was trans-Atlantic. General DeGaulle called in the late 1960s for a "policy of participation" for French laborers. *See* Kaufman, *supra* note 15, at 210–11. A decade later the British government committed itself "to strengthen our democracy by providing new opportunities for citizens to take part

in the decisions that affect their lives." The Queen's Speech, 396 PARLIAMENTARY DEBATES (HANSARD) 1, 4 (Nov. 1, 1978).

43. Kaufman, *supra* note 15, at 211. Nixon also used the rhetoric of participatory democracy to support the conservative strategy of shifting power from the federal government to states, localities, and the private sector. *See* NIXON, *supra* note 41, at 16; State of the Union, *supra* note 42, at 94.

44. *Id.*

45. *Id.*

46. *See* Freeman, *supra* note 38, at 378.

47. Cohen, *supra* note 38, at 407.

48. Post, *supra* note 38, at 282.

49. Cohen, *supra* note 38, at 415.

50. *See, e.g.*, Freeman, *supra* note 38, at 383.

51. JOHN DEWEY, THE PUBLIC AND ITS PROBLEMS 217 (1946 ed.) (1927); *see also* MILLER, *supra* note 12, at 84–85; MILLS, *supra* note 20, at 298–301; Port Huron Statement, *supra* note 13, at 336.

52. DEWEY, *supra* note 51, at 208.

53. PATEMAN, *supra* note 30, at 1.

54. JACK LIVELY, DEMOCRACY 82 (1975).

55. Post, *supra* note 38, at 281–82 (emphasis added).

56. *See* GUTMANN & THOMPSON, *supra* note 38, at 41–42.

57. Freeman, *supra* note 38, at 380.

58. *E.g.*, GUTMANN & THOMPSON, *supra* note 38, at 16.

59. *See, e.g., id.* at 358–69; Schroeder, *supra* note 38, at 111–13. On the tendency of arguments for deliberative democracy to finesse the problem of the second best, see Jon Elster, *The Market and the Forum: Three Varieties of Political Theory, in* DELIBERATIVE DEMOCRACY, *supra* note 38, at 3, 18; Frederick Schauer, *Talking as a Decision Procedure, in* DELIBERATIVE POLITICS: ESSAYS ON *DEMOCRACY AND DISAGREEMENT* 17, 20–26 (Stephen Macedo ed., 1999).

60. GUTMANN & THOMPSON, *supra* note 38, at 359. Joshua Cohen may be an exception in this regard. *See* Cohen, *supra* note 38, at 412–13.

61. Schroeder, *supra* note 38, at 116–17.

62. This is a trade-off Schroeder stresses. *See id.* at 121–23.

63. Stephen Breyer, *Our Democratic Constitution*, 77 N.Y.U. L. REV. 245, 248 (2002) (reprinting 2001 James Madison Lecture at New York University Law School); *see also* STEVEN BREYER, ACTIVE LIBERTY: INTERPRETING OUR DEMOCRATIC CONSTITUTION (2005) (reprinting 2004 Tanner Lectures on Human Values at Harvard University).

64. Breyer, *supra* note 63, at 249.

65. *Id.* at 263; *see also* BREYER, *supra* note 63, at 70–71.

66. Breyer, *supra* note 63, at 253 (emphasis added).

67. BREYER, *supra* note 63, at 70. Something like Breyer's watered-down, status

quo version of participatory democracy forms a key part—probably the rhetorical core—of "contented republicanism," one of the four democratic "discourses" that political scientists John Dryzek and Jeffrey Berejikian identified in the cross section of Americans they studied in the early 1990s. John S. Dryzek & Jeffrey Berejikian, *Reconstructive Democratic Theory*, 87 AM. POL. SCI. REV. 48, 52 (1993). Contented republicans treat "political equality as an established fact," perceive "no structural impediments" to more extensive participation, and believe that politics is "already pervaded by public spirit," so that "all that needs to be done is to make the most of it." *Id.* at 55, 58. Tellingly, none of the four discourses found by Dryzek and Berejikian include the key tenets of pluralism: "the aggregation and articulation of preferences through organized interest groups, leavened by a democracy that can be only representative, never direct." *See* John S. Dryzek, *The Informal Logic of Institutional Design, in* THE THEORY OF INSTITUTIONAL DESIGN (Robert E. Goodwin ed., 1996), at 103, 117.

68. MILLER, *supra* note 12, at 147. On this theme, see also KENNETH KENISTON, YOUNG RADICALS: NOTES ON COMMITTED YOUTH 275–77 (1968).

69. Port Huron Statement, *supra* note 13, at 366.

70. JANE JACOBS, THE DEATH AND LIFE OF GREAT AMERICAN CITIES 379 (1961) (Vintage Books ed. 1992); *see also id.* at 50, 116, 150, 289–90, 340, 374, 379, 444.

71. *See, e.g.*, MILLS, *supra* note 20, at 350–61. On Mills's use of "classical democracy" as a Weberian ideal-type, see MILLER, *supra* note 12, at 83–91.

72. STAUGHTON LYND & TOM HADEN, THE OTHER SIDE 200 (1966).

73. *See, e.g.*, MANSBRIDGE, *supra* note 36; PATEMAN, *supra* note 30.

74. *See* MILLER, *supra* note 12, at 6. On the resurgence in the 1970s of the "antimodern" themes of "tradition, order, hierarchy, and authority," see DAVID GARLAND, THE CULTURE OF CONTROL: CRIME AND SOCIAL ORDER IN CONTEMPORARY SOCIETY 98–102 (2001).

NOTES TO CHAPTER 4

1. WILLIAM BRATTON WITH PETER KNOBLER, TURNAROUND: HOW AMERICA'S TOP COP REVERSED THE CRIME EPIDEMIC (1998); Eric Pooley & Elaine Rivera, *One Good Apple*, TIME, Jan. 15, 1996, at 1, 54.

2. William J. Bratton, *Dispelling New York's Latest Fear*, N.Y. TIMES, Feb. 28, 1999, § 4, at 19.

3. See, for example, the photographs opposite page 274 of Benjamin Barber's 1974 book, *The Death of Communal Liberty: A History of Freedom in a Swiss Mountain Canton.* An outdoor assembly of thoughtful alpine villagers, photographed heroically from below, appears over the caption "Direct Democracy." To illustrate "Representative Democracy," Barber selected a photograph of police dragging away a protester.

4. Richard Flacks, *The Liberated Generation: An Exploration of the Roots of Student Protest*, 23 J. Soc. Issues 52, 56–57 (1967); *see also, e.g.*, James Miller, Democracy is in the Streets: From Port Huron to the Siege of Chicago 7 (paperback ed. 1994) (setting student politics of the 1960s in the context of a broader, "unfettered cultural spirit," in which "musicians, movie directors, and student radicals all tried to lay waste to some part of the old order: no more melody, no more narrative, no more governing structure; no taste, no reason, no law and order").

5. *See, e.g.*, Robert M. Fogelson, Big-City Police 243–68 (1977).

6. James Baldwin, Nobody Knows My Name: More Notes of a Native Son 66 (1962).

7. *See, e.g.*, Fogelson, *supra* note 5, at 239–42; Christopher Lasch, The Agony of the American Left 206 (1969); Jerome H. Skolnick, The Politics of Protest 274–78 (Ballantine Books 1969).

8. John Thomas Delaney & Peter Feuille, *Police, in* Collective Bargaining in American Industry: Contemporary Perspectives and Future Directions 265, 301 (David B. Lipsky & Clifford B. Donn eds., 1987); *see also, e.g.*, Stephen C. Halpern, Police-Association and Department Leaders: The Politics of Co-Optation 93–99 (1974).

9. *See, e.g.*, Fogelson, *supra* note 5, at 284–86.

10. Samuel Walker, Police Accountability: The Role of Citizen Oversight 40 (2002).

11. *See, e.g.*, Michael Fehr, *The 1992 Police Civilian Review Board Controversy in San Jose, in* Police Association Power, Politics, and Confrontation: A Guide for the Successful Police Labor Leader 259 (John Burpo, Ron DeLord & Michael Shannon eds., 1997).

12. *See, e.g.*, Fogelson, *supra* note 5, at 296–300.

13. *See, e.g.*, Herman Goldstein, Policing a Free Society 145 (1977).

14. Jerome Skolnick, *Neighborhood Police*, The Nation, Mar. 22, 1971, at 372.

15. *See* Fogelson, *supra* note 5, at 300.

16. *See* Michael E. Buerger, *The Limits of Community, in* The Challenge of Community Policing: Testing the Promises 270 (Dennis P. Rosenbaum ed., 1994); Gerald Frug, *City Services*, 73 N.Y.U. L. Rev. 23, 81 (1998).

17. *See, e.g.*, David Jenkins, Job Power: Blue and White Collar Democracy (1973); Jane J. Mansbridge, Beyond Adversary Democracy 278–302 (1980); Carole Pateman, Participation and Democratic Theory 109–10 (1970); Philip Selznick, Law, Society, and Industrial Justice (1969).

18. William A. Westley, Violence and the Police: A Sociological Study of Law, Custom, and Morality xvii (1970).

19. George E. Berkley, The Democratic Policeman 29–39 (1969).

20. John E. Angell, *Toward an Alternative to the Classic Police Organizational Arrangements: A Democratic Model*, 9 Criminology 185, 187, 193–95 (1971).

21. *See* Lawrence W. Sherman, *Middle Management and Police Democratization: A*

Reply to John E. Angell, 12 CRIMINOLOGY 363 (1975); John E. Angell, *The Democratic Model Needs a Fair Trial: Angell's Response*, 12 CRIMINOLOGY 379 (1975).

22. *See, e.g.*, PETER B. BLOCH & DAVID SPECHT, NEIGHBORHOOD TEAM POLICING (1973); WILLIAM G. GAY, H. TALMADGE DAY & JANE P. WOODWARD, NEIGHBORHOOD TEAM POLICING (1977); LAWRENCE W. SHERMAN, CATHERINE H. MILTON & THOMAS V. KELLY, TEAM POLICING: SEVEN CASE STUDIES (1973).

23. *See* EGON BITTNER, THE FUNCTIONS OF THE POLICE IN MODERN SOCIETY: A REVIEW OF BACKGROUND FACTORS, CURRENT PRACTICES, AND POSSIBLE ROLE MODELS (1970), *reprinted in* EGON BITTNER, ASPECTS OF POLICE WORK 89, 162–68 (1990). On Bittner's impact, see William D. Darrough, Book Review, 70 SOC. FORCES 846 (1992); P. K. Manning, Book Review, 20 CONTEMP. SOC. 435 (1991).

24. WILLIAM KER MUIR, JR., POLICE: STREETCORNER POLITICIANS (1977).

25. *Id.* at 253.

26. *Id.*

27. HANS TOCH, J. DOUGLAS GRANT & RAYMOND T. GALVIN, AGENTS OF CHANGE: A STUDY IN POLICE REFORM (1975). The study was reprinted and expanded in HANS TOCH & J. DOUGLAS GRANT, POLICE AS PROBLEM SOLVERS (1991). The Peer Review Panel and many of Gain's other innovations were eliminated by Gain's successor for budgetary reasons. *See* JEROME K. SKOLNICK & DAVID H. BAYLEY, THE NEW BLUE LINE: POLICE INNOVATION IN SIX AMERICAN CITIES 151–52 (1986). Toch and Grant note that "[t]he Oakland police began to experience violence problems almost soon as the interventions were discontinued." *Id.* at 85.

28. *See also, e.g.*, DAVID H. BAYLEY & HAROLD MENDELSOHN, MINORITIES AND THE POLICE: CONFRONTATION IN AMERICA 198–200 (1969) (calling police officers "exceedingly knowledgeable . . . about the requirements for successful police work," noting that their knowledge remained "unorganized and unexploited," and arguing that officers "must begin openly and creatively to study and discuss the discretionary aspects of their work").

29. *See* Reinhard Bendix, *Industrialization, Ideologies, and Social Structure*, 24 AM. SOC. REV. 613, 619–22 (1959), *reprinted in* REINHARD BENDIX, WORK AND AUTHORITY IN INDUSTRY: IDEOLOGIES OF MANAGEMENT IN THE COURSE OF INDUSTRIALIZATION 434, 444–48 (Harper Torchbook ed. 1963) (1956). On Bendix, see Paul Hollander, *In Pursuit of the Great Questions of History: Reinhard Bendix and American Sociology*, 20 CONTEMP. SOC. 726 (1991).

30. JEROME H. SKOLNICK, JUSTICE WITHOUT TRIAL: LAW ENFORCEMENT IN DEMOCRATIC SOCIETY 231–32 (1966).

31. *Id.* at 230.

32. In this regard, see also John M. Jermier & Leslie J. Berkes, *Leader Behavior in a Police Command Bureaucracy: A Closer Look a the Quasi-Military Model*, 24 ADMIN. SCI. Q. 1, 16–19 (1979) (finding that "participative leadership" raised the morale of police officers, and suggesting that "much of police authoritarianism and perhaps police brutality" might be traceable to "the authoritarian command model").

33. Among the holdouts were Dorothy Guyot, Policing as Though People Matter (1991) and Toch & Grant, *supra* note 27.

34. Skolnick & Bayley, *supra* note 27, at 214–15. Writing in 1986, Skolnick and Bayley identified "three dimensions of strategic change" lumped together by the phrase "team policing": "decentralization of command, integration of service delivery, and mobilization of communities in their own defense." *Id.* at 215.

35. *See, e.g., id.* at 160.

36. Gary T. Marx, *Police Power, in* Encyclopedia of Democracy 954 (Seymour Martin Lipset ed., 1995). A revised version of the essay appears as Gary T. Marx, *Police and Democracy, in* Policing, Security and Democracy: Theory and Practice 35 (Menachem Amir & Stanley Einstein eds., 2001).

37. Fogelson, *supra* note 5, at 301.

38. Steve Herbert, Citizens, Cops, and Power: Recognizing the Limits of Community 134 (2006).

39. For a sympathetic overview of the new orthodoxy, see Debra Livingston, *Police Discretion and the Quality of Life in Public Places: Courts, Communities, and the New Policing,* 97 Colum. L. Rev. 551 (1997).

40. Paul Jacobs, *The Los Angeles Police,* Atlantic, Dec. 1966, at 95, 101.

41. *Id.*

42. *See, e.g.,* Buerger, *supra* note 16, at 270–71; Frug, *supra* note 16, at 81.

43. Peter K. Manning, *Community Policing as a Drama of Control, in* Community Policing: Rhetoric or Reality 27, 43 (Jack R. Green & Stephen D. Mastrofski eds., 1988); *see also, e.g.,* Michael C. Dorf & Charles F. Sabel, *A Constitution of Democratic Experimentalism,* 98 Colum. L. Rev. 267, 327–32 (1998).

44. *See, e.g.,* Herbert, *supra* note 38, at 55–93; Buerger, *supra* note 16, at 272–73; Carl B. Klockars, *The Rhetoric of Community Policing, in* Community Policing: Rhetoric or Reality, *supra* note 43, at 239, 247–50; *cf.* Robert Weisberg, *Restorative Justice and the Danger of "Community,"* 2003 Utah L. Rev. 343 (2003). Not all arguments for community policing are vulnerable to this objection. David Thacher, for example, praises community policing for "exposing police more systematically to a diversity of values" and "putting a premium on their ability to secure cooperation from the groups that are committed to those values." David Thacher, *Conflicting Values in Community Policing,* 35 Law & Soc'y Rev. 765, 795 (2001). But much of what makes Thacher's views interesting is precisely that they are unconventional. I discuss Thacher's views in more detail in Chapter 6.

45. Toch & Grant, *supra* note 27, at 248. On the nostalgia of the community policing movement for a cleaner, more orderly past, see also Herbert, *supra* note 38, at 18, 23, 92; Buerger, *supra* note 16, at 272; Manning, *supra* note 43, at 30, 35.

46. *See, e.g.,* Bernard E. Harcourt, Illusion of Order: The False Promise of Broken Windows Policing 10, 19, 173–75, 177–78 (2001); Dan M. Kahan & Tracey L. Meares, *The Coming Crisis of Criminal Procedure,* 86 Geo. L.J. 1153, 1163 (1998).

47. *See* Tracey L. Meares & Bernard E. Harcourt, *Foreword: Transparent Adjudication*

and Social Science Research in Constitutional Criminal Procedure, 90 J. CRIM. L. & CRIM-
INOLOGY 733 (2000); Tracey L. Meares, *Three Objections to the Use of Empiricism in
Criminal Law and Procedure—And Three Answers,* 2002 U. ILL. L. REV. 851.

48. *See* Robert Weisberg, *Criminal Law, Criminology, and the Small World of Legal
Scholars,* 63 U. COLO. L. REV. 521, 530–31 (1992).

49. Ronald F. Wright, Book Review, 14 CONS. COMMENT. 557 (1997) (reviewing
AKHIL REED AMAR, THE CONSTITUTION AND CRIMINAL PROCEDURE: FIRST PRINCIPLES
(1997)); *see also, e.g.,* Louis Michael Seidman, *Akhil Amar and the (Premature?) Demise
of Criminal Procedure Liberalism,* 107 YALE L.J. 2281, 2282 (1998) (arguing that
Amar's work "simultaneously symbolizes and helps propel the flood tide away from
criminal procedure liberalism," and therefore forms "part of a significant movement
that has produced a secular change in the politics of criminal procedure"). For com-
parable reactions to the work of Kahan and Meares, see, e.g., HARCOURT, *supra* note
46, at 37–45; David Cole, *Discretion and Discrimination Reconsidered: A Response to the
New Criminal Justice Scholarship,* 87 GEO. L.J. 1059 (1999); Richard Pildes, *The New
Progressives,* BOSTON REV., April/May 1999, at 21.

50. *E.g.,* Akhil Reed Amar, *Fourth Amendment First Principles,* 107 HARV. L. REV.
757, 817–19 (1994) [hereinafter Amar, *Fourth Amendment First Principles*]; *see also*
Akhil Reed Amar, *Reinventing Juries: Ten Suggested Reforms,* 28 U.C. DAVIS L. REV.
1169 (1995) [hereinafter Amar, *Reinventing Juries*].

51. ALEXIS DE TOCQUEVILLE, DEMOCRACY IN AMERICA 262 (Harvey C. Mansfield &
Delba Winthrop trans. & eds., 2000) (1835).

52. Amar, *Fourth Amendment First Principles, supra* note 50, at 818; *cf.* Akhil Reed
Amar, *Foreword: The Document and the Doctrine,* 114 HARV. L. REV. 26 (2000) (praising "the sound instincts of ordinary Americans"); Akhil Reed Amar, *Three Cheers
(and Two Quibbles) for Professor Kennedy,* 111 HARV. L. REV. 1256, 1265 n.26 (1998)
[hereinafter Amar, *Three Cheers*] (arguing that juries "should function as the democratic lower house of a bicameral judiciary," facilitating "a common conversation
affirming and nurturing a deliberative democracy"). Amar's work is part of a
broader academic trend toward renewed appreciation for the virtues of juries as instruments of participatory and deliberative democracy. For other notable examples,
see JEFFREY ABRAMSON, WE, THE JURY: THE JURY SYSTEM AND THE IDEAL OF
DEMOCRACY 6 (1994) (praising juries for reflecting "the values and common sense
of the people"); Lani Guinier, *No Two Votes: The Elusive Quest for Political Equality,*
77 VA. L. REV. 1413, 1485–87 (1991) (proposing "to promote the deliberative process" by restructuring local legislative bodies "in the image of the ideal, consensus-
driven jury"); Jenia Iontcheva, *Jury Sentencing as Democratic Practice,* 89 VA. L. REV.
311 (2003) (describing the jury as a "model deliberative democratic body"); Laurie
L. Levenson, *Change of Venue and the Role of the Criminal Jury,* 66 S. CAL. L. REV.
1533 (1993) (arguing that juries can and should provide "community representation
in criminal trials"); Richard A. Primus, *When Democracy Is Not Self-Government:
Toward a Defense of the Unanimity Rule for Criminal Juries,* 18 CARDOZO L. REV. 1417

(1997) (arguing that "[t]he conception of democracy most appropriate to juries" is "a form of deliberative democracy . . . that sees deliberation as a means to the accurate discovery of exogenous facts"). The Supreme Court, too, now inclines toward seeing the jury as a model instrument of democracy. *See* Blakely v. Washington, 124 S. Ct. 2531, 2539 (2004) (reasoning that "[j]ust as suffrage ensures the people's ultimate control in the legislative and executive branches, jury trial is meant to ensure their control in the judiciary").

53. *See, e.g.*, Kahan & Meares, *supra* note 46; Dan M. Kahan, *Reciprocity, Collective Action, and Community Policing*, 90 CAL. L. REV. 1513 (2002); Tracey L. Meares, *Praying for Community Policing*, 90 CAL. L. REV. 1593 (2002). For a more qualified argument along similar lines, see Livingston, *supra* note 39, at 646–50, 653–70.

54. *See* Dan M. Kahan & Tracey L. Meares, *The Wages of Antiquated Procedural Thinking: A Critique of* Chicago v. Morales, 1998 U. CHI. LEGAL F. 197.

55. *Id.* at 207; *see also, e.g.*, Dan M. Kahan & Tracey L. Meares, *When Rights Are Wrong: Chicago's Paradox of Unwanted Rights*, BOSTON REV., April/May 1999, at 4, 5; *cf.* Craig Bradley, *The Middle Class Fourth Amendment*, 6 BUFF. CRIM. L. REV. 1123, 1126–28 (2003) (suggesting that rising political power of racial minorities has rendered increasingly irrelevant "the great theme of the Warren Court—that the criminal justice system had to be massively reformed to protect the constitutional rights of all citizens").

56. This assumption is also shared by another important strand of contemporary criminal procedure scholarship: the strand calling for greater participation of victims in the criminal justice system. George Fletcher, for example, argues for increased participation of victims in criminal trials in order to "facilitate the public's expressing solidarity with victims." GEORGE P. FLETCHER, WITH JUSTICE FOR SOME: VICTIMS' RIGHTS IN CRIMINAL TRIALS 257 (1995). On the growing use of criminal victimization to build social solidarity, see DAVID GARLAND, THE CULTURE OF CONTROL: CRIME AND SOCIAL ORDER IN CONTEMPORARY SOCIETY 143–44 (2001); Jonathan Simon, *Governing Through Crime Metaphors*, 67 BROOK. L. REV. 1035, 1042–43 (2002); Jonathan Simon, *Megan's Law: Crime and Democracy in Late Modern America*, 25 L. & SOC. INQUIRY 1111, 1128–35 (2000).

57. Dan M. Kahan & Tracey L. Meares, *Meares and Kahan Respond*, BOSTON REV., April/May 1999, at 22.

58. Kahan & Meares, *supra* note 55, at 6.

59. *Id.*; *accord*, Kahan & Meares, *supra* note 46, at 1179.

60. The health metaphor is also found in many discussions of community policing. The Oakland Police Department's early effort at community policing, for example, used the slogan "Beat Health." *See* SKOLNICK & BAYLEY, *supra* note 27, at 159–62. The idea of neighborhood "health" resonates strongly with the theme of orderliness, to which we will return below.

61. Kahan & Meares, *supra* note 46, at 1154.

62. New Jersey v. T.L.O., 469 U.S. 325, 340 (1985).

63. *Id.* at 336.

64. *Id.*

65. Vernonia Sch. Dist. 47J v. Acton, 515 U.S. 646, 650, 654–55, 665 (1995). Kahan and Meares read *Vernonia* to stand, in fact, for the proposition that "random drug-testing of student athletes is exempted from the warrant requirement" because parents, "who naturally take their children's interests to heart," have "significant influence in the political process." Kahan & Meares, *supra* note 46, at 1173. Well, yes and no. The political participation of parents played no role in the formal, doctrinal explanation the Court gave for its decision, but it surely was part of the rhetorical atmosphere of the Court's opinion.

66. Board of Education v. Earls, 536 U.S. 822, 841 (2002) (Breyer, J., concurring). Predictably, Justice Breyer is also impressed with the democratic function juries serve in representing the moral sense of the community. *See* Ring v. Arizona, 536 U.S. 584, 615–16 (2002) (Breyer, J., concurring).

67. Compare, e.g., the textualist manifesto in ANTONIN SCALIA, A MATTER OF INTERPRETATION: FEDERAL COURTS AND THE LAW (1977), with the call for greater attention to "real-world consequences" in Stephen Breyer, *Our Democratic Constitution*, 77 N.Y.U. L. REV. 245, 246–47, 249, 269–71 (2002).

68. 527 U.S. 41 (1999).

69. Kahan & Meares, *supra* note 54, at 198; *see also* Kahan & Meares, *supra* note 46, at 1166; Tracey L. Meares, *Place and Crime*, 73 CHICAGO-KENT L. REV. 669, 700 (1998); Tracey L. Meares & Dan M. Kahan, *Law and (Norms of) Order in the Inner City*, 32 L. & SOC'Y REV. 805, 820–21 (1998). When the Supreme Court took up *Morales*, Kahan and Meares filed an amicus brief on behalf of twenty Chicago neighborhood groups supporting the loitering law. *See* Brief Amicus Curiae of the Chicago Neighborhood Associations in Support of Petitioner at 2, Chicago v. Morales, 527 U.S. 41 (1999) (No. 97–1121). Other neighborhood groups, and several prominent organizations representing members of racial minorities, joined amicus briefs opposing the ordinance. *See* Brief of Chicago Alliance for Neighborhood Safety, U.S. Representative Jesse Jackson, Jr., Community Renewal Society, National Association for the Advancement of Colored People, National Council of La Raza, Mexican-American Legal Defense Fund, Chicago Council of Lawyers, Cook County Bar Association, Puerto Rican Bar Association of Illinois, The Black Leadership Forum, Inc., Chicago Conference of Black Lawyers and Chicago Community Organizations as Amici Curiae in Support of Respondents; Brief of National Law Center on Homelessness and Poverty, National Alliance to End Homelessness, National Coalition for the Homeless, Chicago Coalition for the Homeless and National Network for Youth as Amici Curiae Supporting Respondents; Brief Amicus Curiae of See Forever/The Maya Angelou Public Charter School in Support of Respondents; Brief of Amicus Curiae National Black Police Association, Chicago NBPA, Hispanic National Law Enforcement Association, and NAACP Legal Defense & Educational Fund, Inc., in Support of Respondents.

70. 527 U.S. at 60–64; *see also id.* at 70 (Breyer, J., concurring).

71. *Id.* at 100–01 (Thomas, J., dissenting); *see also id.* at 97–98 (Scalia, J., dissenting). Chief Justice Rehnquist and Justice Scalia joined the dissent by Justice Thomas.

72. *Id.* at 87 (Scalia, J., dissenting); *see also id.* at 98 (Thomas, J., dissenting) (charging that the Court had "unnecessarily sentenced law-abiding citizens to lives of terror and misery").

73. Professor Raymond points to other evidence that the trope of the police state may be going out of fashion in criminal procedure jurisprudence, or at least that consensus regarding the rhetoric's acceptability may be breaking down. *See* Margaret Raymond, *Rejecting Totalitarianism: Translating the Guarantees of Constitutional Criminal Procedure*, 76 N.C. L. Rev. 1193, 1223–24 (1998).

74. 527 U.S. at 65 (O'Connor, J., concurring) (quoting *id.* at 109 (Thomas, J., dissenting)). Justice Breyer joined Justice O'Connor's concurrence. That opinion was also notable for its pointed suggestions regarding how the Chicago ordinance might be redrafted to cure its vagueness. *Id.* at 66. The ordinance was subsequently reenacted in a form that incorporated most of Justice O'Connor's suggestions. *See* Harcourt, *supra* note 46, at 51–52; Eric Luna, *Constitutional Road Maps*, 90 J. Crim. L. & Criminology 1125, 1141–43 (2000). On the equivocal tone taken by the justices in the majority, see, e.g., Debra Livingston, *Gang Loitering, The Court, and Some Realism About Police Patrol*, 1999 Sup. Ct. Rev. 141, 144–45.

75. Eric Luna, *Transparent Policing*, 85 Iowa L. Rev. 1107, 1120 (2000).

76. Jerome H. Skolnick, *On Democratic Policing* 2 (Police Foundation, Aug. 1999); William J. Bratton, *Dispelling New York's Latest Fear*, N.Y. Times, Feb. 28, 1999, § 4, at 19. For other echoes of Luna's argument, see, for example, William J. Stuntz, *Local Policing After the Terror*, 111 Yale L.J. 2137, 2167, 2180 (2002).

77. *See* United States v. Wade, 388 U.S. 218 (1967); Miranda v. Arizona, 384 U.S. 436 (1966).

78. *See, e.g.*, Amy Gutmann & Dennis Thompson, Democracy and Disagreement 95–127 (1996).

79. Luna, *supra* note 75, at 1120. Luna strives for a degree of catholicity regarding democratic theory; he claims that transparent policing is important under any plausible view of collective self-rule. *Id.* at 1130–31. But he sees only "two rough approaches to democratic decisionmaking in American politics: populism and progressivism." *Id.* at 1127. That framework blurs the differences between varieties of participatory democracy, and it hides the significance of democratic pluralism by reducing it to simply another version of progressivism. The heart of Luna's argument, in any event, appeals to the need to build trust and legitimacy by giving people a "voice" in decision making—the characteristic agenda of what I have been calling status quo participatory democracy.

80. Kahan & Meares, *supra* note 55, at 5; Tracey L. Meares, Terry *and the Relevance of Politics*, 72 St. John's L. Rev. 1343, 1344 (1998); *see also, e.g.*, Livingston, *supra* note 39, at 650–70.

81. Jonathan Simon, *Crime, Community, and Criminal Justice*, 90 CAL. L. REV. 1415, 1418 (2002); *see also* GARLAND, *supra* note 56, at 150–52; Franklin E. Zimring, *Populism, Democratic Government, and the Decline of Expert Authority: Some Reflections on 'Three Strikes' in California*, 28 Pac. L.J. 243, 253–56 (1996). Tellingly, the federal sentencing guidelines, which are an important part of the trend that these scholars describe (*see* GARLAND, *supra* note 56, at 151; Zimring, *supra*, at 256), have themselves been attacked as an exercise in anti-democratic "technocracy." William J. Stuntz, *The Pathological Politics of Criminal Law*, 100 MICH. L. REV. 505, 586 (2001). Stuntz probably reflects the general view among scholars today when he suggests that "[t]o the extent that criminal law deals with contestable, and contested, moral questions, one might imagine trading a good deal of expertise for a little democracy." *Id.*

82. *See* Meares, *supra* note 47; Meares & Harcourt, *supra* note 47.

83. *See* Kahan & Meares, *supra* note 46, at 1163.

84. *Id.* at 1176–80; *see also, e.g., id.* at 1168.

85. *See* Amar, *Reinventing Juries*, *supra* note 50, at 1182; *see also, e.g.,* Akhil Reed Amar & Jonathan L. Marcus, *Double Jeopardy Law After Rodney King*, 95 COLUM. L. REV. 1, 50–51 (1995); Akhil Reed Amar, *Sixth Amendment First Principles*, 84 GEO. L.J. 641, 681–82 (1996).

86. Akhil Reed Amar, *Confrontation Clause First Principles: A Reply to Professor Friedman*, 86 GEO. L.J. 1045, 1048 (1998).

87. *See, e.g.,* Kahan & Meares, *supra* note 46, at 1184; *see also* Dan M. Kahan, *Privatizing Criminal Law: Strategies for Private Norm Enforcement in the Inner City*, 46 UCLA L. REV. 1859 (1999); Kahan, *supra* note 53, at 1531–35; Meares, *supra* note 53, at 1612–29.

88. *See, e.g.,* Tracey L. Meares, *Norms, Legitimacy and Law Enforcement*, 79 OR. L. REV. 391 (2000).

89. *See, e.g., id.* at 414; Kahan, *supra* note 53, at 1530, 1536–37; Meares, *supra* note 53, at 1629; Tracey L. Meares, *What's Wrong with* Gideon, 70 U. CHI. L. REV. 215, 216 (2003). Luna, similarly, stresses the importance of trust in the police. Transparent policing, he explains, is not itself trust, but is "a process that helps build trusting relationships." Luna, *supra* note 75, at 1194. This is also why William Bratton values openness in policing: "A police organization that willfully shuts itself off from scrutiny and public exposure can lose public trust." Bratton, *supra* note 76.

90. *See, e.g.,* REPORT OF THE RAMPART INDEPENDENT REVIEW PANEL: A REPORT TO THE LOS ANGELES BOARD OF POLICE COMMISSIONERS CONCERNING THE OPERATIONS, POLICIES, AND PROCEDURES OF THE LOS ANGELES POLICE DEPARTMENT IN THE WAKE OF THE RAMPART SCANDAL 56–62 (2000) [hereinafter REPORT OF THE RAMPART INDEPENDENT REVIEW PANEL].

91. *See, e.g.,* Morgan Cloud, *Searching Through History, Searching for History*, 63 U. CHI. L. REV. 1707 (1996); Thomas Y. Davies, *Recovering the Original Fourth Amendment*, 98 MICH. L. REV. 547 (1999); Tracey Maclin, *The Complexity of the Fourth Amendment: A Historical Review*, 77 B.U. L. REV. 925 (1997).

92. Ronald J. Allen & Ross M. Rosenberg, *The Fourth Amendment and the Limits of Theory: Local Versus General Theoretical Knowledge*, 72 St. John's L. Rev. 1149, 1169 (1998); *see also, e.g.*, William J. Stuntz, *The Uneasy Relationship Between Criminal Procedure and Criminal Justice*, 107 Yale L.J. 1, 3 n.1 (1997) (noting that history "is becoming the dominant subject matter" of Fourth Amendment studies).

93. Wyoming v. Houghton, 526 U.S. 295, 299 (1999); *accord*, Florida v. White, 526 U.S. 559, 563 (1999); Wilson v. Arkansas, 514 U.S. 927, 931 (1995). For discussions of this development, *see* David A. Sklansky, *The Fourth Amendment and Common Law*, 100 Colum. L. Rev. 1739 (2000); Kathryn R. Urbonya, *Determining Reasonableness Under the Fourth Amendment: Physical Force to Control and Punish Students*, 10 Cornell J.L. & Pub. Pol'y 397, 411–12 (2001).

94. *E.g.*, Amar, *Fourth Amendment First Principles*, *supra* note 50, at 759, 761; Amar, *supra* note 85, at 712; Akhil Reed Amar, *The Future of Constitutional Criminal Procedure*, 33 Am. Crim. L. Rev. 1123, 1126 (1996); Akhil Reed Amar, *Double Jeopardy Law Made Simple*, 106 Yale L.J. 1807, 1814 (1997).

95. Akhil Reed Amar, *A Few Thoughts on Constitutionalism, Textualism, and Populism*, 65 Fordham L. Rev. 1657, 1659, 1662 (1997); *see also, e.g.*, Akhil Reed Amar, *Architexture*, 77 Ind. L.J. 671, 684 (2002). Amar recognizes that the Constitution is not "a mere objet d'art," Akhil Reed Amar, *Intratextualism*, 112 Harv. L. Rev. 747 (1999); and that "proper constitutional interpretation must in the end be more than merely aesthetically pleasing," Akhil Reed Amar, 33 U. Rich. L. Rev. 579, 582 (1999). But he has a plain preference for interpretations that clear away "jumble," *e.g.*, Amar, *Fourth Amendment First Principles*, *supra* note 50, at 758, and that make text and doctrine "beautifully cohere[]," Akhil Reed Amar, *The Constitution Versus the Court: Some Thoughts on Hills on Amar*, 94 Nw. U.L. Rev. 205, 214 (1999).

96. *See, e.g.*, Wayne LaFave, *Search and Seizure: "The Course of True Law . . . Has Not . . . Run Smooth,"* 1966 U. Ill. L.F. 255.

97. Amar, *Fourth Amendment First Principles*, *supra* note 50, at 793. On Amar's overarching effort "to reorient criminal procedure toward questions of factual guilt and innocence," see Seidman, *supra* note 49, at 2283.

98. David Luban, *The Adversary System Excuse*, in The Good Lawyer: Lawyers' Roles and Lawyers' Ethics 83, 92 (David Luban ed., 1983) ("no tangible harm"); Murray L. Schwartz, *The Zeal of the Civil Advocate*, 1983 Am. Bar Found. Res. J. 543, 553 ("basic purpose").

99. *See, e.g.*, Mary E. Becker, *The Politics of Women's Wrongs and the Bill of Rights: A Bicentennial Perspective*, 59 U. Chi. L. Rev. 453, 507–09 (1992); Robin West, *Equality Theory, Marital Rape, and the Promise of the Fourteenth Amendment*, 42 U. Fla. L. Rev. 45, 46–48 (1990).

100. Jane Jacobs, The Death and Life of Great American Cities 150, 223, 255, 286, 332–33, 329 (1961) (Vintage Books ed. 1992).

101. *See, e.g.*, Kahan & Meares, *supra* note 46, at 1163–64; Kahan & Meares, *supra* note 69, at 822–24; Dan M. Kahan, *Between Economics and Sociology: The New*

Path of Deterrence, 95 MICH. L. REV. 2477, 2488 (1997); Dan M. Kahan, *Social Influence, Social Meaning, and Deterrence*, 83 VA. L. REV. 349, 367–73 (1997).

102. *See, e.g.*, Livingston, *supra* note 39, at 578–91. Dorothy Roberts exaggerated but little in 1999 when she described scholarly, political, and media support for the broken windows theory as "virtually unanimous." Dorothy Roberts, *Foreword: Race, Vagueness, and Social Meaning of Order-Maintenance Policing*, 89 J. CRIM. L. & CRIMINOLOGY 775, 778 (1999).

103. For a particularly important critique, see Harcourt, *supra* note 46, at 59–216, which draws in part on Robert J. Sampson & Stephen W. Radenbush, *Systematic Social Observation of Public Spaces: A New Look at Disorder in Urban Neighborhoods*, 105 AM. J. SOC. 603 (1999). Kahan gives broken windows policing a "mixed" assessment in Kahan, *supra* note 53, at 1527–30. Even Wilson now calls the broken windows theory "speculation" and is unsure whether "improving order will or will not reduce crime." Dan Hurley, *On Crime as a Science (One Neighbor at a Time)*, N.Y. TIMES, Jan. 6, 2004, at F1 (quoting Wilson).

104. HARCOURT, *supra* note 46, at 27.

105. *See, e.g., id.* at 180; JONATHAN SIMON, GOVERNING THROUGH CRIME: HOW THE WAR ON CRIME TRANSFORMED AMERICAN DEMOCRACY AND CREATED A CULTURE OF FEAR (2007); Bernard E. Harcourt, *After the 'Social Meaning Turn': Implications for Research Design and Methods of Proof in Contemporary Criminal Law Policy Analysis*, 34 L. & SOC'Y REV. 179, 202 n.7 (2000).

106. *See, e.g.*, Frug, *supra* note 16, at 81.

107. *Id.*

108. *See* JAMES Q. WILSON, VARIETIES OF POLICE BEHAVIOR: THE MANAGEMENT OF LAW AND ORDER IN EIGHT COMMUNITIES 291 (1968).

109. *See, e.g.*, FOGELSON, *supra* note 5, at 306–07.

110. *See* Sarah E. Waldeck, *Cops, Community Policing, and the Social Norms Approach to Crime Control: Should One Make Us More Comfortable with the Others?* 34 GA. L. REV. 1253, 1295–96 (2000).

111. WESTLEY, *supra* note 18, at xvii, 193; *see also* BERKLEY, *supra* note 19, at 39.

112. BERKLEY, *supra* note 19, at 29; *see also* WESTLEY, *supra* note 18, at xvii–xviii.

113. EDWARD R. MAGUIRE, ORGANIZATIONAL STRUCTURE IN AMERICAN POLICE AGENCIES 39 (2003).

114. Barbara E. Armacost, *Organizational Culture and Police Misconduct*, 72 GEO. WASH. L. REV. 453, 458 n.18 (2004).

115. *See, e.g.*, REPORT OF THE RAMPART INDEPENDENT REVIEW PANEL, *supra* note 90, at 48–71.

116. Armacost, *supra* note 114, at 6; *see also, e.g.*, Waldeck, *supra* note 110, at 1263–71. Eric Luna's recent call for greater attention to the "institutional design" of policing is noteworthy in two respects: first, because his attention to institutional questions is unusual; and second, because so many of his institutional recommenda-

tions turn out to be aimed, in fact, at altering the culture of policing—modifying "social norms," facilitating "discourse and deliberation," creating a "sense of empathy," etc. Eric Luna, *Race, Crime, and Institutional Design*, 66 L. & CONTEMP. PROBS. 183 (2003). On the "social meaning turn" in criminal law scholarship, see Harcourt, *supra* note 105; Robert Weisberg, *Norms and Criminal Law, and the Norms of Criminal Law Scholarship*, 93 J. CRIM. L. & CRIMINOLOGY 467 (2003).

117. *E.g.*, Kahan & Meares, *supra* note 46, at 1160–61, 1167, 1177, 1183.

118. *Id.* at 1159.

119. *Id.* at 1179.

120. *Id.* at 1183; *see also id.* at 1170.

121. For criticism of Kahan and Meares on this score, particularly in connection with the Chicago loitering law, *see, e.g.*, Reenah L. Kim, *Legitimizing Community Consent to Local Policing: The Need for Democratically Negotiated Community Representation on Civilian Advisory Panels*, 36 HARV. C.R.-C.L. L. REV. 461, 482–88 (2001); Roberts, *supra* note 102, at 822–26.

122. *Id.* at 1163, 1165–67, 1170, 1178.

123. *E.g.*, Amar, *Reinventing Juries*, *supra* note 50, at 1182; Amar, *Three Cheers*, *supra* note 52, at 1265 n.26.

124. Kahan, *supra* note 53, at 1527, 1531–34; *see also* Kahan, *supra* note 87, at 1862–66; Meares, *supra* note 53; Meares, *supra* note 88, at 413–14. Both Kahan and Meares stress, in particular, the mantle of trust and legitimacy that Black church leaders can give to the police.

125. Kahan has recently qualified his enthusiasm, but only with the warning that collaborations with the clergy can "embroil the state in . . . religious rivalries" and thereby "extinguish trust." *See* Kahan, *supra* note 53, at 1535.

126. *See* Kahan, *supra* note 87, at 1870.

127. See Kahan, *supra* note 53, at 1535–38.

128. For notable exceptions, see WALKER, *supra* note 10; Kim, *supra* note 121; Luna, *supra* note 75, at 1167–69.

129. *See* WALKER, *supra* note 10, at 40.

130. *See* Kim, *supra* note 121, at 476–77.

131. *See, e.g.*, BERKLEY, *supra* note 19, at 146–47; GOLDSTEIN, *supra* note 13, at 142, 150–51. Chief Bratton has made the same complaint about the system under which serious disciplinary actions against Los Angeles police officers are adjudicated by a Board of Rights, consisting of two command officers and a civilian: "[A]s chief of police, I lack the necessary ability to control and impose discipline on my staff. Giving the chief—a chief who is directly accountable to civilian management—that power would help ensure the proper delivery of the appropriate message." William J. Bratton, *Power to Discipline LAPD Officers Is Out of the Chief's Hands*, L.A. TIMES, July 1, 2003, at B13.

132. *See* DOUGLAS W. PEREZ, COMMON SENSE ABOUT POLICE REVIEW (1994);

Douglas W. Perez & William Ker Muir, *Administrative Review of Alleged Police Brutality*, *in* POLICE VIOLENCE: UNDERSTANDING AND CONTROLLING POLICE ABUSE OF FORCE 213 (William A. Geller & Hans Toch eds., 1996).

133. *See, e.g.,* Armacost, *supra* note 114.

134. Ian Shapiro, *Three Ways to Be a Democrat*, 22 POL. THEORY 124, 138 (1994). The essay is reprinted in IAN SHAPIRO, DEMOCRACY'S PLACE 109–36 (1996).

135. IAN SHAPIRO, DEMOCRATIC JUSTICE 30 (1999) [hereinafter SHAPIRO, DEMOCRATIC JUSTICE]; *see also* IAN SHAPIRO, THE STATE OF DEMOCRATIC THEORY 3–4, 50–52 (2003).

136. SHAPIRO, DEMOCRATIC JUSTICE, *supra* note 135, at 1.

137. TOCQUEVILLE, *supra* note 51, at 3–6. On Tocqueville's use of old-world aristocracy as the "contrast-model" for democracy, see William E. Connolly, *The Challenge to Pluralist Theory*, *in* THE BIAS OF PLURALISM 3, 22 (William E. Connolly ed., 1969).

138. 2 COLLECTED WORKS OF ABRAHAM LINCOLN 532 (Roy Basler ed., 1953). On the rhetorical tradition invoked by Lincoln's definition of democracy—a tradition that saw slavery less as the antithesis of freedom than as "the antipode of democratic equality"—see David Brion Davis, *American Equality and Foreign Revolutions*, 76 J. AM. HIST. 729, 744–46 (1989).

139. W. B. Gallie, *Essentially Contested Concepts*, *in* THE IMPORTANCE OF LANGUAGE 121, 136 (Max Black ed., 1962) (reprinted from 56 PROC. ARISTOTELIAN SOC'Y 167 (1955–56).

140. *Id.* at 134.

141. Shapiro, *supra* note 134, at 138.

142. On the tendency of recent democratic theory to overlook the value of dissensus, see SHAPIRO, DEMOCRATIC JUSTICE, *supra* note 135, at 14–15; Stephen A. Gardbaum, *Broadcasting, Democracy, and the Market*, 82 GEO. L.J. 373, 386–87 (1993); Shapiro, *supra* note 134, at 133–34.

143. On the lost subtext of racial equality in criminal procedure jurisprudence, see, e.g., Devon W. Carbado, *(E)racing the Fourth Amendment*, 100 MICH. L. REV. 946, 974–1034 (2002); David A. Sklansky, *Traffic Stops, Minority Motorists, and the Future of the Fourth Amendment*, 1997 SUP. CT. REV. 271, 316–23.

144. Shapiro, *supra* note 134, at 139.

NOTES TO CHAPTER 5

1. IAN SHAPIRO, DEMOCRACY'S PLACE 11 (1996).

2. Ian Shapiro, *Three Ways to Be a Democrat*, 22 POL. THEORY 124, 137–38 (1994).

3. *See, e.g.,* SHAPIRO, *supra* note 1, at 7. Shapiro sometimes breaks down democracy into two separate commitments, one to collective self-government and one to the continued opposition to arbitrary exercises of power, and he ties broad opportunities

for participation to the first commitment, not the second. *See id.* at 220–61. Elsewhere, though, he treats inclusive decision making as a means of "empowering the disempowered," *id.* at 7, a view consistent with his suggestion that "democracy is about the structuring power relations so as to limit domination," IAN SHAPIRO, THE STATE OF DEMOCRATIC THEORY 52 (2003).

4. Shapiro, *supra* note 2, at 134; *see also, e.g.*, SHAPIRO, *supra* note 3, at 14–15. For a similar argument, see Stephen A. Gardbaum, *Broadcasting, Democracy, and the Market*, 82 GEO. L.J. 373, 386–87 (1993). Roberto Unger has taken the idea of institutionalizing conflict and destabilization much further. *See, e.g.*, ROBERTO MANGABEIRA UNGER, THE CRITICAL LEGAL STUDIES MOVEMENT (1986). In Shapiro's view, Unger goes too far, naïvely supposing that "every form of context smashing will undermine entrenched hierarchy and fuel greater democratic freedom." Shapiro, *supra* note 2, at 143; *see also* Ian Shapiro, *Constructing Politics*, 17 POL. THEORY 475 (1989).

5. Shapiro, *supra* note 2, at 143–44.

6. *See, e.g., id.* at 135.

7. IAN SHAPIRO, DEMOCRATIC JUSTICE 26 (1999).

NOTES TO CHAPTER 6

1. Willard M. Oliver, *The Third Generation of Community Policing: Moving Through Innovation, Diffusion, and Institutionalization, in* CONTEMPORARY POLICING: STRATEGIES, CHALLENGES, AND SOLUTIONS 39, 40 (Quint C. Thurman & Jihong Zhao eds., 2004); *see also, e.g.*, William F. Walsh & Gennaro F. Vito, *The Meaning of Compstat: Analysis and Response*, 20 J. CONTEMP. CRIM. JUST. 51, 57 (2004).

2. GENE E. CARTE & ELAINE H. CARTE, POLICE REFORM IN THE UNITED STATES: THE ERA OF AUGUST VOLLMER 108 (1975) (quoting PRESIDENT'S COMMISSION ON LAW ENFORCEMENT AND THE ADMINISTRATION OF JUSTICE, TASK FORCE REPORT: THE POLICE 20–21 (1967)).

3. JAMES S. KAKALIK & SORREL WILDHORN, THE PRIVATE POLICE INDUSTRY 34 (1971).

4. On the growth of private security, see David A. Sklansky, *The Private Police*, 46 UCLA L. REV. 1165, 1171–82 (1999). The trend in the United States has been mirrored throughout much of the developed world. *See id.* at 1181.

5. INT'L ASS'N OF CHIEFS OF POLICE, NATIONAL POLICY SUMMIT: BUILDING PRIVATE SECURITY/PUBLIC POLICING PARTNERSHIPS TO PREVENT AND RESPOND TO TERRORISM AND PUBLIC DISORDER 4, 19 (2004) [hereinafter BUILDING PRIVATE SECURITY/PUBLIC POLICING PARTNERSHIPS].

6. *See, e.g.*, Ian Loader, *Thinking Normatively About Private Security*, J.L. & SOC'Y 377, 380 (1997); James P. Murphy, *The Private Sector and Security: A Bit on BIDs*, 9 SECURITY J. 11, 13 (1997); James J. Vardalis, *Privatization of Public Police: Houston, Texas*, 3 SECURITY J. 210, 211 (1992).

7. Lawrence W. Sherman, *The Police, in* Crime 327, 338–39 (James Q. Wilson & Joan Petersilia eds., 1995); *see also, e.g.,* William F. Walsh & Edwin J. Donovan, *Private Security and Community Policing: Evaluation and Comment,* 17 J. Crim. Just. 187, 194 (1989).

8. Building Private Security/Public Policing Partnerships, *supra* note 5, at 1. On the proliferating links between private security firms and public law enforcement agencies, see Elizabeth Joh, *The Paradox of Private Policing,* 96 J. Crim. L. & Criminology 49, 83–95 (2004).

9. For elaboration of this point, see Steve Herbert, Citizens, Cops, and Power: Recognizing the Limits of Community (2006); Reenah L. Kim, *Legitimizing Community Consent to Local Policing: The Need for Democratically Negotiated Community Representation on Civilian Advisory Boards,* 36 Harv. C.R.-C.L. L. Rev. 461 (2001). For evidence that Chicago's community policing programs have been less successful and less popular among the city's burgeoning Latino population than among blacks, see Wesley G. Skogan et al., Community Policing and "The New Immigrants": Latinos in Chicago (2002).

10. David Thacher, *Conflicting Values in Community Policing,* 35 Law & Soc'y Rev. 765, 765, 768 [hereinafter Thacher, *Conflicting Values*]. Elsewhere, Thacher has given a slightly different account of community policing, suggesting that the partnerships it forges function as "sites of public deliberation about the common good." David Thacher, *Equity and Community Policing: A New View of Community Partnerships,* 20 Crim. Just. Ethics 3, 5 (2001). I prefer the account focusing on a reduction in institutional segregation: among its attractions is precisely that it avoids reliance on the vague, Rousseauian notion of "the common good." I am influenced, here as elsewhere, by Ian Shapiro, who points out that an anti-inegalitarian conception of democracy has the advantage, among others, that it "does not revolve around trying to render Rousseau's project coherent." Ian Shapiro, Democracy's Place 6–7 (1996); *see also, e.g.,* Ian Shapiro, The State of Democratic Theory 10–34 (2003).

11. Thacher, *Conflicting Values, supra* note 10, at 791–92.

12. *See id.*

13. *See id.* at 722, 792–95; William Ker Muir, Jr., Police: Streetcorner Politicians (1977).

14. *See* Thacher, *Conflicting Values, supra* note 10, at 767 & n.3.

15. *See* Wesley G. Skogan et al., Taking Stock: Community Policing in Chicago 8–11 (2002); Archon Fung, Street Level Democracy: Pragmatic Popular Sovereignty in Chicago Schools and Policing 14, 30–33 (1999) (unpublished manuscript).

16. *See* Skogan et al., *supra* note 15, at 10; Robert J. Sampson et al., *Neighborhoods and Violent Crime: A Multilevel Study of Collective Efficacy,* 277 Sci. 918 (1997); Robert J. Sampson & Stephen W. Raudenbush, *Systematic Social Observation of Public Spaces: A New Look at Disorder in Urban Neighborhoods,* 105 Am. J. Soc. 603 (1999).

17. Skogan et al., *supra* note 15, at 12.

18. WESLEY G. SKOGAN ET AL., CHICAGO COMMUNITY POLICING EVALUATION CONSORTIUM, COMMUNITY POLICING IN CHICAGO, YEAR SEVEN: AN INTERIM REPORT 6 (2002); *see also id. at* 96–103.

19. *Id.* at 6.

20. SKOGAN ET AL., *supra* note 15, at 12.

21. "During the 1990s, an average of seven police officers attended each beat meeting, including the beat sergeant, the beat officers on duty, and a few beat team members from other shifts. To encourage attendance by the latter, they are paid overtime at a yearly cost of nearly $1 million." *Id.* at 8. The department also trained both officers and civilian participants in decision making and interpersonal skills, and the city paid for "roving teams of community organizers and trainers" to "mobilize residents around public safety issues." Fung, *supra* note 15, at 19. Whether support at these levels can be expected in the future is uncertain. *See id.*; SKOGAN ET AL., *supra* note 15, at 30.

22. On the reasons to think that order maintenance might be "an intrinsically appropriate goal for policing," regardless whether the strategy actually reduces serious crime, see David Thacher, *Order Maintenance Reconsidered: Moving Beyond Strong Causal Reasoning*, 94 J. CRIM. L. & CRIMINOLOGY 381 (2004).

23. BERNARD HARCOURT, ILLUSION OF ORDER: THE FALSE PROMISE OF BROKEN WINDOWS POLICING 27 (2001).

24. HERMAN GOLDSTEIN, POLICING A FREE SOCIETY 146 (1977).

25. *Id.*

26. JAMES Q. WILSON, VARIETIES OF POLICE BEHAVIOR: THE MANAGEMENT OF LAW AND ORDER IN EIGHT COMMUNITIES 290 (1968).

27. Jerome H. Skolnick, *Neighborhood Police*, THE NATION, Mar. 22, 1971, at 372, 373.

28. *See, e.g.*, HERBERT, *supra* note 9, at 76.

29. David Weisburd, *Hot Spots Policing Experiments and Criminal Justice Research: Lessons from the Field*, 559 ANNALS AM. ACAD. POLIT. & SOC. SCI. 220, 221 (2005).

30. *See, e.g.*, Erik Luna, *Transparent Policing*, 85 IOWA L. REV. 1107, 1172–74 (2000); Weisburd, *supra* note 29, at 221.

31. *See* Weisburd, *supra* note 29.

32. *See id.*; David Weisburd & John E. Eck, *What Can Police Do to Reduce Crime, Disorder, and Fear?* 593 ANNALS AM. ACAD. POL. & SOC. SCI. 42, 54–55 (2004).

33. Peter Manning, *Problem Solving?*, 4 CRIMINOLOGY & PUB. POL'Y 149, 150 (2005).

34. Mark Harrison Moore, *Problem-Solving and Community Policing, in* MODERN POLICING 99, 123, 126 (Michael Tonry & Norval Morris eds., 1992); *see also* Debra Livingston, *Police Discretion and the Quality of Life in Public Places: Courts, Communities, and the New Policing*, 97 COLUM. L. REV. 551, 573–75 (1997).

35. HERMAN GOLDSTEIN, PROBLEM-ORIENTED POLICING 43 (1990).

36. *See id.* at 24–27; John E. Eck & William Spelman, *Who Ya Gonna Call? The Police as Problem-Busters*, 33 CRIME & DELINQUENCY 31, 36–37 (1987).

37. *See, e.g.*, Herbert, *supra* note 9; James Forman, Jr., *Community Policing and Youth as Assets*, 95 J. CRIM. L. & CRIMINOLOGY 1 (2004); Kim, *supra* note 9; Dorothy E. Roberts, *Foreword: Race, Vagueness, and the Social Meaning of Order-Maintenance Policing*, 89 J. CRIM. L. & CRIMINOLOGY 775, 822–26 (1999); WESLEY G. SKOGAN ET AL., COMMUNITY POLICING AND "THE NEW IMMIGRANTS": LATINOS IN CHICAGO (2002).

38. Louis Michael Seidman, *Akhil Amar and the (Premature?) Demise of Criminal Procedure Liberalism*, 107 YALE L.J. 2281, 2315 (1998) (book review).

39. *See, e.g.*, ARCHON FUNG, EMPOWERED PARTICIPATION: REINVENTING URBAN DEMOCRACY 3–4 (2004).

40. *Id.* at 53–56, 63–68.

41. For thoughtful proposals along these lines, see Kim, *supra* note 9.

42. Luna, *supra* note 30.

43. *Hearings Regarding Private Security Guards Before the Subcomm. on Human Resources of the House Comm. on Education and Labor*, 103d Cong., at 132 (1993) (statement of Ira Lipman, President of Guardsmark, Inc.).

44. Elizabeth E. Joh, *Conceptualizing the Private Police*, 2005 UTAH L. REV 573 (2005).

45. For a noteworthy exception—albeit one focused on Britain rather than the United States—see Ian Loader, *Plural Policing and Democratic Governance*, 9 SOC. & LEGAL STUD. 323 (2000).

46. *See, e.g.*, Loader, *supra* note 6, at 380; Vardalis, *supra* note 6, at 211.

47. *See, e.g.*, Clifford J. Rosky, *Force, Inc.: The Privatization of Punishment, Policing, and Military Force in Liberal States*, 36 CONN. L. REV. 879, 947–50 (2004).

48. According to one estimate, 45 percent of all local governments were contracting out at least some of their security work by the late 1990s, up from 27 percent a decade earlier. *See* Mercer Group, Inc., *1997 Privatization Survey* 14–15 (unpublished study). Much of the outsourcing involved humdrum tasks like data processing or parking enforcement. *See, e.g.*, MARCIA CHAIKEN & JAN CHAIKEN, PUBLIC POLICING—PRIVATELY PROVIDED 3 (1987). It is increasingly common, though, for private firms to patrol government buildings, housing projects, or public parks, and a few municipalities have experimented with even broader reliance on private police. *See* Joh, *supra* note 44, at 613–15; Sklansky, *supra* note 4, at 1177.

49. *See* MARTHA MINOW, PARTNERS, NOT RIVALS: PRIVATIZATION AND THE PUBLIC GOOD (2002); Jody Freeman, *Extending Public Law Norms Through Privatization*, 116 HARV. L. REV. 1285 (2003); Gillian Metzger, *Privatization as Delegation*, 103 COLUM. L. REV. 1367 (2003); Martha Minow, *Public and Private Partnerships: Accounting for the New Religion*, 116 HARV. L. REV. 1229 (2003).

50. Murphy, *supra* note 6 at 13.

51. Port Huron Statement, *reprinted in* JAMES MILLER, DEMOCRACY IS IN THE STREETS: FROM PORT HURON TO THE SIEGE OF CHICAGO 329, 333 (paperback ed. 1994).

52. Sklansky, *supra* note 4, at 1178 & n.57.

53. Robert B. Reich, *Secession of the Successful*, N.Y. TIMES, Jan. 20, 1991, § 6, at 16.

54. *See* Sklansky, *supra* note 4, at 1224 n.342.

55. Murray Kempton, *Son of Pinkerton*, N.Y. REV. OF BOOKS, May 20, 1971, at 22.

56. *See, e.g.*, Steven Spitzer & Andrew T. Scull, *Privatization and Capitalist Development: The Case of the Private Police*, 25 SOC. PROBS. 18 (1977).

57. *See, e.g.*, MUIR, *supra* note 13, at 73–77 (discussing tactics employed by private police in Oakland's skid row in the early 1970s); Heather Barr, *More Like Disneyland: State Action, 42 U.S.C. § 1983, and Business Improvement Districts in New York*, 28 COLUM. HUM. RTS. L. REV. 393, 400–03 (1997) (describing similar tactics by private security personnel in midtown Manhattan in the 1990s); William Wan & Erin Ailworth, *Flak over Downtown Security Guards*, L.A. TIMES, June 8, 2004, at B1, B10 (reporting allegations of similar conduct by private guards patrolling downtown Los Angeles).

58. Joh, *supra* note 8, at 15.

59. Wan & Ailworth, *supra* note 57, at B10 (quoting Carol Schatz, president of the Downtown Center Improvement District).

60. David H. Bayley & Clifford D. Shearing, *The Future of Policing*, 30 L. & SOC'Y REV. 585, 594, 602 (1996).

61. *See* Sklansky, *supra* note 4, at 1199–1200, 1216–17 & n.305.

62. Joh, *supra* note 8, at 65–66; *see* PHILIP SELZNICK, LAW, SOCIETY, AND INDUSTRIAL SOCIETY 75–120 (1969); PHILIP SELZNICK, THE MORAL COMMUNITY 289–318 (1978).

63. *See* DAVID GARLAND, THE CULTURE OF CONTROL 114–17, 188–90 (2001); *cf.* Ian Loader, *Democracy, Justice and the Limits of Policing: Rethinking Police Accountability*, 3 SOC. & LEGAL STUD. 521, 521–22 (1994) (discussing the "managerialist turn" in British policing).

64. *See* Thacher, *Conflicting Values*, *supra* note 10, at 765, 765, 768, 772, 792–95.

65. *See, e.g.*, GEORGE S. RIGAKOS, THE NEW PARAPOLICE: RISK MARKETS AND COMMODIFIED SOCIAL CONTROL 119–46 (2002).

NOTES TO CHAPTER 7

1. Alexandra Natapoff, *Underenforcement*, 75 FORDHAM L. REV. 1715 (2006).

2. For a helpful overview, see Samuel R. Gross & Debra Livingston, *Racial Profiling Under Attack*, 102 COLUM. L. REV. 1413 (2002).

3. *See* Whren v. United States, 517 U.S. 806 (1996); David A. Sklansky, *Traffic Stops, Minority Motorists, and the Future of the Fourth Amendment*, 1997 SUP. CT. REV. 271, 277–79, 284–91, 307–23.

4. GARY S. BECKER, THE ECONOMICS OF DISCRIMINATION 16–17 (2d ed. 1971). For a helpful overview and critique of studies of racial profiling proceeding from this

assumption, see Bernard E. Harcourt, *Rethinking Racial Profiling: A Critique of the Economics, Civil Liberties, and Constitutional Literature and of Criminal Profiling More Generally*, 71 U. CHI. L. REV. 1275 (2004).

5. *See* Harcourt, *supra* note 4. On the consequences of high rates of arrest and incarceration on minority neighborhoods, see also, e.g., Richard Banks, *Beyond Profiling: Race, Policing, and the Drug War*, 56 STAN. L. REV. 571, 594–97 (2003); Dorothy Roberts, *Foreword: Race, Vagueness, and Social Meaning of Order-Maintenance Policing*, 89 J. CRIM. L. & CRIMINOLOGY 775, 815–16 & n.143 (1999).

6. The best discussion of this problem I know is Devon W. Carbado, *(E)racing the Fourth Amendment*, 100 MICH. L. REV. 946, 974–1034 (2002). On the ways in which criminal justice practices can help to shape self-identity, particularly with respect to race, see also IAN F. HANEY LÓPEZ, RACISM ON TRIAL: THE CHICANO FIGHT FOR JUSTICE (2003). "More and more," Haney López argues, "we know ourselves by how the police and the courts treat us. If we receive respect, courtesy, fair treatment, and due process, we are white; if we are harassed, beaten, arrested or detained by executive fiat, we are black, brown, yellow, or red." *Id.* at 11.

7. *See, e.g.*, Banks, *supra* note 5, at 577–78, 598.

8. *See* Harcourt, *supra* note 4.

9. *See* Carbado, *supra* note 6, at 982.

10. At least from the standpoint of democracy, therefore—and probably from any other standpoint—the Justice Department has been on thin ice in distinguishing sharply between "racial profiling," which it continues to condemn, and profiling based on nationality, which it defends. *See* Gross & Livingston, *supra* note 2, at 1419–21. There is a difference, of course, between discriminating on the ground of *nationality* and discriminating among United States citizens on the ground of *national origin*. But Gross and Livingston seem right that "[t]he Department's focus on visitors from countries with an active al Qaeda presence . . . raises the specter of ethnic profiling," by producing "an interview list that is dominated by Middle Eastern men." *See id.* at 1419–20.

11. *See, e.g.*, Banks, *supra* note 5, at 593–98.

12. Whren v. United States, 517 U.S. 806, 813 (1996).

13. Personnel Admin'r v. Feeney, 442 U.S. 256, 279 (1979); *see also, e.g.*, McCleskey v. Kemp, 481 U.S. 279, 298 (1987).

14. *See, e.g.*, Sklansky, *supra* note 3.

15. *See, e.g.*, Natapoff, *supra* note 1.

16. *E.g.*, Robert Goldstein, Blyew: *Variations on a Jurisdictional Theme*, 41 STAN. L. REV. 469 (1989).

17. DeShaney v. Winnebago County Dep't of Soc. Servs., 489 U.S. 189, 195 (1989)

18. *Id.* at 197 n.3.

19. *See* David A. Sklansky, *The Private Police*, 46 UCLA L. REV. 1165, 1281–82 (1999).

20. Archie v. City of Racine, 847 F.2d 1211, 1218 (7th Cir. 1988) (en banc); *see*

also, e.g., Barbara E. Armacost, *Affirmative Duties, Systemic Harms, and the Due Process Clause*, 94 MICH. L. REV. 982, 1014 (1996).

21. *See* Gerald Frug, *City Services*, 73 N.Y.U. L. REV. 23, 81 (1998).

22. *See, e.g.*, John Dayton, *Examining the Efficacy of Judicial Involvement in Public School Funding Reform*, 22 J. EDUC. FIN. 1 (1996); Phil Weisser, *What's Quality Got to Do with It? Constitutional Theory, Politics, and Education Reform*, 21 N.Y.U. REV. L. & SOC. CHANGE 745, 787–89 (1994–95).

23. *See* Frug, *supra* note 21.

24. JANE JACOBS, THE DEATH AND LIFE OF GREAT AMERICAN CITIES 410 (Vintage 1992) (1961).

25. *See* Justin McCrary, The Effect of Court-Ordered Hiring Quotas on the Composition and Quality of Police, 44 (Nov. 30, 2003) (unpublished manuscript).

26. *See* BRIAN A. REAVES & MATTHEW J. HICKMAN, BUREAU OF JUSTICE STATISTICS, U.S. DEP'T OF JUSTICE, POLICE DEPARTMENTS IN LARGE CITIES, 1990–2000, at 3 (2002). This report compiles figures from the 2000 Law Enforcement Management and Administrative Statistics (LEMAS) survey.

27. Jennifer 8. Lee, *In Police Class, Blue Comes in Many Colors*, N.Y. TIMES, July 8, 2005, at B2.

28. *See* LOS ANGELES POLICE DEPARTMENT ANNUAL REPORT 2000, at 27; REAVES & HICKMAN, *supra* note 26.

29. *See, e.g.*, Lee, *supra* note 27.

30. *See* LOS ANGELES POLICE DEPARTMENT ANNUAL REPORT 2000, *supra* note 28, at 27. Latino officers in Los Angeles remain strongly concentrated in the lower ranks— at least in part, presumably, because the Latino percentage of the city population has been steadily growing over the past several decades, and with it the Latino percentage of new officers hired by the department. Nationwide, as in Los Angeles, the Latino officer-to-resident ratio lags behind the black officer-to-resident ratio, but leads the corresponding figure for other minorities. *See* REAVES & HICKMAN, *supra* note 26, at 3.

31. *See* KIM LONSWAY ET AL., NATIONAL CENTER FOR WOMEN & POLICING, EQUALITY DENIED: THE STATUS OF WOMEN IN POLICING: 2001 (2001). Women comprise a much larger share of the civilian workforce in large police departments. In departments with over one hundred sworn officers, women hold more than two-thirds of the civilian positions, which generally are lower paid and offer fewer opportunities for advancement. *See id.* at 8. Chiefly to save money, American police departments have greatly increased their reliance on civilian employees in recent years; large departments now employ more civilians than sworn officers. *See, e.g.*, REAVES & HICKMAN, *supra* note 26, at 2. The stark gender difference between the two groups—the vast majority of officers are men, and the vast majority of civilian employees are women—both exacerbates and makes more troubling the way in which "civilianization" has tended to create two-tier departments, with civilian employees treated as second-class citizens.

32. *See* STEPHEN LEINEN, GAY COPS 11 (1993); Katy Butler, *The Gay Push for S.F.*

Police Jobs, S.F. CHRON., Apr. 9, 1979, at A1; Randy Shilts, *Gay Police—"We're Not All That Different*," POLICE MAGAZINE, July 1980, at 32. The novelist Jonathan Kellerman recalls that he created the character of a gay Los Angeles homicide detective in the early 1980s "because I wanted to avoid cliches, and a gay officer was a revolutionary concept." Jonathan Kellerman, *Two Identities, but One Compulsion*, N.Y. TIMES, Mar. 31, 2003, at E1. Most police chiefs at the time adamantly opposed hiring gay officers. Shilts, *supra*, at 32.

On the growing but still incomplete acceptance of gay officers, see, e.g., Aaron Belkin & Jason McNichol, *Pink and Blue: Outcomes Associated with the Integration of Open Gay and Lesbian Personnel in the San Diego Police Department*, 5 POLICE Q. 63 (2002); Susan L. Miller, Kay B. Forest & Nancy C. Jurik, *Diversity in Blue: Lesbian and Gay Police Officers in a Masculine Occupation*, MEN & MASCULINITIES 355 (2003); Kristen A. Myers, Kay B. Forest & Susan L. Miller, *Officer Friendly and the Tough Cop: Gays and Lesbians Navigate Homophobia and Policing*, 47 J. HOMOSEXUALITY 17 (2004); Tracy Gordon Fox, *Seminar to Focus on Gay Officers*, HARTFORD COURANT, May 5, 2004, at B11; James Sterngold, *Possible Candidate for LAPD's Top Job Is Gay— So What?*, S.F. CHRON., Aug. 26, 2002, at A1.

33. *See, e.g.*, DAVID E. BARLOW & MELISSA HICKMAN BARLOW, POLICE IN A MULTI-CULTURAL SOCIETY 275–76 (2000).

34. Belkin & McNichol, *supra* note 32, at 78; *see also, e.g.*, SUSAN L. MILLER, GENDER AND COMMUNITY POLICING: WALKING THE TALK 134 (1999).

35. Belkin & McNichol, *supra* note 32, at 77–83.

36. *See* Fox, *supra* note 32, at B11; Laurel J. Sweet, *O'Toole Aims for Gay Cops' Acceptance at Powwow*, BOSTON HERALD, June 21, 2004, at 12.

37. PRESIDENT'S COMM'N ON LAW ENF'T & ADMIN. OF JUSTICE, THE CHALLENGE OF CRIME IN A FREE SOCIETY 107 (1967).

38. *See, e.g.*, KENNETH BOLTON, JR., & JOE R. FEAGIN, BLACK IN BLUE: AFRICAN-AMERICAN POLICE OFFICERS AND RACISM 6–7, 215–16, 250 (2003).

39. *See* James J. Fyfe, *Who Shoots? A Look at Officer Race and Police Shooting*, 9 J. POLICE SCI. & ADMIN. 367, 372 (1981); William A. Geller & Kevin J. Karales, *Shootings of and by Chicago Police: Uncommon Crises Part I: Shootings by Chicago Police*, 72 J. CRIM. L. & CRIMINOLOGY 1813, 1815 (1981); Mark Blumberg, The Use of Firearms by Police Officers: The Impact of Individuals, Communities, and Race 72–80 (1982) (unpublished dissertation on file with author); *cf.* Albert J. Reiss, *Police Brutality*, *in* CRIME AND JUSTICE: THE CRIMINAL IN THE ARMS OF THE LAW 157 (Leon Radzinowicz & Marvin E. Wolfgang eds., 2d ed. 1977) (finding little difference in the likelihood of black and white officers to use force).

40. *See* Robert E. Worden, *Situational and Attitudinal Explanations of Police Behavior: A Theoretical Reappraisal and Empirical Assessment*, 23 L. & SOC. REV. 667, 700 n.42 (1989).

41. *See* Jack L. Kuykendall & D. E. Burns, *The Black Police Officer: An Historical Perspective*, 4 J. CONTEMP. CRIM. J. 4, 9–10 (1980).

42. *See* Stephen D. Mastrofski et al., *Compliance on Demand: The Public's Response to Specific Police Requests*, 33 J. Res. Crime & Tech. 269, 289 & tbl. 2 (1996).

43. *See* Bernard Cohen & Jan Chaiken, Police Background Characteristics And Performance xii & tbl. 24 (1972); Antony Pate & Lorie Fridell, Police Use of Force: Official Reports, Citizen Complaints, and Legal Consequences 102, 155 (1993); Liqun Cao & Bu Huang, *Determinants of Citizen Complaints Against Police Abuse of Power*, 28 J. Crim. Just. 203, 209 (2000); Cohen & Chaiken 1972; Kim Lersch & Tom Mieczkowski, *Who Are the Problem-Prone Officers? An Analysis of Citizen Complaints*, 15 Am. J. Police 23, 33 (1996).

44. *See* Albert J. Reiss, Jr., *Career Orientations, Job Satisfaction, and the Assessment of Law Enforcement Problems by Police Officers* 81, *in* 2 Studies of Crime and Law Enforcement in Major Metropolitan Areas (Albert J. Reiss ed., 1967).

45. *See* Donald J. Black & Albert J. Reiss, *Patterns of Behavior in Police and Citizen Transactions* 132–37, *in* 2 Studies of Crime and Law Enforcement in Major Metropolitan Areas, *supra* note 44.

46. *See* Rita M. Kelly & Gorman West, *The Racial Transition of a Police Force: A Profile of White and Black Policemen in Washington, D.C.*, *in* The Urban Policeman in Transition 354, 374–77 (John R. Snibbe & Homa M. Snibbe eds., 1978) [hereinafter The Urban Policeman in Transition].

47. *See* John J. Donohue III & Steven D. Levitt, *The Impact of Race on Policing and Arrests*, 44 J. L. & Econ. 367, 371 & tbl. 2 (2001).

48. Samuel Walker, Cassia Spohn & Miriam DeLone, The Color of Justice: Race, Ethnicity and Crime in America 111 (2d ed. 2000); *see also, e.g.*, Barlow & Barlow, *supra* note 33, at 249.

49. Edward Conlon, Blue Blood 320 (2004).

50. Herman Goldstein, Policing a Free Society 259 (1976).

51. Walker, Spohn & DeLone, *supra* note 48, at 111; *see also, e.g.*, John L. Cooper, The Police and the Ghetto 29–53, 116–19, 125–28 (1980); Ellis Cashmore, *Black Cops Inc.*, *in* Out of Order?: Policing Black People 87, 104–08 (Ellis Cashmore & Eugene McLaughlin eds., 1991); Reiss, *supra* note 39, at 157; *cf.* Janet Chan, *Changing Police Culture*, 36 Brit. J. Criminology 109, 110 (1996) ("Conspiracy theory aside, the most powerful and currently popular explanation for the recalcitrance of police organizations to change has been to postulate the existence of a 'police culture.'")

52. *Id.*; *see also* Committee to Review Research on Police Policy & Practices, National Research Council, Fairness and Effectiveness in Policing: The Evidence 147 (Wesley Skogan & Kathleen Frydl eds., 2004) [hereinafter Fairness and Effectiveness in Policing] (reporting the "received wisdom from the research community . . . that whatever influence race and gender may exert on behavior is overwhelmed by the unifying effects of occupational socialization").

53. *See* Peter B. Bloch & Deborah Anderson, Policewomen on Patrol: Final Report 2–3 (1974); Joyce Sichel, Women on Patrol: A Pilot Study of Police

PERFORMANCE IN NEW YORK CITY 28–31 (1978); Lewis J. Sherman, *An Evaluation of Policewomen on Patrol in a Suburban Police Department*, 3 J. POLICE SCI. & ADMIN. 434, 435 (1975).

54. *See* John R. Snortum & John C. Beyers, *Patrol Activities of Male and Female Officers as a Function of Work Experience*, 6 POLICE STUD. 36, 41 (1983); Sean A. Grennan, *Findings on the Role of Officer Gender in Violent Encounters with Citizens*, 15 J. PoLICE SCI. & ADMIN., 78, 83–4 (1987); Alissa Pollitz Worden, *The Attitudes of Women and Men in Policing: Testing Conventional and Contemporary Wisdom*, 31 CRIMINOLOGY 203, 227–29 (1993).

55. *See* REPORT OF THE INDEPENDENT COMMISSION ON THE LOS ANGELES POLICE DEPARTMENT 83–84 (1991); Frank Horvath, *The Police Use of Deadly Force: A Description of Selected Characteristics of Intrastate Incidents*, 15 J. POLICE SCI. & ADMIN. 226, 229 (1987).

56. *See* Robert J. Homant & Daniel B. Kennedy, *Police Perceptions of Spouse Abuse: A Comparison of Male and Female Officers*, 13 J. CRIM. JUST. 29, 42–43 (1985).

57. *See* John R. Lott, Jr., *Does a Helping Hand Put Others at Risk? Affirmative Action, Police Departments, and Crime*, 38 ECON. INQUIRY 260 (2000); Brad W. Smith, *The Impact of Police Officer Diversity on Police-Caused Homicides*, 31 POLICY STUD. J. 147, 155 (2003).

58. *See* Houmant & Kennedy, *supra* note 56, at 34–35.

59. KIM LONSWAY ET AL., NATIONAL CENTER FOR WOMEN & POLICING, HIRING AND RETAINING MORE WOMEN: THE ADVANTAGES TO LAW ENFORCEMENT 2–4 (2003).

60. *See, e.g.*, ROBIN A. BURKE, A MATTER OF JUSTICE: LESBIANS AND GAY MEN IN LAW ENFORCEMENT 25–131 (1996); Belkin & McNichol, *supra* note 32, at 87; Brittany Wallman, *Police Try to Recruit More Gay Officers*, SUN-SENTINEL (Ft. Lauderdale, Fla.), Dec. 18, 2005, Community News, at 1.

61. Miller, Forest & Jurik, *supra* note 32, at 378; *see also id.* at 370–71, 376; Myers, Forest & Miller, *supra* note 32, at 34.

62. Myers, Forest & Miller, *supra* note 32, at 35; Shilts, *supra* note 32, at 32–33.

63. PRESIDENT'S COMM'N ON LAW ENF'T & ADMIN. OF JUSTICE, *supra* note 37, at 107.

64. Belkin & McNichol, *supra* note 32, at 87.

65. *See supra* notes 42 & 44.

66. *See* Irving A. Wallach & Colette C. Jackson, *Perception of the Police in a Black Community*, *in* THE URBAN POLICEMAN IN TRANSITION, *supra* note 46, at 382, 401; Ronald Weitzer, *White, Black, or Blue Cops? Race and Citizen Assessments of Police Officers*, 28 J. CRIM. JUST. 313, 316 (2000).

67. *See* BARLOW & BARLOW, *supra* note 33, at 249.

68. NICHOLAS ALEX, BLACK IN BLUE: A STUDY OF THE NEGRO POLICEMAN 20–21 (1969); *accord, e.g.*, COOPER, *supra* note 51, at 111–15, 119–25; Cashmore, *supra* note 51, at 96; Edward Palmer, *Black Police in America*, BLACK SCHOLAR, Oct. 1973, at 19, 21–23.

69. Susan E. Martin, Breaking and Entering: Policewomen on Patrol 197–98 (1980).

70. Marc Burke, *Homosexuality as Deviance: The Case of the Gay Police Officer*, 34 Brit. J. Criminology 192 (1994); *see also, e.g.*, Myers, Forest & Miller, *supra* note 32, at 31.

71. *See, e.g.*, Bolton & Feagin, *supra* note 38, at 22.

72. *See, e.g.*, Belkin & McNichol, *supra* note 32, at 77–79.

73. *See* Robert J. Friedrich, *Police Use of Force: Individuals, Situations, and Organizations*, 452 Annals Am. Acad. Pol. & Soc. Sci. 82, 90 (1980).

74. *See* Michael Cassidy, Caroline G. Nicholl, Carmen Ross & Kimberly A. Lonsway, The Victims' View: Domestic Violence and Police Response, at 4–15 (August 2003) (unpublished paper available at <http://perso.wanadoo.fr/societe.internationale.de.criminologie/pdf/Intervention%20 Cassidy%20et%20ocie.pdf>).

75. Cynthia Estlund, Working Together: How Workplace Bonds Strengthen a Diverse Democracy 84 (2003); *see also id.* at 60–101.

76. *See, e.g.*, Barlow & Barlow, *supra* note 33, at 235–41; Erin Aubry Kaplan, *Rethinking the LAPD Black and Blue*, L.A. Weekly, Sept. 6, 2002.

77. *See, e.g.*, Samuel Walker & Charles M. Katz, The Police in America 433 (4th ed. 2002); Cashmore, *supra* note 51, at 96.

78. *See, e.g.*, *Latino Group Opposes Parks' Bid for Second Term*, L.A. Times, Mar. 12, 2002, at B5; Jill Leovy, *Review of Parks Will Be Private*, L.A. Times, Apr. 2, 2002, at B1.

79. Melissa Hickman Barlow, David Barlow & Stan Stajkovic, *The Media, The Police and the Multicultural Community: Observations of a City in Crisis*, 17 J. Crime & Just. 133, 137, 140, 144–45 (1994).

80. Robin N. Haarr, *Patterns of Interaction in a Police Patrol Bureau: Race and Gender Barriers to Integration*, 14 Justice Q. 53, 66 (1997).

81. *Id.* at 53; *see also, e.g.*, Barlow & Barlow, *supra* note 33, at 205; Fairness and Effectiveness in Policing, *supra* note 52, at 80–82; Steven Maynard-Moody & Michael Musheno, Cops, Teachers, Counselors: Stories from the Front Lines of Public Service 64–76 (2003). Samuel Walker has been pressing this point for twenty years. *See* Walker, Spohn & DeLone, *supra* note 48, at 115; Samuel Walker, *Racial Minority and Female Employment in Policing: The Implications of "Glacial" Change*, 31 Crime & Delinq. 555, 556, 565 (1985).

82. Samuel L. Williams, *Law Enforcement and Affirmative Action*, Police Chief, Feb. 1975, at 72.

83. *See, e.g.*, Myers, Forrest & Miller, *supra* note 32, at 34.

84. *See, e.g.*, Barlow, Barlow & Stajkovic, *supra* note 79, at 140.

85. *See* Trish Oberweis & Michael Musheno, *Policing Identities: Cop Decision Making and the Constitution of the Citizen*, 24 L. & Soc. Inquiry 897, 901–02, 904 (1999).

86. *See id.* at 910–17; Barlow & Barlow, *supra* note 33, at 235–41.

87. I owe this point to Michael Musheno.

88. *See* Lott, *supra* note 57.

89. Using data regarding hiring of police officers in New York City, Justin Mc-
Crary has found that "even aggressive hiring quotas change the test score distribution of new hires only minimally." McCrary, *supra* note 25, at 26–31, 33. McCrary
also did a time series comparison of crime rates in cities that had been sued for discriminatory police hiring and in cities that had not, and an "event study" analysis of
crime rates before and after litigation. He found little evidence that litigation was related to crime rates. *See id.* at 26–29.

90. *Cf.* FAIRNESS AND EFFECTIVENESS IN POLICING, *supra* note 52, at 80 (noting
that "in important respects" the new employment of openly gay and lesbian officers
"represents an even greater transformation of the traditional police subculture than
the employment of female officers as equals in the 1970s").

91. WILLIAM A. WESTLEY, VIOLENCE AND THE POLICE: A SOCIOLOGICAL STUDY OF
LAW, CUSTOM, AND MORALITY 61–63, 89–90, 107 (1970); William Westley, *Violence
and the Police*, 59 AM. J. Soc. 34, 37–38 (1953). Seven of fifteen law enforcement
agencies in Los Angeles County interviewed by law students in 1966 admitted en-
gaging in organized, extralegal harassment of homosexuals. *See* Project, *The Consent-
ing Adult Homosexual and the Law: An Empirical Study of Enforcement and
Administration in Los Angeles County*, 13 UCLA L. REV. 643, 719 (1966).

92. KIM LONSWAY ET AL., NATIONAL CENTER FOR WOMEN & POLICING, UNDER
SCRUTINY: THE EFFECT OF CONSENT DECREES ON THE REPRESENTATION OF WOMEN IN
SWORN LAW ENFORCEMENT 1 (2003).

93. McCrary, *supra* note 25, at 8.

94. *See id.* at 9.

95. *See id.* at 7, 14, 26.

96. *See id.* at 47.

97. William G. Lewis, *Toward Representative Bureaucracy: Blacks in City Police Organizations, 1975–1985*, 49 PUB. ADMIN. REV. 257 (1989).

98. *See* Lott, *supra* note 57, at 244.

99. Susan E. Martin, *The Effectiveness of Affirmative Action: The Case of Women in
Policing*, 8 JUSTICE Q. 489 (1991). Martin ran a series of regressions to control for the
effects of region, city size, and minority representation. The results indicated that
"both court-ordered and voluntary affirmative action were significantly associated
with the proportion of women in a department," after controlling for other variables. *Id.* at 494.

100. LONSWAY ET AL., *supra* note 92.

101. Tim R. Sass & Jennifer Troyer, *Affirmative Action, Political Representation,
Unions, and Female Police Employment*, 20 J. LAB. RES. 571 (1999). They found no
similar effect on hiring rates in 1991, a result they speculated might reflect the fact
that most of the decisions were handed down in the early 1980s: "[o]f the 65 decisions in gender-related cases against municipal police departments decided by 1991,
only 16 decisions occurred in the 1986–1991 period." *Id.* at 579 & 585 n.14.

102. *See* Lott, *supra* note 57, at 244.

103. On the impact, in particular, of a lawsuit filed by a gay LAPD officer in 1988, see Belkin & McNichol, *supra* note 32, at 69; Marita Hernandez, 2 *LAPD Officers Join Homosexual Bias Suit*, L.A. TIMES, Nov. 22, 1989, at B3.

104. *See* LONSWAY ET AL., *supra* note 31, at 6.

NOTES TO CHAPTER 8

1. On "the dominant view of police unions," see George L. Kelling & Robert B. Kliesmet, *Police Unions, Police Culture, and Police Abuse of Force, in* POLICE VIOLENCE: UNDERSTANDING AND CONTROLLING POLICE ABUSE OF FORCE 191 (William A. Geller & Hans Toch eds., 1996).

2. EDWARD CONLON, BLUE BLOOD 243 (2004).

3. *See* Debra Livingston, *Police Discretion and the Quality of Life in Public Places: Courts, Commentators, and the New Policing*, 97 COLUM. L. REV. 551, 573–74 (1997).

4. HANS TOCH & J. DOUGLAS GRANT, POLICE AS PROBLEM SOLVERS: HOW FRONT-LINE WORKERS CAN PROMOTE ORGANIZATIONAL AND COMMUNITY CHANGE 81 (2d ed. 2005); Thomas J. Cowper, *The Myth of the "Military Model" of Leadership in Law Enforcement, in* CONTEMPORARY POLICING: CONTROVERSIES, CHALLENGES, AND SOLUTIONS 113 (Quint C. Thurman & Jihong Zhao eds., 2004).

5. *See, e.g.,* Gerald Frug, *City Services*, 73 N.Y.U. L. REV. 23, 81 (1998); Jerome Skolnick, *Neighborhood Police*, THE NATION, Mar. 22, 1972, at 372; Arthur L. Waskow, *Community Control of the Police*, TRANS-ACTION, Dec. 1969, at 4.

6. JOHN DEWEY, THE PUBLIC AND ITS PROBLEMS 217 (1946 ed.) (1927).

7. *See, e.g.,* DAVID MONTGOMERY, THE FALL OF THE HOUSE OF LABOR: THE WORKPLACE, THE STATE, AND AMERICAN LABOR ACTIVISM, 1865–1925, at 214–56 (1987).

8. *See, e.g.,* BARBARA GARSON, ALL THE LIVELONG DAY: THE MEANING AND DE-MEANING OF ROUTINE WORK 214–18 (1975); MIKE ROSE, THE MIND AT WORK: VALUING THE INTELLIGENCE OF THE AMERICAN WORKER 142–47 (2004); JOHN FABIAN WITT, THE ACCIDENTAL REPUBLIC: CRIPPLED WORKINGMEN, DESTITUTE WIDOWS, AND THE REMAKING OF AMERICAN LAW 109 (2004).

9. FREDERICK WINSLOW TAYLOR, THE PRINCIPLES OF SCIENTIFIC MANAGEMENT (1911); *see also, e.g.,* FRANK BARKLEY COPLEY, FREDERICK W. TAYLOR: FATHER OF SCIENTIFIC MANAGEMENT (1923).

10. *See, e.g.,* CYNTHIA ESTLUND, WORKING TOGETHER: HOW WORKPLACE BONDS STRENGTHEN A DIVERSE DEMOCRACY 56–59 (2003).

11. DEWEY, *supra* note 6, at 217.

12. *See, e.g.,* HARRY BRAVERMAN, LABOR AND MONOPOLY CAPITALISM: THE DEGRADATION OF WORK IN THE TWENTIETH CENTURY (1974); GARSON, *supra* note 8; William H. Simon, *Ethics, Professionalism, and Meaningful Work*, 26 HOFSTRA L. REV. 445, 447–57 (1997).

13. *See, e.g.*, JAMES MILLER, DEMOCRACY IS IN THE STREETS: FROM PORT HURON TO THE SIEGE OF CHICAGO (paperback ed. 1994).

14. *See, e.g.*, DAVID JENKINS, JOB POWER: BLUE AND WHITE COLLAR DEMOCRACY (1973); JANE J. MANSBRIDGE, BEYOND ADVERSARY DEMOCRACY (1980); CAROLE PATEMAN, PARTICIPATION AND DEMOCRATIC THEORY (1970); PHILIP SELZNICK, LAW, SOCIETY, AND INDUSTRIAL JUSTICE (1969).

15. *See, e.g.*, WELLFORD W. WILMS, RESTORING PROSPERITY: HOW WORKERS AND MANAGERS ARE FORGING A NEW CULTURE OF COOPERATION (1996); Mark Barenberg, *Democracy and Domination in the Law of Workforce Cooperation: From Bureaucratic to Flexible Production*, 94 COLUM. L. REV. 753, 881–904 (1994); William H. Simon, *The Politics of "Cooperation" at the Workplace*, RECONSTRUCTION, Winter 1990, at 18.

16. *See* Barenberg, *supra* note 15, at 870–79, 904–18; Simon, *supra* note 15, at 18, 20–21, 55–57.

17. *See* Simon, *supra* note 15, at 18–19, 59–61; Graham Sewell, *The Discipline of Teams: The Control of Team-Based Industrial Work Through Electronic and Peer Surveillance*, 43 ADMIN. SCI. Q. 397 (1998). "Quality circles" are "periodic meetings at which small groups of employees are encouraged to discuss workplace issues and to make 'suggestions' to management." Simon, *supra* note 15, at 18; *see also, e.g.*, WILMS, *supra* note 15, at 34.

18. *See, e.g.*, JEROME H. SKOLNICK, JUSTICE WITHOUT TRIAL: LAW ENFORCEMENT IN DEMOCRATIC SOCIETY (3d ed. 1994); Joseph Goldstein, *Police Discretion Not to Invoke the Criminal Process: Low-Visibility Decisions in the Administration of Justice*, 69 YALE L.J. 543 (1960); Sanford H. Kadish, *Legal Norm and Discretion in the Police and Sentencing Processes*, 75 HARV. L. REV. 904, 906–15 (1962); Charles A. Reich, *Police Questioning of Law Abiding Citizens*, 75 YALE L.J. 1161, 1164–70 (1966).

19. For the argument for regulating the police by legislation, see, e.g., CRAIG M. BRADLEY, THE FAILURE OF THE CRIMINAL PROCEDURE REVOLUTION (1993). For suggestions that the police should be regulated through rules promulgated by police agencies themselves, see KENNETH CULP DAVIS, DISCRETIONARY JUSTICE 65, 95 (1969); Anthony G. Amsterdam, *Perspectives on the Fourth Amendment*, 58 MINN. L. REV. 349, 380 (1974). On civilian oversight, see, e.g., SAMUEL WALKER, POLICE ACCOUNTABILITY: THE ROLE OF CITIZEN OVERSIGHT (2002).

20. *See, e.g.*, Egon Bittner, *The Police on Skid-Row: A Study of Peace Keeping*, 5 AM. SOC. REV. 699, 699–700 (1967).

21. *See, e.g.*, HERMAN GOLDSTEIN, PROBLEM-ORIENTED POLICING xii (1990).

22. *See, e.g.*, EGON BITTNER, *The Functions of the Police: A Review of Background Factors, Current Practices, and Possible Role Models, in* ASPECTS OF POLICE WORK 89 (1990) (reprinting monograph originally published in 1970); WILLIAM KER MUIR, JR., POLICE: STREETCORNER POLITICIANS (1977); JAMES Q. WILSON, VARIETIES OF POLICE BEHAVIOR: THE MANAGEMENT OF LAW AND ORDER IN EIGHT COMMUNITIES (1968).

23. BITTNER, *supra* note 22, at 131.

24. *Id.* at 148–49.

25. *See, e.g.,* STEVE HERBERT, CITIZENS, COPS, AND POWER: RECOGNIZING THE LIMITS OF COMMUNITY 103–04 (2006).

26. *See, e.g., id.* at 153 ("Whenever police officers are furnished an opportunity to discuss their work problems around a conference table, they generally display a thoughtful approach that amazes outsiders. Naturally not all policemen contribute to discussions nor do all benefit from them. But in this respect they are not very different from teachers, some of whom might also not attend faculty meetings without much loss.").

27. HANS TOCH, J. DOUGLAS GRANT & RAYMOND T. GALVIN, AGENTS OF CHANGE: A STUDY IN POLICE REFORM (1975). A revised account of the study appears in TOCH & GRANT, *supra* note 4.

28. GOLDSTEIN, *supra* note 21, at 28.

29. *See, e.g.,* WILMS, *supra* note 15.

30. *See* Justin McCrary, The Effect of Court-Ordered Hiring Quotas on the Composition and Quality of Police 9 (Nov. 30, 2003) (unpublished manuscript).

31. *See* CONLON, *supra* note 2, at 74 ("For cops, there was never any shortage of complaints, formal and otherwise: the crime reports we wrote were called complaints, and when the DA wrote up a charge, it was called a complaint, and when a civilian accused a cop of wrongdoing, it was also a complaint. We complained among ourselves, about bad food, hurting feet, lousy bosses, long hours, and little money. We complained about the sun and the rain. We did have a lot to complain about, within the Job and without, but some cops seemed to lose the power of speech altogether, except for complaining."); *see also, e.g., id.* at 284–85.

32. This is a major subject of Edward Conlon's recent memoir of his work as a New York City police officer. *See, e.g., id.* at 307–404.

33. *See, e.g.,* MUIR, *supra* note 22.

34. CONLON, *supra* note 2, at 312.

35. *See, e.g.,* Herbert, *supra* note 25, at 97; SUSAN EHRLICH MARTIN, BREAKING AND ENTERING: POLICE WOMEN ON PATROL (1980); MUIR, *supra* note 22.

36. *See, e.g.,* CONLON, *supra* note 2, at 291–94, 322–30; STEVEN MAYNARD-MOODY & MICHAEL MUSHENO, COPS, TEACHERS, COUNSELORS: STORIES FROM THE FRONT LINES OF PUBLIC SERVICE 57 (2003). This, too, is a large theme of Conlon's book.

37. *E.g.,* Jack Dunphy, *Betrayal, Not Bullets, Is What Cops Fear,* L.A. TIMES, Sept. 4, 2005, at M3; *see also* REPORT OF THE RAMPART INDEPENDENT REVIEW PANEL: A REPORT TO THE LOS ANGELES BOARD OF POLICE COMMISSIONERS CONCERNING THE OPERATIONS, POLICIES, AND PROCEDURES OF THE LOS ANGELES POLICE DEPARTMENT IN THE WAKE OF THE RAMPART SCANDAL 55 (2000).

38. *See* GOLDSTEIN, *supra* note 21, at 149.

39. *See* David L. Carter & Allen D. Sapp, *The Evolution of Higher Education in Law Enforcement: Preliminary Findings from a National Study,* 1 J. CRIM. JUST. EDUC. 59 (1990).

40. *See id.* at 62–63.

41. *See* GOLDSTEIN, *supra* note 21, at 150.

42. Jordan v. City of New London, 2000 U.S. App. LEXIS 22195 (2d Cir. 2000) (unpublished opinion); *see also* Mike Allen, *Help Wanted Invoking the Not-Too-High-IQ Test*, N.Y. TIMES, Sept. 19, 1999, at D4.

43. *Jordan*, *supra* note 42, at *2.

44. Allen, *supra* note 42.

45. *Id.*

46. *Id.* (quoting New London Deputy Police Chief William C. Gavitt).

47. *Id.* (quoting Charles F. Wonderlic, Jr.).

48. TAYLOR, *supra* note 9, at 59.

49. Allen, *supra* note 42 (quoting Gilbert G. Gallegos, national president of the Fraternal Order of Police).

50. *See* Simon, *supra* note 12 (citing sources).

51. *See, e.g.*, CONLON, *supra* note 2, at 313 (discussing officers who "left the Job with the taste of ashes in their mouths").

52. *See, e.g.*, SKOLNICK, *supra* note 18, at 57–62; WILLIAM A. WESTLEY, VIOLENCE AND THE POLICE: A SOCIOLOGICAL STUDY OF LAW, CUSTOM, AND MORALITY (1970); Maureen Cain, *Some Go Forward, Some Go Back: Police Work in Comparative Perspective*, 22 COMP. SOC. 319, 320 (1993).

53. *See, e.g.*, SKOLNICK, *supra* note 18, at 41–68.

54. *See* Michael G. Aamodt & Nicole A. Stalnaker, *Police Officer Suicide: Frequency and Officer Profiles, in* SUICIDE AND LAW ENFORCEMENT (Donald C. Sheehan & Janet I. Warren eds., 2001); Melissa J. Erwin et al., *Reports of Intimate Partner Violence Made Against Police Officers*, 20 J. FAM. VIOLENCE 13 (2005); Erlend Hem, Anne Marie Berg & Oivind Dkeberg, *Suicide in the Police—A Critical Review*, 31 SUICIDE & LIFE-THREATENING BEHAVIOR 224 (2001).

55. *See, e.g.*, Akiva M. Liberman et al., *Routine Occupational Stress and Psychological Distress in Police*, 21 POLICING 421 (2002).

56. *See* MARY ANN WYCOFF & WESLEY K. SKOGAN, U.S. DEP'T OF JUSTICE, COMMUNITY POLICING IN MADISON: QUALITY FROM THE INSIDE OUT 46 (1993).

57. Todd Wuestewald & Brigitte Steinheider, *Shared Leadership: Can Empowerment Work in Police Organizations?* THE POLICE CHIEF, Jan. 2006, at 48.

58. On Mill and Cole, see PATEMAN, *supra* note 14, at 33–44.

59. *See, e.g.*, *id.*; MANSBRIDGE, *supra* note 14.

60. *See, e.g.*, HERMAN GOLDSTEIN, POLICING A FREE SOCIETY 1 (1977).

61. *See* MUIR, *supra* note 22, at 3–4, 79–80, 99, 119, 144, 268.

62. *See, e.g.*, SKOLNICK, *supra* note 18, at 249–56; Byron Michael Jackson, Leadership and Change in a Public Organization: The Dilemmas of an Urban Police Chief (1979) (unpublished Ph.D. dissertation, University of California, Berkeley) (on file with author).

63. MUIR, *supra* note 22, 253. All of the officers Muir studied were men. Oakland's police force at the time was 97 percent male; the nationwide figure was 98 per-

cent. *See* FEDERAL BUREAU OF INVESTIGATION, UNIFORM CRIME REPORTS FOR THE UNITED STATES 160, 249 (1971). Today, of course, the figures are far different—a matter discussed in Chapter 7.

64. MUIR, *supra* note 22, at 253.

65. *Id.* at 281.

66. *See id.*

67. WESTLEY, *supra* note 52, at xvii.

68. GEORGE E. BERKLEY, THE DEMOCRATIC POLICEMAN 29–39 (1969).

69. *Id.* at 29, 30.

70. John E. Angell, *Toward an Alternative to Classic Police Organizational Arrangements: A Democratic Model*, 9 CRIMINOLOGY 185, 187, 193–95 (1971); *see also* John E. Angell, *The Democratic Model Needs a Fair Trial: Angell's Response*, 12 CRIMINOLOGY 379 (1975).

71. The theme is entirely absent, for example, from a recent, otherwise balanced encyclopedia article on police and democracy by the sociologist Gary Marx, despite the fact that both Berkley and Muir appear in the bibliography. *See* Gary T. Marx, *Police Power, in* ENCYCLOPEDIA OF DEMOCRACY 954 (Seymour Martin Lipset ed., 1995), *reprinted with revisions as* Gary T. Marx, *Police and Democracy, in* POLICING, SECURITY, AND DEMOCRACY: THEORY AND PRACTICE 35 (Menachem Amir & Staley Einstein eds., 2000).

72. Compare, for example, Carole Pateman's influential argument for workplace democracy, published in 1970, PATEMAN, *supra* note 14, with Jane Mansbridge's equally famous but much more qualified defense of the same ideal in 1980, MANSBRIDGE, *supra* note 14.

73. *See* David Alan Sklansky, *Not Your Father's Police Department: Making Sense of the New Demographics of Law Enforcement*, 96 J. CRIM. L. & CRIMINOLOGY 1209 (2006).

74. *See, e.g.,* ROBERT M. FOGELSON, BIG-CITY POLICE 239–42 (1977); CHRISTOPHER LASCH, THE AGONY OF THE AMERICAN LEFT 206–07 (1969); JEROME H. SKOLNICK, THE POLITICS OF PROTEST 278–81 (1969); WALKER, *supra* note 19, at 27–29.

75. Kelling & Kliesmet, *supra* note 1, at 193; *see also, e.g.,* TOCH & GRANT, *supra* note 4, at 33–37; Albert J. Reiss, *Police Organization in the Twentieth Century, in* MODERN POLICING 51, 68–72 (Michael Tonry & Norval Morris eds., 1992).

76. *See* Gary T. Marx, *When the Guards Guard Themselves: Undercover Tactics Turned Inward*, 2 POLICING & SOC. 151 (1992).

77. Kelling & Kliesmet, *supra* note 1, at 193. They were inconsistent, too, with the thinking of August Vollmer, the pioneering police reformer of the early twentieth century, who encouraged his officers to think for themselves and held weekly sessions for officers to discuss and debate departmental matters. *See id.* at 205–06.

78. *See, e.g.,* MAX LERNER, AMERICA AS A CIVILIZATION: LIFE AND THOUGHT IN THE UNITED STATES TODAY 433 (1957) ("The American is not overly impressed by police

authority, considering the police officer as a badly paid job holder, not above being 'fixed' by a bribe.").

79. T. W. ADORNO ET AL., THE AUTHORITARIAN PERSONALITY (1950); *see, e.g.*, SKOL-NICK, *supra* note 74, at 259–62; ARTHUR NIEDERHOFFER, BEHIND THE SHIELD: THE POLICE IN URBAN SOCIETY 103–51 (1967); JAMES Q. WILSON, VARIETIES OF POLICE BE-HAVIOR 33–34, 47 (1968); Robert W. Balch, *The Police Personality: Fact or Fiction?* 63 J. CRIM. L. CRIMINOLOGY & POLICE SCI. 106, 107 (1972) (noting that "the typical po-liceman, as he is portrayed in the literature, is almost a classic example of the au-thoritarian personality").

80. John Thomas Delaney & Peter Feuille, *Police, in* COLLECTIVE BARGAINING IN AMERICAN INDUSTRY: CONTEMPORARY PERSPECTIVES AND FUTURE DIRECTIONS 265, 301 (David B. Lipsky & Clifford B. Donn eds., 1987); *see also, e.g.*, STEPHEN C. HALPERN, POLICE-ASSOCIATION AND DEPARTMENT LEADERS: THE POLITICS OF CO-OPTATION 93–99 (1974).

81. GOLDSTEIN, *supra* note 21, at 156.

82. GOLDSTEIN, *supra* note 60, at 264.

83. *See* DAVID C. COUPER & SABINE H. LOBITZ, QUALITY POLICING: THE MADISON EXPERIENCE (1991); WYCOFF & SKOGAN, *supra* note 56. Regarding similar but more limited initiatives elsewhere, see TOCH & GRANT, *supra* note 4, at 47–67. For recent academic attention to the attractions of workplace democracy in policing, see *id.*; Ian Loader, *Democracy, Justice and the Limits of Policing: Rethinking Police Accountability*, 3 SOC. & LEGAL STUD. 521, 538 (1994) (hesitantly suggesting that line police officers in Britain "may provide a potential resource upon which deliberative problem-solving mechanisms can draw"); Monique Marks, *Democratizing Police Organizations from the Inside Out: Police-Labor Relations in Southern Africa, in* COMPARATIVE AND INTERNA-TIONAL CRIMINAL JUSTICE: TRADITIONAL AND NONTRADITIONAL SYSTEMS OF LAW AND CONTROL 109, 110 (Charles B. Fields & Richter H. Moore Jr. eds., 2005) (linking "internal" and "external" democratization of the police in Southern Africa); Monique Marks, *Transforming Police Organizations from Within: Police Dissident Groupings in Southern Africa*, 40 BRIT. J. CRIMINOLOGY 557 (2000) (same) [hereinafter Marks, *Transforming Police Organizations from Within*].

84. GOLDSTEIN, *supra* note 21, at 27.

85. *See, e.g.*, Livingston, *supra* note 3, at 574–78.

86. Jonathan Simon, *Speaking Truth and Power*, 36 LAW & SOC. REV. 37, 40 (2002).

87. SKOLNICK, *supra* note 18, at 226–30.

88. *See id.* at 11 ("In the abstract, the rule of law embodies rational restraints on authority as it defines criminal conduct. There must be specificity, clarity, prospec-tivity, and strict construction in favor of the accused. There must be procedural reg-ularity and fairness, and so forth. In practice, however, such standards may not be clear.") Phrases like "and so forth" are quite typical in discussions of the rule of law.

89. LON L. FULLER, THE MORALITY OF THE LAW 39 (1964).

90. *See, e.g.*, Joseph Raz, *The Rule of Law and Its Virtue, in* The Authority of the Law 210, 214 (1979); Richard H. Fallon, Jr., *"The Rule of Law" as a Concept in Constitutional Discourse*, 97 Colum. L. Rev. 1, 8 & n.27 (1997); Margaret Jane Radin, *Reconsidering the Rule of Law*, 69 B.U. L. Rev. 781, 785 (1989).

91. *See* Fallon, *supra* note 90, at 10–24.

92. Fuller, *supra* note 89, at 81; *cf., e.g.*, Jerome H. Skolnick & James J. Fyfe, Above the Law: Police and the Excessive Use of Force xvi (1993) (arguing that "in a free society, especially in the United States, where police derive their authority from law and take an oath to support the Constitution, they are obliged to acknowledge the law's moral force and to be constrained by it").

93. Fuller, *supra* note 89, at 39.

94. F. A. Hayek, The Road to Serfdom 54 (1944) (quoted in, *e.g.*, Raz, *supra* note 90, at 210); *cf., e.g.*, Raz, *supra* note 90, at 219 (noting that "the rule of law is often rightly contrasted with arbitrary power").

95. *See* Raz, *supra* note 90, at 210–11.

96. William Kornblum, *Drug Legalization and the Minority Poor*, 69 Milbank Q. 415, 422 (1991).

97. *See, e.g.*, Emily J. Sack, *Battered Women and the State of the Law: The Struggle for the Future of Domestic Violence Policy*, 2004 Wisc. L. Rev. 1657.

98. *See, e.g.*, Selznick, *supra* note 14, at 29.

99. Tom R. Tyler, *Enhancing Police Legitimacy*, 593 Annals Am. Acad. Pol. & Soc. Sci. 84, 94 (2004); *see also, e.g.*, Tom R. Tyler, Why People Obey the Law (1990).

100. *See* William H. Simon, *Toyota Jurisprudence: Legal Theory and Rolling Rules Regimes, in* Law and New Governance in the EU and the US 37, 47–48 (Grainne de Burca & Joanne Scott eds., 2006).

101. This is the point stressed by Raz: the rule of law is a political virtue, but it is not the only political virtue, and sometimes it should yield. *See* Raz, *supra* note 90.

102. *See, e.g.*, Michael E. Buerger, *The Limits of Community, in* The Challenge of Community Policing: Testing the Premises 270, 270–71 (Dennis P. Rosenbaum ed., 1994); Frug, *supra* note 5, at 81.

103. *See, e.g.*, Samuel Walker, Police Accountability: The Role of Citizen Oversight (2001).

104. *See, e.g.*, Frug, *supra* note 5, at 81; Jerome Skolnick, *Neighborhood Police*, The Nation, Mar. 22, 1972, at 372; Arthur L. Waskow, *Community Control of the Police*, Trans-Action, Dec. 1969, at 4.

105. I thank Monique Marks for helping me to see the importance of these distinctions.

106. *See* Michael J. Yelnosky, *Title VII, Mediation, and Collective Action*, 1999 U. Ill. L. Rev. 583, 614.

107. *See, e.g.*, Estlund, *supra* note 10, at 54–56; Alan Hyde, *Employee Caucus: A*

Key Institution in the Emerging System of Employment Law, 69 CHI.-KENT L. REV. 149, 160 (1993).

108. *See* COUPER & LOBITZ, *supra* note 83, at 18, 33–34.

109. Outside of law enforcement, too, informal, overlapping "employee caucuses" appear to many observers to be "the growing, lively, vital mode of employee representation." Hyde, *supra* note 107, at 187; *see also, e.g.*, Yelnosky, *supra* note 106, at 614.

110. *Cf., e.g.*, Hyde, *supra* note 107, at 161–62 (arguing that "[a]n active caucus system could encourage participation, provide loyal opposition to union leadership, and create a richer internal union political life").

111. *See, e.g.*, MARKS, *Transforming Police Organizations from Within*, *supra* note 83.

112. *See, e.g.*, BERKLEY, *supra* note 68.

113. *See, e.g.*, ROBERT REINER, THE BLUE-COATED WORKER: A SOCIOLOGICAL STUDY OF POLICE UNIONISM (1978); Jenny Fleming & Monique Marks, *Reformers or Resisters? The State of Police Unionism in Australia*, 4 EMPLOYMENT RELATIONS REC. 1 (2004); Jenny Fleming, Monique Marks & Jennifer Wood, *"Standing on the Inside Looking Out": The Significance of Police Unions in Networks of Police Governance*, 39 AUSTRL. & N.Z. J. CRIMINOLOGY 71 (2006).

114. *See* Erwin Chemerinsky, *An Independent Analysis of the Los Angeles Police Department's Board of Inquiry Report on the Rampart Scandal*, 34 LOY. L.A. L. REV. 545 (2001). The PPL had earlier supported Chemerinsky's successful bid to serve on the Los Angeles Charter Reform Commission. *See* Erwin Chemerinsky, *On Being a Framer: The Los Angeles Charter Reform Commission*, 2 GREENBAG 131, 134 (1999).

115. *See* Nancy Cleeland & Jill Leovy, *Teamsters Seeking to Represent the LAPD*, L.A. TIMES, Feb. 12, 2002, at B1. The decertification drive failed, and the PPL remains and affiliate of the IUPA.

116. Simon, *supra* note 100, at 38.

117. *See* TOCH, GRANT & GALVIN, *supra* note 27.

118. *See* Simon, *supra* note 100, at 47–48.

119. *Id.* (quoting AMERICAN SOCIETY FOR QUALITY, THE ISO 14000 HANDBOOK 196 (Joseph Cascio ed., 1996)).

120. *Id.* at 45, 48.

121. *See, e.g.*, Michael C. Dorf & Charles F. Sabel, *A Constitution of Democratic Experimentalism*, 98 COLUM. L. REV. 267 (1998).

122. Simon, *supra* note 100, at 58–59 (quoting JOSEPH REES, HOSTAGES TO EACH OTHER: THE TRANSFORMATION OF NUCLEAR SAFETY SINCE THREE MILE ISLAND 82 (2003), in turn quoting INSTITUTE OF NUCLEAR POWER PLANT OPERATION, GOOD PRACTICE, CONDUCT OF OPERATIONS 18–19 (1984)).

123. *See* Simon, *supra* note 100, at 58.

124. *See* Kelling & Kliesmet, *supra* note 1, at 196–99.

125. *See, e.g.*, LASCH, *supra* note 74, at 203.

126. *See, e.g.*, GOLDSTEIN, *supra* note 21, at 155–57.

127. *See, e.g.*, *id.* at 157–59.

128. Gillian Metzger, in fact, has suggested that due process might be re-imagined to include a duty on the part of government to assure adequate supervision of its agents, both public and private. *See* Gillian E. Metzger, Private Delegations and Due Process 32 (Mar. 12, 2005) (unpublished manuscript).

129. *See, e.g.*, Tennessee v. Garner, 471 U.S. 1, 18–19 (1985); Illinois v. Lafayette, 462 U.S. 640, 648 (1983); South Dakota v. Opperman, 428 U.S. 364 (1976); Miranda v. Arizona, 384 U.S. 436, 483–86 (1966).

130. *Cf.* Bd. of Educ. v. Earls, 536 U.S. 822, 841 (Breyer, J., concurring) (arguing for deferring to views of local school board regarding drug testing of students, in part because the school board had used a "democratic, participatory process to uncover and to resolve differences").

131. *See* GEORGE S. RIGAKOS, THE NEW PARAPOLICE: RISK MARKETS AND COMMODIFIED SOCIAL CONTROL 98–146 (2002).

132. Some of the same technological developments that allow patrol officers to communicate more easily and more privately also allow their employers to monitor them more closely. *See, e.g.*, PETER K. MANNING, POLICING CONTINGENCIES 123–74 (2003); RIGAKOS, *supra* note 131. In policing as in other occupations, advances in communications technology can make the choice between the democratic and authoritarian norms of work that Bendix described more pressing than ever.

133. Steven Greenhouse, *Borrowing Language of Civil Rights Movement, Drive Is On to Unionize Guards*, N.Y. TIMES, July 26, 2006, at A13.

134. RIGAKOS, *supra* note 131, at 148.

135. Police officer bills of rights—statutory guarantees of procedural rights to sworn law enforcement personnel—warrant a brief discussion. If there is anything to the notion that police officers who experience democracy at work will be more comfortable with and respectful of democracy in the broader society, one might expect that officers who enjoy procedural protections—e.g., the right to representation when questioned by internal affairs investigators—will be more understanding and supportive of similar rights enjoyed by criminal suspects. Whether this in fact happens is largely unknown. There is some evidence that police officers, like other government workers, think more legalistically about their own treatment than about their treatment of others. *See* MAYNARD-MOODY & MUSHENO, *supra* note 36, at 57. But it may not be coincidence that it was a police chief famous for his heavy hand in disciplinary matters who helped push the Los Angeles Police Protective League into its novel partnership with a civil libertarian law professor.

136. *See* DAVID GARLAND, THE CULTURE OF CONTROL 114–17, 188–90 (2001); Ian Loader, *Democracy, Justice and the Limits of Policing: Rethinking Police Accountability*, 3 SOC. & LEGAL STUD. 521, 521–22 (1994).

NOTES TO CONCLUSION

1. *See, e.g.,* PUBLIC SECURITY AND POLICE REFORM IN THE AMERICAS (John Bailey & Lucía Dammert eds., 2005).

2. ROBERT A. DAHL, DEMOCRACY AND ITS CRITICS 2 (1989); *see also, e.g.,* JACK LIVELY, DEMOCRACY 1 (1975).

3. *See* Daniel C. Richman, *The Right Fight: Local Police and National Security,* BOSTON REV., Dec. 2004/Jan. 2005, at 6.

Index